D1237514

# HEMINGWAY ON LOVE

# HEMINGWAY on LOVE

*ROBERT W. LEWIS, JR.*

UNIVERSITY OF TEXAS PRESS
AUSTIN & LONDON

Library of Congress Catalog Card No. 65–21297

Manufactured in the United States of America

Acknowledgment of permissions to quote from copyrighted materials appears on a Permissions page.

*For my parents*

# PREFACE

Every reader of Ernest Hemingway knows that "love" is a central subject of his work, and many readers have been struck by what seemed to be different and changing treatments of that subject in his work. The purpose of this study is to consider the subject of love as treated by Hemingway in major and representative works, with the end of describing as exactly as possible the terms of his "love ethic." My conclusion is that Hemingway's concept of love and its role in the lives of his characters gradually changed and matured from a negativistic disillusionment with romantic love to an acceptance of agape or brotherly love. In Hemingway, erotic love is at all times a source of pleasure that is commendable but morally neutral. Admittedly, to say that Hemingway "matured" is to use a relative word that involves an ethical judgment, but the judgment is as much Hemingway's as it is mine. If I have read him rightly, I am merely presenting his changing views.

Many of Hemingway's critics have furnished me with suggestions relevant to my analysis. The suggestions have ranged from passing hints to entire articles or sections of books on one or another aspect of the subject of love. If they often concurred in accepting the centrality of the subject, they did not always concur in my particular understanding of specific points. By writing an extended analysis of this aspect of Hemingway's work, I hope I can work out the discrepancies or at least clarify the differences. Major themes and images emerge more clearly the more one reads Hemingway, and to my mind, he is that kind of writer whose total production is greater than the sum of the parts.

Evaluating and applying the literature that deals with love in general were more difficult tasks than evaluating the relevant criticism of Hemingway alone. Because the topic of love is so broad, I have almost certainly missed some useful essay or book, but I have tried to inform myself of all major views and works on this strangest and perhaps strongest of all human emotions. That I differ with some of this literature about love, in my interpretation of terms and in my attitudes, will be apparent to anyone familiar with that literature, and if I play loose with some of my sources, I can only plead that Hemingway is my concern, and not they.

All writers inevitably write about love of one kind or another. Love, like air or water, is of the essence, and it would not be rash to think that every modern writer has an implicit or explicit love ethic. Of course some writers, like Hemingway, treat love more centrally, sometimes even obsessively. Yet seeing beyond Hemingway's exciting stories to his love ethic is not the end of an examination of his work. The development of his love ethic from romance through eros to agape is a reflection of his entire art, but the study of this change is, I think, a dominant and perhaps the essential way of grasping his art.

An ever-growing body of secular and religious thought concerning the achievement of love considers it the way out of a no-exit world. For example, a rediscovery of the role of love in Christianity may begin with a view of Christ as the great lover. He is still being crucified and resurrected in Western art. Modern psychology has come to some harmony with Christian love through a rediscovery of Greek and Christian agape and through a failure to find any other exits.

Only its intrinsic merits can justify a critical study, but this study—in purpose, at least—benefits from the importance and high seriousness of its subject:

> Love of man for man is perhaps the most difficult task that has been laid upon us, the ultimate, final test, the one undertaking that renders all other labor a mere preliminary preparation for it.[1]

Whatever my success or failure in reading Hemingway, it is with consciousness of temerity that I approach the subject of love, and I claim no intrinsic benefits simply because of the use in my criticism of the agape that is not simply a virtue but a means of endurance and perhaps salvation.

A number of persons besides those acknowledged in the bibliography have contributed directly or indirectly to this book. It gives me pleasure

[1] Rainer Maria Rilke, as quoted by August Adam, *The Primacy of Love,* p. 117.

to remember the encouragement and instruction of professors at the University of Illinois, where this study began taking shape in various courses and as a dissertation. I especially wish to thank Professor Sherman Paul, my adviser at the University of Illinois, for his direction and encouragement. My colleagues at The University of Texas, Professors C. L. Cline, William J. Handy, and Gordon H. Mills, have been kind in their aid, and a research grant from The University of Texas enabled me to complete work on this book. Professor Max R. Westbrook of The University of Texas read parts of the manuscript and was particularly helpful in matters of both style and interpretation. For their presence in crisis and their forbearance, I also fondly remember both former fellow students at the University of Illinois and my own students in various classes both there and at The University of Texas. To my wife, my children, and my parents I owe a different but deeper debt for other points of instruction.

R. W. L.

## PERMISSIONS

Permission to quote copyrighted materials is acknowledged as follows:

CHARLES SCRIBNER'S SONS

Quotations from the following works of Ernest Hemingway are used by permission of Charles Scribner's Sons: *Across the River and into the Trees, Death in the Afternoon, A Farewell to Arms, For Whom the Bell Tolls, Green Hills of Africa, A Moveable Feast, The Old Man and the Sea, The Short Stories of Ernest Hemingway, The Sun Also Rises,* and *To Have and Have Not.* Copyright 1926, 1929, 1932, 1935 Charles Scribner's Sons; renewal copyright 1954, © 1957, 1960 Ernest Hemingway; renewal copyright © 1963 Mary Hemingway. Copyright 1937, 1938, 1940, 1952 Ernest Hemingway. Copyright © 1964 Ernest Hemingway, Ltd.

HARCOURT, BRACE & WORLD, INC.

From "The Waste Land" in *Collected Poems, 1909–1962* by T. S. Eliot, copyright, 1936, by Harcourt, Brace & World, Inc.; copyright, ©, 1963, 1964, by T. S. Eliot. Reprinted by permission of the publishers.

LITTLE, BROWN AND COMPANY

From "Argonauts" and from "Stratis the Sailor among the Agapanthi" in *Poems* by George Seferis. English translation (c) Rex Warner 1960.

HARPER & ROW, PUBLISHERS, INC.

Excerpts by E. B. White from *Is Sex Necessary?* by James Thurber and E. B. White. Copyright 1929 by Harper & Brothers; renewed 1957 by James Thurber and E. B. White. Reprinted with the permission of Harper & Row, Publishers.

## CONTENTS

*And for the soul*
*If it is to know itself*
*It is into a soul*
*That it must look.*
*The stranger and the enemy, we have seen him in the mirror.*

—George Seferis, "Argonauts"

# 1 ~ AN OVERWHELMING QUESTION

The word "love" is used loosely by writers, and they know it. Furthermore, the word "love" is accepted loosely by readers, and *they* know it. There are many kinds of love, but for the purpose of this article I shall confine my discussion to the usual hazy interpretation: the strange bewilderment which overtakes one person on account of another person. Thus, when I say love in this article, you will take it to mean *the pleasant confusion which we know exists.* When I say passion, I *mean* passion.

—James Thurber and E. B. White,
*Is Sex Necessary?*

THAT ERNEST HEMINGWAY was an obsessed writer who wrote chiefly to relieve his psychic distress is a widely held belief, and his jesting comment that his typewriter was his psychiatrist lends credence to the theory.[1] Perhaps more interesting than this Freudian view itself are the parallels between psychoanalysis and the course of Hemingway's writing career. In the five-step process of curing the sick psyche, the first step is relieving repressed aggressiveness, often through transference.[2] Such is a possible extraliterary function of stories like "The Doctor and the Doctor's Wife" and "Soldier's Home," that is, stories which have a strong autobiographical basis and which tell of a young man caught up in a world of hostility or violence. The second stage of psychoanalysis is making the patient capable of love by abolishing the guilt feelings attached to his erotic impulses (his libido). In order to have life, the forces of life must be accepted, and thus one group of stories emphasizes the near death of Nick Adams when he was blown up on the Italian front, while another group of stories emphasizes either persons who cannot love in a sexually "normal" way or who do have normal feelings or experiences but worry about them or are made to suffer for them. A number of the short stories have homosexuals in them—for instance, "The Battler," "Mr. and Mrs. Elliot," "A Simple Enquiry," and "The Sea Change." A good example in which

1 Philip Young, *Ernest Hemingway*, p. 136.

2 Georges Parcheminey, "The Problem of Ambivalence," *Love and Violence*, pp. 94–95. Each of the five stages is noted by Parcheminey in his essay.

eros is suppressed is the nightmarish "God Rest You Merry, Gentlemen" in which a sixteen-year-old "religious" boy amputates his penis in order to subdue " 'that awful lust'."[3] Other examples of eros denied or, though experienced, distorted by romance or into romance occur in "Up in Michigan," "The Three-Day Blow," "Cat in the Rain," and "Hills Like White Elephants."

The very early "Up in Michigan" (1923) may be examined as this second kind of love story. It is an interesting variation of Hemingway's theme in that the protagonist is a young girl rather than a young man, but her initiation and disillusionment are very similar to those of male protagonists like Nick Adams. And like Nick, the girl Liz is guilty of *thinking* about love. She and her lover, Jim, like each other, but while she loses sleep and is otherwise distracted through thinking about him, "he never thought of her"(81). When he finally seduces her, any potential sensitivity is further inhibited by his being drunk, but her thoughts on love are only heightened by the act of sex. That is, innocence is not unthinking by any means.

On the other hand, though Jim's sensual feelings are gratified, they are short-lived. Love-making for him comes between work and the more important sport of the deer hunt (in which each of the masterly male characters kills a deer, an animal symbolically akin to the medieval unicorn, representative of agape). There is no hint that the rough seduction will affect Jim at all, but Liz, whose story it is, has had dreams of Jim and longed for him, and she thought of him most when he was away from her on his hunting trip. She was sure something romantic, though unimaginable, would happen when he returned, but "nothing had happened"(83), and nothing desirable happens when in erotic climax her Tristan lies on top of her, and romance fades, fades away; although she did "want it," she is frightened and hurt and protests. Neither is the setting exactly ideal. They lay on "hard and splintery" "hemlock planks of the dock," planks a bit harder for the romantic Liz than for the realistic "lover" on top of her.

No vestige of dreamland is spared the young girl: Jim falls asleep, still lying on top of her. "Jim was heavy on her and he had hurt her. Liz pushed him, she was so uncomfortable and cramped"(85). Yet after she

[3] Ernest Hemingway, *The Short Stories of Ernest Hemingway,* p. 394. Subsequent references in this chapter to the short stories will be in the text itself.

squeezes out from under him, she kisses his open-mouthed face. She shakes him. He rolls his head and swallows, and then she cries. "She was cold and miserable and everything felt gone"(85). After one last gesture of love—wrapping her coat around him—she walks home alone.

Liz has lost her romantic dream of love, but what endures in spite of Jim's coarseness is an admirable, even a heroic love. Her gesture of care in wrapping Jim in her coat gives us hope for her survival in an unromantic world. Her gesture represents the kind of love that Hemingway's heroes (and heroines) often have: it is the agape that outlives the eros.

The story is also interesting as one of Hemingway's first love stories which contains motifs that will reoccur with variations throughout his work. Jim is a hunter; Liz is pretty and passive; the setting is idyllic; the action counters the setting in its rudeness and coarseness; the protagonist, Liz, is set off against one variety of realist, though Jim is hardly intelligent enough to have a conscious point of view; and it is the romantic who suffers and, one hopes, learns.

In the third stage of psychoanalysis, an "adult" morality is substituted for an archaic one; hence the analyst—and in this analogous case, Hemingway—must have a certain moral attitude toward life or, if you will, an ideal that can peacefully coexist with reality and provide the guiding tension that checks but does not overcome the eruptive, chaotic forces of life; the ideal of romance cannot do either. While the first two stages are best illustrated by Hemingway's short stories and his two novels of the twenties, the third stage begins with the death of Catherine Barkley, at the end of *A Farewell to Arms*, and with the publication of the pivotal works of the late thirties: *Green Hills of Africa* (1935), "The Snows of Kilimanjaro" (1936), "The Short Happy Life of Francis Macomber" (1936), and *To Have and Have Not* (1937). In similar chronological order, the fourth and fifth stages of psychoanalysis are the next steps in Hemingway's developing love ethic: the renunciation of narcissistic satisfactions and the final stage of an ever-increasing capacity for love. These last two stages are best represented by the last three novels: *For Whom the Bell Tolls* (1940), *Across the River and into the Trees* (1950), and *The Old Man and the Sea* (1952). Hemingway himself gave some validation for this division of his work into increasingly refined stages, when in 1950 he was quoted as saying, "I have moved through arithmetic, through plane geometry and algebra, and now I am in calculus."[4]

This development in Hemingway's writings is closely related to the twentieth-century search for values—for simple things like peace and the good—through love. His idea of love, however, changes. First he writes in reaction to romantic love without quite accepting his own rejection of it (*The Sun Also Rises* and *A Farewell to Arms*). He accepts eros at all points, in all his works, but eventually he supplements it with agape and finally sees agape as "the way out." There is a chronological development from the first two novels to the five-year period beginning with *Green Hills of Africa* and ending with *For Whom the Bell Tolls*. This middle period is pivotal for Hemingway's love ethic, and thus I emphasize the works in it rather than the earlier and later works, although this emphasis is clearly not meant to represent an esthetic judgment. His last two novels mark a culmination, a maturity of view in regarding love that is strongly emphasized in the most recently published book, *A Moveable Feast*.

The general critical view of Hemingway's work reverses this pattern of growth and sees his writing as almost steadily deteriorating, with the exception of *The Old Man and the Sea*, but still not nearly so good as his first two novels. Certainly his style changes, and perhaps his work "deteriorates" as his love view matures, because he is somehow overwhelmed by the complexity of mature love. He cannot cope with it in the same artistic way. His early work contrasted the world of men and women with a simpler, strictly male world of war, hunting, and bullfighting. Violence also provided protection from the complexity of love. One could kill the heroine (Catherine Barkley) or desex the hero (Jake Barnes). Later Hemingway could not accept these patent though dramatic simplifications. In any case, this analysis is not biographical or primarily esthetic, though I would argue that the social significance of some of his generally depreciated work—chiefly *To Have and Have Not* and *Across the River and into the Trees*—elevates it esthetically also, inasmuch as art may have a moral or social meaning inseparable from its form or esthetic dimension.

[4] Harvey Breit, "Talk with Mr. Hemingway," *New York Times Book Review*, LV (September 17, 1950), 14.

This relevancy of love to society was eloquently restated for many readers by Denis de Rougemont's *Love in the Western World*, and while Rougemont's thesis regarding the religious origins of courtly love in the Middle Ages is not widely accepted, he intelligently and provocatively describes the development and influence of that love upon Western society.

I am painfully aware of the abuses and misuses of the words "romance" and "romantic." In this book, the words refer to the archetypal story of Tristan and Iseult and the kind of love they represent (my critique of that love being essentially Rougemont's). Since many ages and cultures reflect the Tristan-Iseult syndrome, the words do not refer to any historical or social context. Romantic love overlaps with and possesses characteristics of the other two key "love" terms used here: "eros" and "agape." There is nothing exclusive about romance; in fact, it often tries to be all-inclusive, all-embracing, and certainly it uses erotic love, though it may better be said that it "elevates" erotic love. Although what I would call "romance" may have characteristics of agape also, in general the two may be thought to stand belligerently at opposite poles with the indifferent eros reclining between them.

As with philosophy, most discussions of love eventually come round to Plato, and especially is this circuit appropriate when one looks for the origins of romance.[5] A possible underlying cause of romance is man's desire for the ideal, which he may look for in art that by its very nature is static, unchanging. One can give himself to admiring (even loving?) a painting or a novel. The artistic fallacy emerges: the lover of art unconsciously asks himself, "If Flaubert (or El Greco) gives me so much pleasure when I attend to him, why should I not find similar pleasure in each phase of my life and similarly beautify my life by finding and admiring, loving, adoring a beautiful woman?" (And of course the object of the love can be quite ugly either physically, mentally, or spiritually, just as great art can have such "ugly" subject matter. There is probably no true or universal ugliness in a woman by any objective criteria, though each society usually prescribes a standard from which the lover deviates at his risk.) Each society also encourages the lover in his artistic

[5] See Maurice Valency, *In Praise of Love*, especially Chapter I, "Love and the Poetry of Love," for a first-rate discussion.

fallacy when it in turn idealizes and even idolizes particular types of women through the insidious media of advertising, motion pictures, popular magazine fiction, and the like.

Man's artistic instinct is expanded to include all of life and love, but a problem, the problem of romance (and romance *is* an art), arises simply because the materials of life are essentially different. Even the musician's materials are ultimately static: a musical note exists in perfect inviolable abstraction and mathematical absolute. The marble once carved is complete, the sonnet once written is in essence unchanging. Of course, with all art the response of the audience is everchanging, and the materials may weather and eventually decay. But still the brides on many a Grecian urn are unravished, and even though the urns be crumbled into dust, the brides will remain forever unravished. That quality of endurance is part of art's unfailing attraction, and the mutilated Plato in man leads inevitably to romance and its ubiquitous consequences, such as the hilarious incongruity of a quotation from Marilyn Monroe, "the world's No. 1 [childless!] Sex Goddess": "I've never liked sex. I don't think I ever will. It seems just the opposite of love."[6] And a nation of unblinking Platos reads on.

The rub is this: not only is the lover, like the audience of art, always changing and perceiving anew the object, but the object itself, in this case the loved one, is also changing and responding quite irregularly and complexly to the not-so-simple audience in the tremendously complex series of actions and reactions that constitute human relations. The romancer wants to simplify, to abstract, to regularlize. With marble or words he may. With a woman he cannot.

This romantic yearning for the absolute has not always been for unattainable woman. It may be present in a longing for anything that can be idealized and that is beyond one's grasp, such as the dream of America, that quest for paradise that was often a more vivid ideal for Europeans and later for New Englanders than it was for the actual hard-nosed pioneers. And no goal has ever been so unreal or so indelibly delineated in literature as that pre-eminently exciting object, Iseult. Does the Tristan ever want a woman, or does he rather not simply want an

[6] Ben Hecht, "The Myth about Marilyn Monroe's Death," *Family Weekly*, September 30, 1962, p. 4.

object—with a face, with a name, and with a body of course, but really, ultimately, without any individuality?

The opposite side of Hemingway's concern with love is his concern with destructive forces, and the biographical emphasis on his traumatic wounding in World War I and his lifetime courting of violence is instructive. Hemingway's climactic exposure to the power of hate was in the dugouts and hospitals of the Italian-Austrian front, and his subsequent woundings, accidents, and near misses with death function as reinforcements of that central lesson of destruction which served him time and time again as a point of reference in his work.

Hemingway's short stories, most of which date from his early writing years, recurrently center on the theme of romantic illusions. The illusions may concern love or other aspects of life, but invariably they tell a story of some pain or loss that comes to those who are deluded. In "Mr. and Mrs. Elliot," "Cat in the Rain," "Out of Season," "Cross-Country Snow," "A Canary for One," and "The Sea Change" young husbands or wives find the hard work of marriage instead of the realization of an eternal, happy approach to erotic fulfillment, with Tchaikovsky playing in the background. In "The Capital of the World," "The End of Something," "The Three-Day Blow," "A Very Short Story," "The Revolutionist," and "Ten Indians," young romantic men begin to test their illusions and begin to pay for them and learn how to function without them. In "Ten Indians" the conflict is not between the protagonist Nick Adams and some outside antagonist but between what Nick really feels about his love affair with the Indian girl and what he is supposed to feel. The romantic notions he harbors are cruelly shattered when he learns that his primitive, unspoiled, Edenic Iseult was "threshing around" in the woods and "having quite a time" with another boy (335). He thinks he cries for the broken heart he is supposed to have, but the greater hurt is probably to his pride, that had swelled during the course of the story. The conclusion is neatly ironic:

> "My heart's broken," he thought. "If I feel this way my heart must be broken."
>
> . . . after a while he forgot to think about Prudence and finally he went to sleep. . . . In the morning there was a big wind blowing and the waves were running high up on the beach and he was awake a long time before he remembered that his heart was broken. (336)

As Shakespeare put it, "Men have died from time to time and worms have eaten them, but not for love."[7]

One more Nick Adams story, "The Three-Day Blow," should be cited, for it dates from 1925 and contains an allusion that without doubt indicates Hemingway's early familiarity with the Tristan and Iseult myth. Nick is older than he was in "Ten Indians," but he is recovering from ending another affair. With his friend Bill he discusses Maurice Hewlett's romantic novel *The Forest Lovers,* " 'the one where they go to bed every night with the naked sword between them,' " just as Tristan and Iseult did in a gesture of hypocritical chastity that Rougemont interprets as the illogical romantic need to love only where barriers to love's satisfaction exist. Nick is still susceptible to the idea of romantic love; he thinks the novel was " 'a swell book'." But he also cannot understand the reason for the sword between them " 'because if it went over flat you could roll right over it and it wouldn't make any trouble' " (118).

Nick is not entirely duped by the romantic myth, and as the story climaxes, we see him in subtle conflict with Bill on the parallel of his recently ended affair and Tristan and Iseult's ever-enduring romance. Bill is an idealist who has apparently induced Nick to break off his affair with Marjorie even though—judging from what we see of her in "The End of Something" and from what we learn of Nick's real feelings about her in these two stories—Nick could be happy with her. Bill thinks that Nick's continuing with Marge would have meant working too hard, marrying not only her but her whole family, demeaning himself by marrying a social inferior, and missing out on life's real pleasures (like fishing with Bill). He sums it all up in an attempt to be terribly wise: " 'Once a man's married he's absolutely bitched' " (122). Nick really doesn't know his own feelings from those of the culturally absorbed Bill, who describes what a lover is "supposed" to feel. When Nick thinks that perhaps the affair is not completely over, he feels happy and no longer alone or *triste.* His healthier attitude has won over Bill's traditionally romantic view. Portentous nature in the form of a windstorm complements Nick's adjustment: " 'There's no use getting drunk,' " Nick says, and "Outside now the Marge business was no longer so tragic. It was not even very important. The wind blew everything like that away"

[7] *As You Like It,* Act IV, scene 1.

(125). He does not *forget* Marge; he simply puts her into a humane perspective. Nick is not a man, but neither is he the adolescent romantic (a phrase that is practically redundant) that Bill is.

These short stories of romantic illusions and the correction and pain of them may be compared with Freud's observations on the same disillusioning process on a broader, culture-wide basis.[8] Freud saw the disillusionment of World War I as a characteristic of intelligent, unsentimental Westerners who had expected that their high degree of civilization and fellowship would not be disrupted by recourse to war, a nationalized embodiment of hate (the opposite of love). Machiavelli was in disrepute, yet even the "rules" of "civilized" war were abandoned in the horror that was the Great War. The new state forbade lying, cheating, and violence among its citizens, yet in the name of patriotism exercised wholesale deceit and slaughter.

Freud saw this silver lining: the disillusionment with the state was good, for it destroyed the illusion that man can eradicate evil and the elemental instincts which are "in themselves . . . neither good nor evil."[9] "Civilization is the fruit of renunciation of instinctual satisfaction, and from each new-comer in turn it exacts the same renunciation."[10] On Hemingway's fictional scale, the newcomer becomes Nick Adams—the Adamic man—and by turns the gradually aging and maturing Hemingway heroes. For Hemingway as well as for Freud, mixing erotic instincts with egoistic instincts gives social instincts. The passionate, happily suffering, world-ignorant, romantic ego is sacrificed because of the need for love. Adolescent illusion, adult neuroses, and national war are related forms of the unyielding ego, and probably the ego wins more often than it loses and the civilized hypocrites outnumber the truly civilized persons. Since art is one of the marks of civilization, it is perfectly fitting that agape is essential to a writing technique. Thus Hemingway advised his young brother: most people are self-centered, but the writers must identify with other people. " 'Forget about yourself and try to get inside other people more and see things from their point of view.' "[11]

[8] Sigmund Freud, "Thoughts for the Times on War and Death," *On Creativity and the Unconscious.*

[9] *Ibid.*, p. 213. [10] *Ibid.*, p. 215.

[11] Leicester Hemingway, *My Brother, Ernest Hemingway*, p. 156.

The conclusion is, then, that a civilized person is a loving person, like Count Greffi in *A Farewell to Arms,* Anselmo in *For Whom the Bell Tolls,* and Santiago in *The Old Man and the Sea.* Men like these are exceptions to the masses of civilized hypocrites. Men like these may live in comparative isolation, as Santiago does, but they demonstrate their fellowship in civilization. The instructive irony here is that each of these three gentlemen has reached an age when the libido is quite naturally subdued. Eros no longer impels them as it does the younger heroes.

Thus, "eros," from the Greek, meaning "sexual desire," refers here simply to that natural appetite. In Hemingway's, and others', hands it may sometimes appear to take on a mystique of its own, not different from the mysteries associated with romantic love, but I wish to keep it free from such burdens. However,

> Eros is not merely a demoniac power who creates chaos and destruction. . . . In all ages, this same power has been a source of irresistible energy. . . . [It] is also one of the greatest inspirations of human culture.[12]

Thinking of the image of the polarity of romance and agape, one would not be wrong in thinking of eros as a kind of prize over which they fight.

Agape, the Greek complement to eros, is also appropriate to Hemingway, and it refers here as in the original Greek to brotherly love or the Christian charity. There is a curious parallel between Old Testament love and romance. In the Old Testament, love is jealous, passionate, willful, and strained. In Genesis, Jacob loves only one of his two wives and only one of his twelve sons. But in his letters in the New Testament, St. Paul uses the word "agape," which was usually translated as "love" or "charity," and he gives the seminal Christian treatment of the problem of love and wrath (his own life, of course, was sharply divided between acts of oppression of the Christians and his conversion). He writes in Romans 12:9–21 of the application of brotherly love and says in I Corinthians 13:1: "Though I speak with the tongues of men and of angels, and have not love [agape], I am become as sounding brass or a tinkling cymbal." The chapter in I Corinthians is justly famous and is the classical statement from which my use of the term derives. Agape is not sublime or spiritual, but something very simple, homely, and human. As it was regarded by the early Christian apostle as the greatest, never-

[12] August Adam, *The Primacy of Love,* p. 130.

failing force of life, so is it today "the only life-force that has a future in this age of death."[13] Perhaps agape as described in its workings by Paul is not the ideal, tranquil love of Plato's *Symposium,* but "it is far more realistic and descriptive of what love really is."[14]

In a negative way, some of Hemingway's short stories deal with this kind of love. The son Joe in "My Old Man" is trying desperately to love his crooked father. Joe is not as ignorant and naive as he pretends to be, but his innocence demands of him that he continue to delude himself, for the loss of faith in and love for his father would be an unimaginable catastrophe. He therefore undergoes the further ironic necessity that he think of George Gardner, his father's crooked friend, as a "son of a bitch," even though Gardner tries to protect and help him when the father dies. Joe is painfully initiated into a world of violence and deceit. Forced to face the fact of his father's crookedness, he thinks he is left with nothing. As yet, this Hemingway hero cannot perceive the slight but nonetheless important care of a friend who to him is a son of a bitch.

Other stories from *In Our Time,* like "The Doctor and the Doctor's Wife" and "The Battler," are about the hatred that destroys agape. In the first story, the loss of love within Nick Adams' family undermines it with extreme subtlety. In "The Battler" Nick witnesses open and violent forms of the same loss of love. This story is also about an effort to regain some small measure of love through kindness and care, but the telling irony is that the lover, Bugs, is queer and the lovers are outcasts of their society. A distorted eros diseases the love. Ad Francis is "crazy"; both he and Bugs had resorted to violence in their past lives; and while Bugs is a homosexual, Ad Francis had married his "sister" and had then broken up the marriage. Together in jail, the punchy ex-prizefighter and the Negro criminal find each other and are able to recover a little of their own human dignity through mutual aid and dependence, even though it means for Bugs merely acting like a human being.

In the second volume of short stories, *Men Without Women* (1927), the love pattern continues: young heroes like Nick Adams are exposed to a world full of destructive forces, and they are often painfully separated from their romantic illusions (as in "Ten Indians"). Older heroes,

[13] Victor White, "Anathema-Maranatha," *Love and Violence,* p. 233.
[14] *Ibid.,* p. 230.

like Manuel in "The Undefeated," may have some measure of success or at least moral victory, but they posit no hopeful view for a world full of hypocrites and phonies, like the bullfight critic; except for Zurito the picador, Manuel is alone, and Zurito's compassion by itself cannot save or protect him. In "In Another Country" the Italian major is destroyed through an accident of fate that kills his young wife, whom he loves; when a man does find love, it is taken away from him one way or another. In "Hills Like White Elephants" the young man chooses to deny the responsibility for his unborn child; the product of eros must be certified by agape, but the commitment—the responsibility, the care, the involvement, the "sacrifice"—is here avoided. In "The Killers" the forces of destruction do not even bear the dignity of hate; they are hired gunmen who carry out impersonal, stereotyped murders. Sam the cook, George the counterman, and Nick Adams represent three increasing degrees of involvement, and only the innocent but concerned Nick is active in trying to avert destruction. Even the victim, the lonely and loveless Ole Andreson, is too far gone to accept the help of brotherhood when Nick brings it. In the ironically titled "An Alpine Idyll," one of the few presumably happy marriages in Hemingway's fiction ends in a grotesque way: the peasant husband, mindlessly and without malice, mutilates the body of his dead wife by hanging a lantern from her frozen jaw. Not every story in the *Men Without Women* volume deals explicitly with isolated men, as the title suggests, but the title is metaphorically appropriate in that the feeling of a lonely man well represents the dominant mood of the collection.

So does the title of the third volume of short stories, *Winner Take Nothing* (1933), suggest the similarly negative feelings of those tales of loss and destruction, of sickness and disintegration. But neither here nor in the earlier stories and novels is Hemingway nihilistic, as is sometimes claimed. "A Clean, Well-Lighted Place" contains the parody of the Lord's Prayer beginning "Our nada who art in nada," but the prayer is not Hemingway's central point (as Wayne C. Booth has pointed out): Hemingway, like the waiter, resists the nothingness, if only by desiring the comfort of a clean, well-lighted place.[15] Any pure nihilism, by definition, would be unreliable, and the waiter does perceive some hope in

[15] Wayne C. Booth, *The Rhetoric of Fiction*, pp. 299–300.

the "certain cleanness and order" that "was all *it* needed" (383; my emphasis). People, the world, everything is turned and twisted. The waiter will go home and try not to think about it, "and finally, with daylight, he would go to sleep. After all, he said to himself, it is probably only insomnia. Many must have it" (383). It is not Hemingway but his character who has insomnia, his characters who establish oppositions of hate (disaster or a world without love and faith) to clean, well-lighted places, to drinking, whoring, fishing, education, ambition, economics, patriotism, liberty, bread, gambling, or playing a radio—to anything that Mr. Frazer in "The Gambler, the Nun, and the Radio" calls an "opium of the people" (485–487). His list significantly omits art, and although education is an opiate, Mr. Frazer does believe in knowledge, perhaps the peculiar kind of nondiscursive knowledge that art conveys. Thinking is painful and generally to be avoided, but Mr. Frazer does think, and his belief in knowledge subsumes thought.

The evolution of heroes like Mr. Frazer into the highly reflective Santiago of Hemingway's last novel is a dangerous passage from a wonderfully evoked world of the concrete into a world where abstractions emerge from the concrete. Actually the earlier world conveys an abstraction—that of the quiet, strong courage to look into nada, or the heart of darkness. In the later world, Hemingway attempts to convey not only the still-necessary courage but also the sustaining spirit of a love that, like Mr. Frazer's felt insight or the waiter's perception of nada, passes all understanding.[16] That love is agape.

The Greek word for "madness in love"—which is what romance is—derives from eros rather than agape, agape being a warmth more of the heart than of the loins. It is perhaps possible to have a brotherly love without some notion of divinity—that is, to have socialism or some kind of mass hypnotic brotherhood—but the idea of agape usually includes the love of God for man (a grace which is not earned) and the love of man for God, as well as the love of man for man—"*caritas fraternitas*." An important distinction between agape and romance is that the former is selfless, the latter full of pride, honor, and self-respect. The sexual urge (eros) may be a "primitive force, but egoism in the long run can

[16] For further refutation of the charge of nihilism, see William Barrett, *Irrational Man,* Appendix I on "A Clean, Well-Lighted Place."

tyrannize in ways which even surpass the tyranny of sex,"[17] the image of sex as a tyrant being a peculiarly modern one. Eros is really creative and active and a love of the actual; romantic love is Oedipean, fearful, and passive (it is passion); it is love of the absolute.[18]

M. C. D'Arcy points out that the term charity had "been spoilt" by careless and too general usage. Thus the terms eros and agape were revived to purify the language of love, but in their turn those newer terms "have failed to keep orthodox and have been twisted to support the theories of original writers."[19] Just as he recognized the problem of meaning but went on to use the terms, so must I, hoping that this attempt at clarification and illustration through the short stories and a consistent use of the terms in the following chapters will induce a full meaning of the ideas behind the words.

[17] Adams, *The Primacy of Love,* p. 118.
[18] Valency, *In Praise of Love,* pp. 32–33.
[19] M. C. D'Arcy, *The Mind and Heart of Love,* p. 28.

# 2 ~ TRISTAN OR JACOB?

My Love is of a birth as rare
As 'tis for object strange and high:
It was begotten by despair
Upon Impossibility.

—Andrew Marvell, "The Definition of Love"

*Love* in her Sunny Eyes does basking play;
  *Love* walks the pleasant Mazes of her Hair;
*Love* does on both her Lips for ever stray;
And *sows* and *reaps* a thousand *kisses* there.
In all her outward parts *Love's* always seen;
  But, oh, He never went within.

—Abraham Cowley, "The Change"

THE SUN ALSO RISES was Hemingway's first serious venture into the craft of the novel, and in some ways the 1926 novel may be his best. The style is wonderfully controlled; there is no self-consciousness, no self-imitation; the characters are well-conceived and executed; and there is the feeling if not the certainty of multiple levels of meaning to the story. In short, the novel is an esthetic success.

As a reflection of its times it is also valuable, providing as it does a detailed historical picture of the expatriates and the self-styled lost generation that Hemingway referred to in his epigraph from Gertrude Stein. (In fact, one of his sensitive readers felt compelled to defend himself from a too-exact identification of himself with the Robert Cohn of the novel.)[1]

But in terms of Hemingway's present canon and the themes of love in his work as a whole, the interest of the novel is more than esthetic or historical. In *The Sun Also Rises,* the dominant themes that run through all of Hemingway's novels begin to emerge. The emphases of the different themes will vary as will the images which he will use to convey them, but basically the subject of Hemingway's novels has been chosen in this first novel, and that subject is love. If it were not for gradually changing attitudes toward that subject, the canon might truly be as monotonous as Hemingway's deprecators say it is, but with each novel some changes are evident, though the themes are familiar from *The Sun Also Rises* on.

[1] See Harold Loeb, *The Way It Was.*

Most simply, the love themes can be divided into three: eros, agape, and romantic love. (Supplementary classifications such as loneliness and love of nature can be seen as variations found from novel to novel in greater or lesser degree.) Using the threefold division in viewing *The Sun Also Rises,* one can see that it is not so much a novel about eros as it is about romantic love. Sex is surely of paramount interest to the characters, but to Hemingway, eros in this novel is secondary. It is as if Hemingway was carefully testing three views of love, and in this first novel romantic love is examined and rejected. Eros will subsequently receive a similar scrutiny, but in *The Sun Also Rises* it is as yet in the background, as is agape, the third and ultimately accepted form of love.

Further, the method of this first novel is much more heavily ironical than that of the work of the middle and later Hemingway. Thus one can see Hemingway destroying romantic illusions much easier than one can see the construction of positive ideals. In terms of the later Hemingway as well as in terms of the second, more hopeful, epigraph from Ecclesiastes, it is possible to read into *The Sun Also Rises* foreshadowing of the rebirth of love; but mainly the impression of the novel is negative. Loss rather than eternal return and renewal is clearly more strongly felt, in spite of the title and the Biblical epigraph. The irony seems a natural shield for this loss as well as for the novelist's and the hero's sensitivity, self-pity, and lack of a constructive, positive faith to fill the void. To keep from blubbering when a Brett presses against one's sexless body and moans, "Oh, Jake . . . we could have had such a damned good time together," one must hide behind the thin hard shield of irony and say, as Jake does, "Isn't it pretty to think so?"[2]

Jake *is* in desperate straits, but Hemingway reminds us, through Bill Gorton, that irony and pity are, after all, a little cheap: "Don't you know about Irony and Pity? . . . They're mad about it in New York. It's just like the Fratellinis [a team of circus acrobats] used to be" (114).

For all his worldly wisdom, his being an *aficionado,* his wide experience and skills, and his interesting friends, Jake Barnes strikes one as almost deserving of being indicted by Bill's jocular observations:

> "You're an expatriate. You've lost touch with the soil. You get precious. Fake European standards have ruined you. You drink yourself to death. You

[2] Ernest Hemingway, *The Sun Also Rises,* p. 247. Subsequent references in this chapter to this novel will be in the text itself.

become obsessed by sex. You spend all your time talking, not working. You are an expatriate, see? You hang around cafes."

"It sounds like a swell life," I said. "When do I work?"

"You don't work. One group claims women support you. Another group claims you're impotent." (115)

In his essay, "The Death of Love in *The Sun Also Rises,*" Mark Spilka explains that Jake as well as Cohn is a romantic, but that Jake's romanticism is a partially hidden weakness while Cohn's is public. Jake, Spilka continues, stands as an unhappy medium between the extremes of the Romantic Hero Cohn and the Code Hero Romero, the young bullfighter. The assumption is, of course, that romantic love is dead and that Cohn's clinging to it and Jake's failure to break away from an old reverence for and delight in it are stupid, silly weaknesses with no place in the "real" world.[3]

It would seem more accurate to say that *The Sun Also Rises* is not so much about the death of love as it is about its sickness, a sickness unto death, but by no means a fatal illness. As has been demonstrated by Denis de Rougemont in *Love in the Western World,* romantic love is still very much alive. More pertinently, in Hemingway's novel the chief proponent of it, Cohn, is complemented by Jake and Brett, whose frustrated love is much more like the traditional love of a Tristan and Iseult than is the idealistic love of Cohn for Brett. Furthermore Spilka fails to point out the survival and strength of agape or brotherly love among the characters. It is a love that is overshadowed by the clearly central romantic love, that is true, but its presence is definite, and in perspective it assumes importance and foreshadows its emergence in the later Hemingway.

The central theme of romantic love is expressed most clearly in the character of Robert Cohn, a well-to-do expatriate and a would-be professional writer. Robert Stephens calls him Hemingway's Don Quixote, but it would be more accurate to call him Hemingway's first Tristan, for

[3] Mark Spilka, "The Death of Love in *The Sun Also Rises,*" *Twelve Original Essays on Great American Novels,* Charles Shapiro, ed., pp. 238–256. See, however, the view of Cohn as the real hero of the novel as expressed by Arthur L. Scott, "In Defense of Robert Cohn," *College English,* 18 (March 1957), 309–314. Robert O. Stephens argues in a similar vein that Cohn's idealism is not entirely foolish or outdated: "Hemingway's Don Quixote in Pamplona," *College English,* 23 (December 1961), 216–218.

he is much more obsessed with love than Don Quixote ever was, and much less concerned with idealism in spheres beyond love's compass. Hemingway explicitly compares Cohn to a medieval chivalric knight when he describes him in the Pamplona brawl with Mike Campbell as "proudly and firmly waiting for the assault, ready to do battle for his lady love" (178). Cohn's view of Brett as a golden-haired angel is of course ridiculous, as Jake and the others see it, but Cohn's whole life with women has been molded on principles different from those of the other expatriates. And Cohn, Jake knows, is very stubborn; he will not surrender his ideals simply because others laugh at him and harbor other, equally misguided, ideals—or anti-ideals.

Lest one think that Cohn is not the pivotal character, if not the central one, Hemingway devotes the first two chapters of this economical novel to a history of Cohn's past and recent life. Like some subsequent Hemingway heroes, from Francis Macomber to Colonel Cantwell, Cohn had been married to a bitch. Presently, he has a mistress, Frances Clyne, to whom Jake satirically refers as Cohn's "lady," and she is another bitch. As Jake views it, Cohn has acquired her, as he did his wife, not because of love but because of convenience and style; as Frances says, "Robert's always wanted to have a mistress"—the idea of a mistress is what appealed to Cohn (51).

> I am sure he had never been in love in his life.
>
> He had married on the rebound from the rotten time he had in college, and Frances took him on the rebound from his discovery that he had not been everything to his first wife. He was not in love yet but he realized that he was an attractive quantity to women, and that the fact of a woman caring for him and wanting to live with him was not simply a divine miracle. This changed him so that he was not so pleasant to have around. (8–9)

Further, Cohn has, like Don Quixote, learned his way of life from books, specifically W. H. Hudson's *The Purple Land.*

> It recounts splendid imaginary amorous adventures of a perfect English gentleman in an intensely romantic land, the scenery of which is very well described. For a man to take it at thirty-four as a guide-book to what life holds is about as safe as it would be for a man of the same age to enter Wall Street direct from a French convent, equipped with a complete set of the more practical Alger books. Cohn, I believe, took every word of "The Purple Land" as literally as though it had been an R. G. Dun report. (9)

It is not unexpected that he would marry the wrong woman and have no forewarning that she might leave him, or that he would acquire Frances, with whom he has so little in common, or that he would fall in love "at first sight" with Brett—like Iseult someone else's woman, and like Quixote's servant girl misunderstood, not seen for the base thing she really is. Love for Cohn, as for all Tristans, is a sickness. It affects the mind and the body. It dominates and one becomes a slave to it. One is in love with love. As in the words of a popular song of the late thirties, "This can't be love because I feel so well." So Jake knows Cohn is in love when the latter's tennis game goes "all to pieces" (45). He must suffer, and the more he suffers, the happier (theoretically) he will be.

Even his break with Frances is needlessly prolonged and painful, almost as if Cohn enjoyed his mistress' acrimony: " 'We have dreadful scenes, and he cries and begs me to be reasonable, but he says he just can't do it [marry Frances]' " (47).

Frances in her turn fails to see the contradiction of her desire to marry Cohn. Now that she sees her prey slipping away, she realizes their two-and-a-half–year courtship has been a waste to her; when Jake defends Cohn to her, she replies that he doesn't know the real selfishness of Cohn, and then she caustically insults Cohn to his face in Jake's presence. In practical terms, her futile pursuit of security and wealth has been a waste of time, and her labeling of Cohn as selfish and cruel is not simply sour grapes. But how such realistic views, that could be reconciled to marriage, contrast with the ideal of wedded bliss! Frances perceives Cohn's real reason for not marrying his mistress: "if he marries me . . . that would be the end of all the romance" (51). And since Frances, aging a bit, her figure and face fading, sees little future as an Iseult, she is not afraid of touching on the truth of Cohn's actions.

In Book II, Cohn's Tristanizing can have free play. He has had his little fling with Brett (a *real* English lady), and now that the preliminary amour is over, he can get down to serious suffering, which is the joy of romantic love. Where Tristan had only King Mark as a rival, Cohn luxuriates in having as rivals for Brett's love Mike, her fiancé; Pedro Romero, her current lover; Jake, her handicapped but constant lover; and assorted peripheral admirers such as Bill Gorton and the ghost of her first true love, dead of dysentery in the War. Just as he endured having Frances berate him in front of Jake, so Cohn endures great abuse from his so-called friends at the Pamplona fiesta. Brett's lovers have various claims on her, but Cohn's claim is honored by the tradition with which he is imbued: he will play his role knowingly and well, accepting ridicule (141–142), but at the same time asserting the superiority earned by his suffering (162). He has no armed battles to fight, no guarded boudoirs to broach, but he is faithful to the principle of love. Mike brutally insults him:

> His face had the sallow, yellow look it got when he was insulted, but somehow he seemed to be enjoying it. The childish, drunken heroics of it. It was his affair with a lady of title. (178)

Finally even Brett is rude to him and drives him off. His best friend, Jake, has come to hate him, and specifically they hate him because he suffers (182).

When Cohn is finally driven to do real combat for his lady love, he then discovers the ineffectuality of his role. Having been a middleweight boxing champion in college, Cohn has no trouble winning separate pugilistic jousts with Jake, Mike, and Pedro Romero, who has displaced Cohn in Brett's affections, Cohn thinks. But the courageous Romero, though beaten badly, refuses to yield graciously. He promises to kill Cohn, and Brett refuses to leave with the Pyrrhic victor. No one plays it as it is in the movies or in W. H. Hudson's *The Purple Land.* The script has been rewritten, and no one told Cohn that his role was thrown out.

> That damn Cohn. He should have hit somebody the first time he was insulted, and then gone away. He was so sure that Brett loved him. He was going to stay, and true love would conquer all. (199)

Jake makes fun of Cohn's chivalric suffering, but his and Brett's notions of love are just as insidious, perhaps more so because of their hypocrisy and their concealment of their notions behind a tough facade. Jake clearly views Cohn as a misguided romantic, and by dating the whore Georgette he denies to Brett that *he* is getting romantic: he is bored, not romantic (23). But Brett and Jake follow the pattern of Tristan and Iseult with little variation. Theirs is a hopeless love, the course of which is filled with the obstacles of love: rivals aplenty, Jake's maiming wound, and Jake's mixed allegiances. Tristan's problems were similar. One could even imagine Georgette as a type of Iseult of the White Hand, the first Iseult's (Brett's) rival.

But the chief parallel is not in action or characters but in the common theme of suffering for love, of being possessed by love and made its slave, of having no love except outside the bonds of marriage, and of the spiritualization of love or its severance from man's animal nature. Cohn's sufferings are academic; he goes literally by the book, and that is, no doubt, why he is scorned. Brett and Jake are really sick with love. And thus the essential comedy of the whole story—of any romantic love story—in which the lovers claim a special role and ask for a special sympathy because they are really crazy (only *they* are entitled, they would seem to plead, to belittle the scapegoat Cohn who plays at insanity but really isn't mad, as they are). Once after extended classroom discussion of this novel, a prettily smiling coed asked, "If Jake and Brett are really in love, why don't they get married?" More worldly students grinned and guffawed, but the coed had, inadvertently, no doubt, asked a very intelligent question on the mythic level.

The success and continued acclaim of the novel is remarkable in that Hemingway has created such a convincing version of an old theme that is usually read as an attack on that old Tristan and Iseult story—the death of love in *The Sun Also Rises*—but this story is of a sick love, a hypochondriac love, of lovers who enjoy poor health, poor love, sick love. But the love never dies.

At Brett and Jake's first meeting in the novel, the lovers escape from their friends at a dance to be alone. The action and tone are greatly restrained, but there is no mistaking the source of Brett's pleading cry: "Oh, darling, I've been so miserable" (24). There is more than frustrated eros in the scenes in which Brett and Jake are alone. After all, Brett has slept with just about whoever pleased her. Jake's wound is presumably not an emasculation but the loss of his penis, and thus he has no accompanying loss or diminution of sexual desire.[4] Tristan's wound was only symbolically castrative, and he voluntarily abstained from intercourse with Iseult even when there were no obstacles to his pleasure. But Jake can never have intercourse with Brett; his predicament is a

[4] See George Plimpton, "Ernest Hemingway," *Paris Review*, 18 (Spring 1958), 61–82. Reprinted in *Writers at Work*, second series, p. 230.

little laughable, as Jake himself points out (26). And to the ancient Greeks who regarded romantic love as a sickness and a calamity, his wound would be funny, but it is not funny to the romanticist who lives for love.

Brett is compelled by her love for Jake; she has no freedom. She kisses him and then she breaks away from him because she "can't stand it." She turns "all to jelly" when he touches her, and she has a look in her eyes as if she were possessed. Apparently they have tried to find some method of mutual physical relief that was a "hell" that ended in failure, but when Jake suggests that they "keep away from each other," Brett insists, " 'But darling, I have to see you. It isn't all that [sex] you know.' "

" 'No, but it always gets to be.' "

Then they discuss Jake's wound:

> "It's funny," I said. "It's very funny. And it's a lot of fun, too, to be in love."
> "Do you think so?" her eyes looked flat again.
> "I don't mean fun that way. In a way it's an enjoyable feeling."
> "No," she said. "I think it's hell on earth."
> "It's good to see each other."
> "No. I don't think it is."
> "Don't you want to?"
> "I have to." (26–27)

Brett is compelled to torture herself and to enjoy her torment. Before rejoining their friends she asks Jake for just one more kiss.

When he retires that night, he looks at his body in the mirror, thinks some more of his problem, thinks that Brett "only wanted what she couldn't have," cries, finally falls asleep, and is shortly awakened, at four-thirty, by the drunken Brett's arrival with Count Mippipopolous. She simply must torture herself about Jake, that unattainable commodity, even if it means being rude and thoughtless, that is, lacking respect for her love object—in effect, having passion, lacking agape. And Jake, though knowing Brett for what she is, is still touched by her presence (30–34).

In short, though Jake perceives the folly of their relationship more sharply than Brett does, he nonetheless submits to the tyranny of romantic love. Telling Cohn about Brett, Jake with conscious irony says that during the war Brett's "own true love . . . kicked off with the dysentery" (39). The idealistic Cohn won't believe Brett would subsequently marry anyone she didn't love, but Jake, accepting the terms of the adulterous Tristan-Iseult love, says that Brett has already married twice without love.

Later that same day it is Brett's turn to use the phrase "true love," and she of course applies it to Jake during one of their frequent scenes of misery. They avow their love for one another, and they think what a "bad time" they have because of their consummate inconsummable love. With her love vow on her lips and unknown to Jake, Brett is planning her trip to San Sebastian where she will have a brief fling with Robert Cohn, Jake's friend, before her fiancé (whom she later admits she hasn't thought of in a week) returns from Britain! Jake wants to try living together with Brett, but, says Brett, it is better for Jake and better for her that they live apart (55).

Jake hates Cohn and is jealous of him when he learns of his tryst with Brett (she herself casually tells Jake of the affair). A King Mark like Mike Campbell is one thing, but Iseult shouldn't "take up social service," as Jake sarcastically says (84). Yet Jake still "loves" her, and his passion again returns to submerge his irony and bitterness. On his fishing trip with Bill Gorton, he reads a romantic novel by A. E. W. Mason, and once more Jake ironically uses the phrase "true love" (120). He realizes the comic stupidity of the "wonderful" story in which a man falls into a glacier and his bride waits twenty-four years "for his body to come out on the moraine," but still he voluntarily chooses to read the story. He begins to protest too much. Like many another denigrator, Jake accompanies his irony with a large amount of pity, in this case, self-pity. Both Jake and Brett have to let others know how they suffer; so Jake tells Bill about his love for Brett, and Brett tells Mike about her affairs, and tells Jake about her new-found passion for Pedro Romero. At the same time, she has to know if *Jake* still loves her (183), for he is still the only person she has (no doubt because he is the only person she has not "had" and never can have). She apparently justifies her promiscuity and torture of Jake, her true love, on the grounds of her unique role; she is the fair lady and, tortured by love herself, her role is to torture, to be, as Cohn calls her, a Circe.

Only after Jake acts as her pimp with Romero does he finally begin to emerge from his passive role, and it is Cohn who has to label Jake for what he is (190). Of course, in resorting to violence, Cohn also plays the fool, but after his Quixotic fights with Jake, Mike, and Romero, Jake's attitudes seem to clear. The progress of the book is toward a frenzied, idiotic climax of action and "romance" at the end of the fiesta. Afterwards there is calmness, cleanliness, catharsis—at least for Jake. His love for Brett has undergone a subtle change. From unreasoning passion it has gone through a period of bitter awareness to an ending which describes a relationship of responsibility and care. Passion is submerged if not subdued.

That is, there is the growing presence of agape in the course of the novel, and it is finally extended to include the two great lovers themselves; the lovers are at last ready to love. In Book I, the epitome of love was Count Mippipopolous, a phony Greek count who is "one of us," (32), as Brett says, because he has taste, manners, the right values, and above all, past sufferings (60). The Count is "always in love" (61), for love too has a place in his system of values. The Count is a charming host, but in spite of his frankness Brett and Jake never become intimate with him. He remains an eccentric.

In Book II, the focus of this other possibility of love is Bill Gorton, Jake's writer friend who goes fishing with him before the fiesta. Gorton is significantly different from the expatriates in that he has remained at home and he works. He is productive as are none of the others except Jake himself. Perhaps the symbol of this difference is the sport of fishing—the fish themselves representing a kind of fertility. Bill and Jake meet a materialistic tourist and a border guard (a representative of authority) who do not care for fishing. Cohn is not keen for it either, and Brett and Mike don't arrive in time to join Bill and Jake as scheduled. Without the parasitic, unloving others, Bill and Jake have a splendid, carefree trip. Their mutual affection is complemented by their easy friendship with the pastoral Basques with whom they ride in a bus into the green, undefiled mountains where the fast, cold trout stream runs. They also meet the pleasant Wilson-Harris, another fisherman, another disciple of the sexless brotherhood of man, who is greatly touched by Bill and Jake's friendliness. The trouble is that the Burguete interlude is just that—an idyllic escape into an unreal world of simple military or boyhood relationships. One must go back to work, and one must go back to a more complicated, sexual society where women rather than fish contest with the lovers.

Back at Pamplona, then, Jake assumes a new social role that can be seen as a maturing of the uncomplicated, male love of fellow fishermen. At the fiesta the parallels between Jake and the sexless steers that herd the fertile bulls have been prepared for by the earlier establishment of parallels between Jake and Ecclesiastes, literally the Preacher or "steer" of the Old Testament.

Because of the title of the novel and its second epigraph, one may assume that Hemingway read the book of Ecclesiastes. Like the Hebrew writer living in another Waste Land, Hemingway too was skeptical and pessimistic, and his hero Jake Barnes had the same doubts and the same sharp awareness of transiency and death.[5] Learning and wisdom are futile, for God's ways are mysterious, the Preacher says (Eccles. 7:16, 8:17, 11:5, 12:12). "Time and chance happeneth to . . . all" (Eccles. 9:11). In the midst of prosperity and life is the seed of desolation and death (Eccles. 12:1–7). There are, however, some positive values to cling to: food and drink are good (Eccles. 2:3, 2:24–26, 5:18–20, 8:15, 9:7, 10:19); companionship and fellowship are good—"two are better than one" (Eccles. 4:9–12); a wise man has heart, but a fool does not (Eccles. 10:2); a good name is desirable—one should live by the "code" (Eccles. 7:1); this means, in part, helping others (Eccles. 11:1–2); in spite of impermanence and futility, life is sweet (Eccles. 9:4–6). The direct parallels are extended and consistent.

Like the author of Ecclesiastes, Jake Barnes is alienated from his faith, Catholicism, which he clings to but cannot sincerely practice. Pragmatically, it does not work, but it seems to offer to fill the void in his spirit, and he wants it to work. In Jake, Hemingway is moving from the even more complete lack of faith of Frederic Henry in *A Farewell To Arms* to the more complete acceptance of Robert Jordan (with a Biblical allusion in his last name) in *For Whom the Bell Tolls* and of the Catholic fisherman Santiago in *The Old Man and the Sea.* The reader is reminded that "Jake" is "a hell of a biblical name" (22), and if one should add up the total of all Hemingway heroes, one could see Jake

[5] Ecclesiastes 3:1, 7:1–4, 8:8. Subsequent references to Ecclesiastes will be in the text itself.

Barnes as the first stage of the composite hero's parallel to Jacob's life, which ran the cycle of sin and fraud in youth, much suffering and then repentance in maturity, and final exaltation of God's ways in his old age.

Another possible parallel occurs in Book II where the setting shifts to San Sebastian. It is there that Brett goes for her fling with Cohn and later for a pre-honeymoon with Mike. It is also the place where Jake goes after the Pamplona fiesta (Book III). Saint Sebastian and Jake have significant ironic similarities: the saint was martyred during a Roman saturnalia—Jake goes through agony because of his impotence and Brett's great sexuality; after being stoned and shot through with arrows (equivalent to Jake's suffering), Sebastian was nursed back to health by a devout woman—Brett has not only destructive but recuperative powers upon Jake, Cohn, and Mike. Of taking Cohn to San Sebastian, she says it was "good for him" (83), and Jake says she was probably good for Pedro Romero too (241). She literally does nurse Romero back to health, just as she had nursed Jake when she first met him in a hospital during the war (38); "She loves looking after people," Mike says (203). Furthermore, in sacred art Sebastian is usually depicted as a young soldier, which Jake once was. In these parallels, even if the details are extravagant, the general image of martyrdom is clear enough, and Brett's complexity is emphasized.

Jake is the one even mildly religious character in the central group of characters. He is, however, only "technically" Catholic, he explains (124). Like the Preacher of Ecclesiastes, he is skeptical and yet devout; he does not believe, but he wants to believe. He goes through the motions of his faith hoping that somehow it will succeed in giving him an anchor in his disintegrating worldly milieu. Jake is world-weary as the Preacher is: "All things have I seen in the days of my vanity" (Eccles. 7:15), but, also like the Preacher, Jakes does not completely abandon his god. Thus Jake, though bitterly, considers the Church's counsel regarding sex—"don't think of it"—and is always noting and visiting churches. Notre Dame in Paris was "squatting against the night sky" (77), a personification picturing Mary in a bestial pose. On his trip to Spain, another Catholic country, he "took a look at the cathedral" in Bayonne, France (90). He notes churches in Spain, and Pamplona is a city of churches with a "great brown cathedral, and the broken skyline of the other churches" (93–94). A monastery dominates Burguete where

Jake and Bill go fishing; it is up in the mountains, like Kilimanjaro "cold" and "high" (108). Jake notes a steel engraving of Nuestra Señora de Roncesvalles in his Burguete room (109), and later Bill, "good old Wilson-Harris," and he visit the monastery. Bill and Harris admit they are "not much on those sort of places," but Jake says nothing (128).

In Pamplona Jake goes to church remarkably often for a skeptic. He first thought the facade of the cathedral ugly, but he later liked it, and it is "dim and dark" and peaceful inside. Jake prays there in a rather naive manner, but at least he prays and thinks about praying, regretting that he is "such a rotten Catholic" but holding out some hope of being a better one in the future (96–97). After returning to Pamplona, Jake casually mentions going to church "a couple of times, once with Brett" (150). Jake implies that he still confesses himself, for Brett wants to witness his confession. Jake says she could not and adds, significantly, that "it would be in a language she did not know" (151). Both literally —it would be in Spanish—and figuratively the Brett who then goes to the pagan rite of having her fortune told cannot understand his faith. Even in the excitement of the festival, Jake continues to go to church; he goes to mass the first day of the fiesta, noting that the saturnalian "San Fermin is also a religious festival" that begins with a big religious procession which Jake apparently followed (153, 155). Once more he goes to church with Brett, and once more the pagan fertility bitch-goddess is rejected: she has no hat, no symbol of deference. But outside in the bright sunlight she realizes her role as the dancing Spaniards form a gay circle of homage around her: "They wanted her as an image to dance around" (155). The church remains as a backdrop for the frenzied action. Jake walks as far as the church, once by himself and once with Brett (156, 182). A third time he and Brett go to church "Where the show started on Sunday" (208). Brett tries to pray for Romero, but she stiffens and becomes "damned nervous. . . . I'm damned bad for a religious atmosphere," she says (208). Jake jokes about praying, but he also says praying works for him and he is "pretty religious" (209). Later Jake tells Brett that "some people have God" (245).

Jake also apparently likes to bathe, to purify or rebaptize himself. Brett too rushes off to bathe several times: "Must clean myself. . . . Must bathe," she says after returning from her vacation with Cohn (74), and after a night in a hotel (that looks like a brothel) with her fiancé Mike, she also "must bathe" (83). Twice during the wild fiesta she also has to bathe (144, 159). The other romantic, Cohn, also tries to wash away his dirt after his brief affair with Brett (81, 96, 97). But it is Jake who makes almost a ritual, like baptism, out of bathing. After the disappointing, fight-marred end of the partly pagan fiesta, Jake returns to the fertile sea for purification. Hemingway describes at length two swims: the water is green, dark, and cold (235); it is also buoyant—"It felt as though you could never sink" (237). After the renewal of the sea, Jake is ready to answer the call of help from those without even his tentative faith, once more to play the role of sexless priest and steer for his friends, his "parish," his "herd."

In addition to these more or less direct allusions to Ecclesiastes in particular and Judeo-Christian attitudes in general—especially to agape—Jake's relation to bullfighting is also fraught with religious overtones, as is bullfighting itself. As with the story of Saint Sebastian, the Roman, or pagan, and Christian elements overlap. Bullfighting was a favorite sport in imperial Rome, and Pedro Romero's last name hints at a Roman root even if there is no etymological connection. The *espadas* pass through a trying novitiate just as priests do before they may perform publicly. The pomp and brilliance of costume and decoration in the *plaza de toros* parallels the richness of dress and the colorful setting of the Catholic Church. In the *corrida de toros* itself there are the trinities of the triple mule team, of the *espadas*, of the *suertes* or divisions of the fight, and of the bulls, each fighter usually getting three in one afternoon. The *suertes* divide into lancing, planting the darts, and killing, with parallels to the Crucifixion that Hemingway would specifically refer to in the later novels *Across the River and into the Trees* and *The Old Man and the Sea.*

Pedro Romero stays in a room whose two beds are "separated by a monastic partition" (163), and, as with a priest, his retinue believes that women will corrupt the young bullfighter. Montoya, Jake's *aficionado* friend, observes that "He shouldn't mix in that stuff" (172). The very word *aficion*—"aficion means passion" (131)—recalls the similarity of love imagery in the language of the Catholic Church since the Middle Ages. Those who are *aficionados* have a secret fellowship that is discovered by "a sort of oral spiritual examination" concluded by a laying on of hands: "nearly always there was the actual touching. It seemed as though they wanted to touch you to make it certain" (132). If you had *aficion*, like faith, anything could be forgiven you, as Montoya initially forgives Jake his friends who lack it. It seems significant that of Jake's friends it is the Jewish Cohn who is the least interested in the *corrida*; he is even afraid he might be bored (162). Like the revered blood of Christ and the symbolic Communion wine, the blood of the bullfights disturbs only the uninitiated; Brett learns from Jake how to watch and then comments, "Funny. . . . How one doesn't mind the blood" (211). Also remindful of the Passion is the sense of tragedy that the *aficionados* derive from the fights: "People went . . . to be given tragic sensations" (214).

Hemingway once circumvented the question of parallels between the bullfight and the characters, but he does have Jake make a comparison between one bull and a boxer, which Cohn once was (139), and the parallels are instructive.[6] Jake's relation to his friends is paralleled by the steers' role in the *corridas*. The sexless steers—"like old maids"—quiet the bulls in the corrals and keep them from fighting. Sometimes the steers are gored by the bulls. "Can't the steers do anything?" Bill asks. "No," Jake answers. "Must be swell being a steer," Bill later adds (133). At the corral Brett observes that the steers don't look happy, but the bull is "beautiful." The bulls, like Jake's sexually active friends, "are only dangerous when they're alone, or only two or three of them together" (140). Bill makes the analogy clear when he says, "Don't you ever detach me from the herd," and Cohn says,"It's no life being a steer" (141). In the end, Jake's role as a steer is once more demonstrated when he rescues Brett. Jake recalls that he was the one who introduced the bitch-goddess to one bull, Cohn, and later to another bull, Romero. Then he must go fetch her back to the custody of still another bull, Mike (239). The Catholic priest is also celibate, also has a role of explaining ritual to the uninitiated, of confirming and blessing (laying on of hands), and of protecting his flock—his "herd," if you will.

Ecclesiastes once more provides the text and enlightening parallels that Hemingway must have been aware of. Men are like beasts: "they themselves are beasts. For that which befalleth the sons of men befalleth beasts . . ." (Eccles. 3:18–19). The Biblical Preacher, like Jake,

[6] See Plimpton's interview (note 4 above), p. 230.

believes it is good to study death, which is the real subject of the bullfight. Further, the Preacher sees that the battle is not to the strong—the bulls—as the race is not to the swift, nor riches to men of understanding (Eccles. 9:11). Thus a good man—a good preacher, a good steer—must help others: "Cast thy bread upon the waters: for thou shalt find it after many days," as Jake does, and a good man must be content in God's wisdom (Eccles. 11:1). All may be vanity, but yet man does not know the ways of God: ". . . thou knowest not what is the way of the spirit . . ." (Eccles. 11:5). Though he may not be a bull, a live steer is better than a dead bull, just as "a living dog is better than a dead lion," another beast symbolic of eros (Eccles. 9:4). Even more startling is the suggestion in Ecclesiastes that a man (Jake) is lucky to be sexless, for woman is a trap: "And I find more bitter than death the woman, whose heart is snares and nets, and her hands as bands: whoso pleaseth God shall escape from her; but the sinner shall be taken by her" (Eccles. 7:26). Jake may be unhappy, but he is not tormented by Brett in the way Mike, Cohn, and Romero are; they know they are able to possess Brett. To Cohn, at least, Brett is quite appropriately a Circe, a goddess who turns men into swine (144).

Like the Preacher of Ecclesiastes and Jake's namesake, the Biblical Jacob, Jake Barnes is passing through a period of doubt and vexation in which superficial values and actions are seen for what they are, even though they may be sanctioned by the Church, like the action of the pilgrims who monopolize the dining car on Jake and Bill's train. Neither Jake nor Hemingway nor the Preacher seem quite sure of what is enduring and valuable, but like Jacob they are learning and perhaps will discover a fuller faith as they grow older. The essence of this faith is perhaps imaged in Jake's description of how Romero fought a good bull especially for his loved one, Brett:

> Pedro Romero had the greatness. He loved bull-fighting, and I think he loved the bulls, and I think he loved Brett. Everything of which he could control the locality he did in front of her all that afternoon. Never once did he look up. He made it stronger that way, and did it for himself, too, as well as for her. Because he did not look up to ask if it pleased he did it all for himself inside, and it strengthened him, and yet he did it for her, too. But he did not do it for her at any loss to himself. He gained by it all through the afternoon. (216)

This doing for another without individual loss is a sign of agape which the simple uncorrupted Romero possesses. Knowing her own self-centeredness and perhaps perceiving this somewhat paradoxical performance as Jake does, Brett can also make a paradoxical sacrifice. In the quiet but climactic Book III, she knows that her selfishness and her bitchery would eventually hurt Romero, as Montoya predicted, and so she selflessly drives him away (241–243).

Jake also seems to have come to a greater knowledge of his condition than at any other time. It is true that the concluding note of the novel is still one of irony and pity, but he does not give way to maudlin tears or resort to bitter invective over Brett's cruelty in using him as a pimp and then a rescuer when she is down and out in Madrid. We are not much, they say by their actions, but we are all that we have. Like the polite bartender of the last chapter, they must exercise some devotion to each other by simple acts of kindness. Such is the skeptical but not nihilistic conclusion of Hemingway's first novel.

# 3 ~ THE TOUGH ROMANCE

Beauty, strength, youth, are flowers but fading seen;
Duty, faith, love, are roots, and ever green.

—George Peele, "Farewell to Arms"

I am giddy; expectation whirls me round.
Th' imaginary relish is so sweet
That it enchants my sense. What will it be
When that the watery palates taste indeed
Love's thrice-repurèd nectar? Death, I fear me,
Sounding destruction, or some joy too fine,
Too subtle, potent, tuned too sharp in sweetness
For the capacity of my ruder powers.

This is the monstrousity in love, lady, that the will is infinite and the execution confined, that the desire is boundless and the act a slave to limit.

—Shakespeare, "Troilus and Cressida," III, ii

IN THE FIRST CHAPTER, Hemingway's early period was divided from his middle and transitional period at the point of Catherine Barkley's death, the event that concludes *A Farewell to Arms.* A common technique of fiction complicates the discussion of this novel in relation to Hemingway's ideas about and dramatization of love, and that technique is the use of Frederic Henry as the first-person narrator.[1] If one reads his story without understanding the direction that the first-person narration gives it, one may very well come to a far different conclusion from the point that Hemingway is making.

While it is true that Catherine's death concludes the novel, her death is really only the end of a beginning as far as Frederic Henry is concerned; he is now ready to reflect on his recent experiences and to present them to the reader, and he is a very sophisticated narrator. He is not merely recounting events in an objective way. (If he were, the advantage of the first-person over a third-person point of view would be questionable.) Like many of the protagonists of the short stories and like Jake Barnes, another first-person narrator, Henry has undergone an initiatory and learning experience that he is now ready to interpret. The wonderful sense of immediacy that Henry can convey in this most brilliantly written of Hemingway's novels should not mislead the reader into thinking that the events transpire and are immediately recorded in a diary or epistolary form.

[1] Earl Rovit, *Ernest Hemingway* (pp. 98–106), has come to similar conclusions about the meaning of the novel as determined by the point of view.

Nor is Henry a naive innocent like a Huckleberry Finn; he looks back on his adventures but without conveying the degree of understanding that Twain, through brilliant use of an ironic "unreliable" narrator, enabled the reader to experience. The vividness of scene and dialogue in *A Farewell to Arms* is countered by the heavy and carefully prepared feeling of doom that makes us see Henry the narrator as strangely detached from and lifeless in the vivid world that he can nonetheless evoke around his immediate past, the subject of his story. His past catatonic state is a brilliant anachronism: all the events that have created his sense of loss and isolation have already occurred when he begins the presentation of his story, and each scene that he recreates for us is distorted by the climactic event of Catherine's death at the end of the novel.

For example, in the mess-hall scenes of Chapters 2 and 3, Henry is set apart from his messmates superficially by his nationality but profoundly by his "tragic" experience, but it is an experience that has not yet happened. His isolation is anachronistic in that he creates the feeling of it by his hindsight into the scenes, just as he "remembers" in Chapter 1 that the soldiers marching to their deaths looked as though they were pregnant (an image that foreshadows, of course, Catherine's death in childbirth). Throughout the novel, Henry uses rain and Catherine's feelings about the rain in the same portentous way. (She sees herself dead in it, and sure enough—) Unlike Huck Finn, Frederic Henry is thus demonstrated to be terribly literary. The clinching passage comes early in the novel and justifiably should arouse the reader's curiosity, as it indirectly informs him that Henry has undergone a learning experience that he is now reflecting on and writing about. In an initially cryptic comment Henry says that the priest in his outfit

> had always known what I did not know and what, when I learned it, I was always able to forget. But I did not know that then, although I learned it later.[2]

What is the "it" he learned but the entire initiatory experience with war and death, Catherine and love that the novel is about? The pattern of the novel, like that of *Adventures of Huckleberry Finn*, is of the nar-

[2] Ernest Hemingway, *A Farewell to Arms,* p. 14. Subsequent references to this novel in this chapter will be in the text itself.

rator's sequential exposure to evil, but unlike Huck Finn (whose "reversion" to adolescence in the last third of the novel many critics do not like), Frederic Henry becomes aware of the nature of the evil that exists around and within him.[3] Henry *thinks* more and more as the novel progresses, though sometimes he thinks against his will because some things, as Joseph Conrad's Winnie Verloc put it, do not bear much looking into. The meaning of the novel must be inherent in the pattern and, again like *Huckleberry Finn,* it involves many disguises and frequent reversals of the expected.[4] In Chapter 1 the disguise motif is set most importantly in the figure of the soldiers who look as if they were pregnant, but it is also present in the literal camouflaging of the mechanized instruments of doom, the big tractor-drawn guns that are disguised by the growth of life, "green leafy branches and vines" (3). This irony is implicit in Henry's view of the war: when seven thousand soldiers die of cholera, he says that "only" seven thousand died (4), and towns are captured "handsomely," and the destructive war is "going well" (5–6).

Images of camouflage enlarge to reinforce a number of ironies central to the theme. Identities are confused, roles are exchanged, motives are misunderstood, and deceit, hypocrisy, and phoniness are rife in a succession of dramatic ironies: Henry is an American in Italian uniform; he pretends to love Catherine, who substitutes him for her dead fiancé; the whole war is theatrical and ridiculous (Chapter 6); Henry learns that some patriots, some singers, and some doctors are phonies (Chapters 15 and 19); he and Catherine conceal their lovemaking in the hospital as he conceals the empty wine and liquor bottles that he accumulates (Chapters 16 and 22); they go to a "fixed" horse race, which has symbolic overtones of a fixed love, especially in view of Hemingway's frequent use of the horse as an erotically symbolic beast (Chapter 20); the two virgin sisters misunderstood Aymo's Italian and his gestures (Chapter 28); in the disaster at Caporetto the Italians greatly fear Germans who have been rumored to be dressed in Italian uniforms, and the battle police are summarily trying and executing their own officers (as Henry had himself shot an Italian sergeant) while the Germans—the enemy—are attacking without any resistance (Chapters 27–30);

[3] Cf. Philip Young, *Ernest Hemingway,* Ch. 6, for an extension of the relation of Huckleberry Finn to the Hemingway hero.

[4] Rovit, (*Ernest Hemingway,* pp. 100–101) also cites the disguise motif.

after his escape from the battle police, Henry disguises himself first as an enlisted man, then as a civilian (Chapters 32–33), and as a civilian he "felt [like] a masquerader" (260); after his reunion with Catherine, they use deceit to escape to Switzerland and there pass themselves off first as cousins and then as a married couple (Chapters 36–37); masked like a doctor, Henry watches helplessly as in the final reversal, the act of birth ends in death (Chapter 41).

All these ironies, reversals, and disguises are metaphors and preparation for Henry's disillusionment—first with the war which he had presumably volunteered to be in, and second with his romance with Catherine, which, to give him credit, he had not initially volunteered for. An intrinsic though literary precedent within the details of the narrative has thus been set for the reader to perceive the tendency and effect of Henry as an extraordinary kind of narrator.

Though it is perhaps easy to accept the idea of an ironic or unreliable narrator or a narrator who tells about a radical change in his own character, in practice the convention is sometimes deceptive, and Hemingway's use of it here has probably caused many misreadings of the love theme in the novel. One such misunderstanding is reflected in Edmund Wilson's passing comments on the novel.[5] He calls it a tragedy in which the lovers are innocent victims, and this view he supports through reference to Hemingway's own comment that *A Farewell to Arms* was a *Romeo and Juliet.* Perhaps having read *A Farewell to Arms* not too sympathetically, Wilson gives evidence of never having read *Romeo and Juliet,* or at least of subscribing rather carelessly to the popular notions of what that play is about. In light of Hemingway's remark, a cursory examination of some parallelisms in the works may be instructive. As Wilson says, both pairs of lovers are star-crossed, but are they tragic? Without further worrying that problem of whether tragedy is possible today or is ever possible in the genre of the novel, one can certainly see the qualitative difference between *Romeo and Juliet* and Shakespeare's great tragedies. Further, Romeo lacks tragic self-awareness; Mercutio with his antiromantic wit keeps the play from

5 Edmund Wilson, "Hemingway: Gauge of Morale," *The Wound and the Bow.* Leslie A. Fiedler, *Love and Death in the American Novel,* gives another brilliant misreading (p. 306) because he assumes the complete Ernestness of Frederic Henry.

slopping over; and even Juliet hints at Shakespeare's realization of the foolishness of the conventions of romantic love. And yet the play can quite rightly be considered as the first great expression of romantic love in English literature. Likewise *A Farewell to Arms* can be wept over—it is truly moving, but largely, I suspect, because most of us have had our sensibilities trained to be moved almost automatically by such stuff. But we also see with Mercutio's eyes (or Rinaldi's and the priest's in the novel) while we *feel* with Romeo's whole being.

Wilson's view is very well, as far as it goes, but Wilson thinks of *A Farewell to Arms* as a limited success because of the flatness or conventionality of the characterizations, a view that indicates that he regards the Frederic Henry of the action of the novel as the same Frederic Henry who is the later narrator. The distinction is crucial for a fair view of Hemingway's skill. Appreciation of this manipulation of point of view doesn't mean that Hemingway has here discovered his love ethic, because the novel is like *The Sun Also Rises* in being negative, a novel of disillusionment that holds only slight hope for the future of a character like Frederic Henry. Thus these two readings of *A Farewell to Arms* are possible, but neither is wholly right by itself. My comments here assume Henry's growing awareness of the emptiness of romance, but the moralist in me despises the earlier, ignorant protagonist; and even at the end of the novel his knowledge is felt rather than intellectualized. Always, however, the important distinction must be remembered that Hemingway is not Henry. While one may deliberately criticize the "ethic" of Frederic Henry, the more impassioned the abuse, the greater the implication of the success, in a technical sense, of Hemingway's novel. The reader becomes completely absorbed and perhaps partisan, either for romance or against it. (And I strongly suspect the judgment of those readers who admire the "emotional impact" of the "love" story. It is a very good novel, but for reasons other than those that Hollywood periodically capitalizes on by producing screen versions of it.)

Chronologically the novel is a flashback in the life history of the Hemingway hero. Frederic Henry is not, of course, Jake Barnes, but he bears many similarities to him, as Philip Young has pointed out. Assuming some continuity between the Hemingway heroes, can one also assume that the protagonist of *A Farewell to Arms* is not only younger but also less mature in his "love ethic," or does the younger hero represent an advancing stage in the development of Hemingway's changing views of love? Perhaps it is best to read *A Farewell to Arms* simply as a complementary, little-changed view of love. The second novel does not repeat the views of the first novel but fills in with different emphases Hemingway's earlier statement. Both *The Sun Also Rises* and this second novel closely parallel T. S. Eliot's *The Waste Land.* There is the emphasis on the seasons and the contrast between natural cycles and symbols and the human cycle of disjointed activities. And just as we can imagine Jake as an older Lieutenant Henry, so do we note that Brett Ashley shares with Catherine her Circe-like powers to ruin her lover. One general difference even strengthens the connection and may be thought of as the difference between Hemingway's epic knight (Jake) and his chivalric knight (Henry). The former held the manly virtues of courage, strength, and loyalty in highest esteem; the latter admired love and gentleness. *The Sun Also Rises* is Hemingway's *chanson de geste,* in which the action and love are violent and the "women are often inclined to evil and always burning with desire while the men are by nature temperate and businesslike."[6]

In general outline, *A Farewell to Arms* is chivalric in its emphasis on the love story, though war provides the background and Hemingway moves back and forth between those strange but time-honored bed-companions, love and war. Against his will, a young officer falls deeply in love with a beautiful nurse—the scenario goes. The horrors of war are contrasted with the wonders of love, but in the end Death the master reaches the hero, who thought he had escaped death by escaping the war. Ironically, it is through love that he is hurt. Still, love is better than war.

But this slightly absurd summary is by no means a complete statement of the essence of the novel that is, rather, about another confusion and distortion of values and love—as in *The Sun Also Rises,* in which the reader does not have to condone the hero and heroine's actions though he must become emotionally involved in their human condition. Also like *The Sun Also Rises, A Farewell to Arms* is one of the best written of Hemingway's books. It is in an examination of the attitudes

[6] Maurice Valency, *In Praise of Love,* p. 54.

of the chief characters—but not perhaps of Hemingway's attitudes—that the reader is frustrated and annoyed. *A Farewell to Arms* hints at the understanding of the values of agape that are to emerge gradually, but its hero and heroine are still mired in the follies and contradictions of "true love." The follies are not as apparent as in *The Sun Also Rises.* The toughness is so deluding that Hemingway seems already to have begun to move from romanticism to agape. But as Joseph Warren Beach has seen: "Hemingway, in his severely 'modern' and unromantic idiom, has given us a view of love as essentially romantic as any of his predecessors in the long line of English novelists."[7]

Beach, however, is generally pleased with the view, "romance" carrying no onus for him. He describes the story as an embodiment of the transcendental values of courage and love, a love neither irresponsible nor one that ends sentimentally or melodramatically. Beach's reasoning is that Catherine Barkley and Lieutenant Henry do plan to marry after the child is born, and their love is sealed by death and suffering if not by marriage vows. Further, if there is any bad love in the story, it is the "whorehouse love" which symbolizes the evil of war. Humane love is impossible under the conditions of war, Beach says, ignoring the wartime love of Robert Jordan and Maria in *For Whom the Bell Tolls.*[8]

In the light of subtle but undeniable evidence in the novel itself, one cannot hold with these views, even though they are tempting to espouse, largely because they coincide with congenital clichés and flatter hard-to-shake ideas about the nobility of romantic love. As Maurice Valency describes it, romantic love is an amatory fixation on a single ideal, and it centers on the courtship stage of a relationship.[9] On the surface of this love, the romantic appears to be concerned only with pleasing his love object.

Within a tough context of modern war not fought according to chivalric rules, the love affair in *A Farewell to Arms* is wildly romantic. An improbable hero and heroine live an adolescent dreamlife full of adventure and sex. When the courtship is over (when Catherine is pregnant), she conveniently dies, as does the baby who would have been so troublesome to the hero. Iseults never have babies. Lieutenant Frederic

[7] Joseph Warren Beach, *American Fiction: 1920–1940,* p. 88.
[8] *Ibid.,* pp. 85–89.
[9] Valency, *In Praise of Love,* pp. 17–18.

Henry falls into a love trap. Initially he says he wants only physical love, and Catherine is preferable to the whores in the army-sponsored bordello whom Henry visited regularly and who might give him another case of gonorrhea. Catherine is, after all, beautiful to him (18) and eminently available, working at the field hospital where he is attached and being "a little crazy" because of the death of her soldier fiancé.

But this knight who had never been in love and who knew he "did not love Catherine Barkley nor had any idea of loving her" (32) swiftly changes his mind. Suddenly the ribaldry of the officers' mess and the romanceless love of the whorehouse is distasteful to him, and he regrets having treated Catherine so lightly. Away from her he feels "lonely and empty," "lonely and hollow" (44). After his wounding—the beginning of the end of his romance with war—Catherine comes to his hospital bed, and "When I saw her I was in love with her" (98). Tristan and Iseult fell in love after drinking a magic love potion. For Henry the magic lay perhaps in Catherine's long blonde hair that he admires so much (19, 27, 276, 312–313, 320, 324).[10]

Henry falls in love hard, but it is interesting to note that he repeats the imagery of "lonely and empty," "lonely and hollow" in quite different contexts. In *To Have and Have Not* this image of emptiness or hollowness becomes a major sign of the lonely and loveless man. One would think that Henry lost his loneliness when he fell in love with Catherine, but subsequent uses of the imagery suggest that she does not quite satisfy his spiritual hunger. After a night of love with her he feels "hollow and hungry" (167) though admittedly the hunger is literally for food. After his escape from the battle police, he feels "hollow and sick," "lonesome inside and alone," seeing things "clearly and emptily" (243, 247–248); he has made his separate peace, and perhaps this hollowness and emptiness is a foretaste of his later not altogether happy isolation with Catherine. After his reunion with her, Henry says that they never wished to be separated from each other as ordinary mortal lovers sometimes wish privacy, but he adds that they were "alone against the others" (266), that their separate peace had left them (or at least Henry) with no defense except each other. Still later, Catherine

[10] J. Huizinga, *The Waning of the Middle Ages*, p. 91. Huizinga refers to the magical power attributed to hair in the chivalric code.

apologizes to Henry because their "marriage" has limited his activities. He had tried to keep from thinking, and he answers:

"My life used to be *full* of everything. . . . Now if you aren't with me I haven't a thing in the world. . . ."

"*Don't think* about me when I'm not here."

"That's the way I worked it at the front. But there was something to do then."

"Othello with his occupation gone," she teased.

". . . I'm not jealous. I'm just so in love with you that there isn't anything else." (274; my emphasis)

We are moved by this loneliness to pity Henry rather than to envy him for the realization of what he thought he longed for.

Other evidence in the novel indicates an understanding of the folly of the romantic view of life. Initially it is not with Catherine that Henry sees folly, but with the war, that other aspect of his current life. In addition to the disguise and reversal motif, there is the well-known passage in which Henry tells of his embarrassment "by the words sacred, glorious, and sacrifice" (196); Hemingway indicates his disillusionment with war as a noble enterprise. Catherine, too, had had romantic notions about war which, like her fiancé, were all blown to bits by reality (20). The "theatrical" war on the "picturesque" Italian front with its noble leaders is a fraud. Toilet paper and a gas mask are more useful than a sword and pistol (29–30, 38–39, 159).

It is one thing to see the mud, pain, sickness, and death of war, and another thing to retreat from an illusion of it to an illusion of escape in those other arms, the arms of a goddess, as Rinaldi the cynical surgeon calls Catherine (71). Henry's escape involves more than a rejection of war; it more seriously entails a loss of agape, both literally and symbolically. In Chapter 1, Henry writes in the first-person plural: he is part of a group. But as the war goes badly and he grows increasingly bitter and restless, his point of view becomes personal. Immediately after first making love with Catherine, Henry is divorced from his role as a participant in the war by his severe wounding. When Catherine is transferred to Henry's rear-echelon hospital, he resumes the "we" point of view once more, but he means in this later case just Catherine and himself, no one else. He is isolated from mankind, and it is but a short step further to the "separate peace" that he declares, knowing full well that it will make him "damned lonely" until he can return to Catherine. Of course, the separate peace is well motivated: Henry will likely be shot as a spy if he does not escape from the singleminded Italian battle police. But after this immediate aversion of a foolish, undeserved fate, Henry continues to run—from war and its commitment to others and to vague, often hypocritical ideals, and its difficult decisions and responsibilities (Henry had shot an Italian sergeant who had refused to help get his ambulances out of the mud). He runs to the simplicity, isolation, and irresponsibility of an idyllic life with his beloved.

And this beloved is a woman who has no self and very little depth as a fictional character. Whether Hemingway could or could not create a lifelike woman character (a question that is often argued) seems beside the point here and elsewhere in his fiction. He had no need for one in a context that demanded a heroine who lacked a self (and lacking a self does not at all mean being selfless). Selfhood or individuality is necessary for one to love and be loved or to be selfless, but Catherine is afraid of herself in a manner that suggests Nick Adams' fear of falling asleep after his traumatic wounding; the background of her fear was the violent death of her first fiancé and her subsequent "craziness." She wants to lose her identity in her lover. She doesn't care what they do or where they go; whatever Henry wants is fine with her; she will be what he wants, and they will never fight because if anything ever came between them they would "be gone"; she doesn't "live at all" when they are apart even briefly, and once after seeing a fox she imagines how lovely it would be for them to be in such a nonhuman condition where thought and individuality would be even more remote than in their Swiss hideout (146, 148–149, 320, 323).

It is to Henry's credit that his solution is felt to be suspect. The lovers have everything their own way up to the very end of the story, but their lives are marred, and not simply by the premonition and foreshadowing of death. They flee Italy and guarantee their safety in Switzerland by a rowboat escape that parallels Tristan and Iseult's honeymoon cruise, but the honeymoon is over for Henry whether he knows it or not. The barriers to their happiness have been met and overcome: Catherine's "craziness" about her dead fiancé, Miss Van Camp (the unsympathetic head nurse), the war itself, Henry's wound, finally even the soldiers of the country Henry served.

The love of Tristan and Iseult feeds on suffering and obstacles; without them, there is no love. And in spite of what Henry says, his solution to the war has been to reject love in the ordinary sense of friendship and kindness. From Tristan and Iseult to Antony and Cleopatra to Frederic and Catherine—living for romantic love is personal and a rejection of the larger, more magnanimous, more perilous agape. In such contexts, the two loves are antithetical. There is a pseudotragic ring to the ending, for in the depths of his mind Henry is really glad that Catherine dies, yet there is a metaphorical appropriateness to the ending, for as a story of self versus antiself, with a movement from commitment to desertion and death, the novel can be read as an exemplary one. Romantic love is not the solution to war or any other human dilemma.

As in *The Sun Also Rises*, the conclusion is negative, but in *A Farewell to Arms* there are more hints of a positive solution than there were in *The Sun Also Rises.* In Henry's friendship with Rinaldi and the priest attached to the army hospital, he finds human affections that are not unrealistic. The fact that he deserts these friends in making his separate peace is merely a sign of Henry's confusion, for he cannot satisfy his longings through them. Both Rinaldi and the priest are in some measure sick of the war too. Rinaldi finds his relief in whores and liquor; the priest clings to his faith and his love of his simple mountain homeland in Abruzzi. They take different medicines, but neither quits, neither reaches the turning point that Henry does, and each has a different view of the love between man and woman (Rinaldi's: 71–72, 179–186; the priest's: Chapter 11, 188–189).

The idea that Henry's decision has not been the best possible one is hinted at as early as Chapter 20, when he and Catherine are fully committed to each other and supposedly living in erotic bliss while he is recuperating from his wounds. At Catherine's suggestion, they leave their friends at a racetrack in order to be by themselves.

The ironic overtones of their conversation seem unmistakable. Just because they bet on an unknown and losing horse (when they could have had the name of the winner from the shady Mr. Meyers), Catherine illogically feels "cleaner." Henry's voice is quiet, and Catherine, who orders some drinks, has assumed the active, male role. He is reduced to domesticity by Catherine's possessiveness; he is reduced to banalities like "It's grand here" and "It's nice" as Catherine has him cornered and all to herself. But apparently she is sensitive to his controlled restiveness, for she soon says, "'Don't let me spoil your fun, darling. I'll go back whenever you want.'" He indulges her, at least until they can finish their drinks, and she is grateful, but the last sentences of the episode are beautifully instructive of the inherent dullness of his life with her: "After we had been alone awhile we were glad to see the others again. We had a good time" (141). Such stylistic flatness belies Henry's statement and gives it an ironic twist. Of course he has had enough of a certain kind of excitement in the war to appreciate a near vacuum of intellectual stimulation, and the nocturnal crestings of his passion must alternate with such troughs of sensation. But there is the tonal hint that Henry has already seen what the realization of romance is like. And by its nature romance cannot be domesticated.

In Book V, after the last obstacle to their peace has been surmounted—they have perilously escaped to Switzerland just before Henry was to have been arrested for desertion—the lovers are so happy that they are bound to be bored, just as Henry had earlier been bored by the kind priest whom he had, nonetheless, liked (8–9, 145). The priest had urged Henry to go to his home in Abruzzi, where men still loved each other. The vision of goodness was attractive to Henry, but he had perversely refused to go there where the land was frozen, the air cold and dry, the peasants kind, and the hunting good. Instead of in this good place purified by the white snow, he had spent his leave in drunken whoring, which he had certainly enjoyed, but he had to face himself alone in the daytime, as he faces Catherine at the racetrack without the blinding stimulation of blind eros or the narcotic of drunkenness. His world was "all unreal in the dark and so exciting." The "night was better" than the day "unless the day was very clean and cold" like the days in Abruzzi. Henry tries to explain to his friend the priest why he had not visited the priest's homeland, but he cannot—for he himself does not quite know why.

> He had always known what I did not know, and what, when I learned it, I was always able to forget. But I did not know that then, although I learned it later. (13–14)

The confusion of eros and the dissatisfaction with it are clear, but Henry never returns to this cryptic comment to say what it was he later learned. Yet if the central story is one of a farewell to arms that turns out badly, one can assume that that farewell was an unfortunate decision. Henry describes a number of little encounters with real people who are both good and bad and who intermittently establish him in a social milieu. There are a street artist (143–144), Meyers and his wife (Chapters 19–20), the hospital porter and his wife who cries when Henry leaves (156), a hotel manager (167), the captain of artillery to whom Henry gives his seat on the train (169–170), the two stray sergeants whom Henry at least has the social involvement to hate and even kill (217–218), his Italian ambulance crew and especially his driver Aymo whom he "had liked as well as anyone" he ever knew (229), the singer Simmons who gives him some clothes (257–259), and the barman in Stresa who is an old friend and helps him escape (Chapter 36). Along with Rinaldi and the priest, the doctors and nurses, and Count Greffi, these minor characters help describe the actual world of little victories and defeats that so sharply contrast with Henry and Catherine's Wagnerian world.

Mixed in with the quiet scenes of their mountain happiness, in Book V, are the undercurrents of the same malaise that touched Henry at the racetrack. He is distracted. Repeatedly he turns his mind back to the war that he had so conclusively left; time after time he picks up the newspapers to read about the war, even when Catherine is in the hospital having her difficult delivery (311, 312, 328, 330, 331, 341, 352). And he admits that sometimes he wonders about the front and people he knows there. He tells the curious Catherine at one moment that he is thinking about nothing, but on being pressed, he says he was thinking about Rinaldi and whether he had syphilis (319).

A curious contradiction of statements and actions develops that is almost painful to read if one senses the waning of the romance. Of course, the loss of idyllic love is no loss at all if it is exchanged for a realistic, conscious harmony of the lovers, but one wonders how deeply Henry understands his own honesty. And that is what is painful—the honesty that permits the hero to reveal the secret unrest that the Tristan feels when he no longer suffers for love. That there is a contradiction between the open expression and the secret expression of Henry's feelings is not hypocrisy; it is rather a dimension of characterization that is seldom realized, and whether or not Hemingway was conscious of what he was doing—as one may feel Henry is not fully conscious—the portrayal is a brilliant tour de force in manipulating point of view.

For example, the slow-moving Book V pictures Catherine and Henry as a happy couple enjoying a well appointed if not luxurious holiday in Switzerland. To Henry, Catherine is a "lovely wife" (314) to whom he says, "Oh, darling, I love you so" (313). Yet he senses trouble in paradise (314–316, 332), and Catherine (with the reader) senses restlessness in him (318–319). His premonitions might very well be instigated by boredom as much as by the desire for new barriers to their love. In any event, they have little to do but express love for one another and their mutual dependence. The canker is subtly depicted:

> "Let's go to sleep at exactly the same moment" [Catherine said].
> "All right."
> But we did not. I was awake for quite a long time thinking about things and watching Catherine sleeping, the moonlight on her face. Then I went to sleep, too. (321)

The "things" Henry thinks of are presumably the war and his friends who have not made their separate peace. Yet when Catherine asks him if he wants to see other people, he flatly answers "no"—the lovers are dependent on each other, but independent of the world; even their baby will not come between them (323).

Henry has attempted to reduce life to its lowest denominator, to make it simple, to make it thoughtless, to destroy consciousness and responsibility in a romantic, orgiastic dream. He does not even want to think of his family because it will make him worry about them (324). But now Iseult is pregnant and possessive. She wishes to consume Henry in destructive love; after the birth " 'You'll fall in love with me all over again,' " Catherine says.

> "Hell," I said, "I love you enough now. What do you want to do? Ruin me?"
> "Yes. I want to ruin you."
> "Good," I said, "that's what I want too." (325)

The dramatic situation does not support an image of happiness. The passage "We had a fine life. We lived through the months of January and February and the winter was very fine and we were very happy" (326) clearly seems ironical, though at that time Henry may have wanted to believe what he said.

During Catherine's difficult delivery Henry thinks of love as a biological trap. Nature is giving Catherine hell, not some deity who is punishing them for illicit love, he thinks. Yet he prays, and the idea of retribution is in his mind. Thinking of the child as a "by-product of good nights in Milan" seems a deliberately casual front for doubt and guilt (342). When he administers anesthetic gas to Catherine, he says of the gauge that he is "afraid of the numbers above two" (345). Literally, he does not want to give Catherine too much gas; metaphorically, he is afraid of the complications the baby will introduce to his simple life, just as he was afraid and yet drawn to the complications of the war—the multiplicity of responsibility, the lack of clear-cut issues, the meaning within meaninglessness, as with the taboo words *sacred* and *glorious*.

Catherine and the baby die. She is killed in the biological trap. As she is drained of her life's blood, Henry too feels an emptying inside of him, a feeling of the hollowness that Jake Barnes had felt and that will grow into a major image for loveliness and loneliness in the pivotal novel *To Have and Have Not*. One's sympathy for Henry is genuine, but it is tempered by the intellectual reservation that he was not, after all, prepared for growth beyond romantic love. He was not psychically ready to be a father and a husband. His last conversation with Catherine is sticky, bitter, and sad:

> "Do you want me to get a priest or any one to come and see you?"
> "Just you," she said. . . .
> "You won't do our things with another girl, or say the same things, will you?"
> "Never."
> "I want you to have girls, though."
> "I don't want them."
> "You are talking too much," the doctor said. "Mr. Henry must go out. He can come back again later. You are not going to die. You must not be silly."
> "All right," Catherine said. "I'll come and stay with you nights," she said. (354)

Their love is hermetic and ritualized, and eros is not central to it (conveniently, one suspects, for the hero's sake: he can enjoy his agony and also an occasional romp).

Catherine is a hard-to-believe dream girl who can be read on the realistic level only as a neurotic but who is better read as a deliberate stylization. Her death carries the hope with it of the destruction of her destructive love that excludes the world, that in its very denial of self possesses selfishly, that leads nowhere beyond the bed and the dream of a mystical transport of ordinary men and women to a divine state of love through foolish suffering. Indeed, the doctor and both of them say that it is foolish and silly to die. But die Catherine does, and the emptiness that Henry feels is the necessary state that must precede a refilling of his spirit with the more substantial stuff of agape. The old love dies with Catherine, and Henry's malaise even when living his idyll before her death is practically a guarantee that the Hemingway hero, having tried one love that has failed, will search for another. The promise of success had been hinted at in the first two novels. It was to be gradually evolved in Hemingway's middle period.

# 4 ~ THAT GULF STREAM FEELING

Love is often a fruit of marriage.

—Moliere

Except sexually only fools can love one another.

—G. Bernard Shaw
(From the inscription in his personal
copy of the *Works of Dante*)

UNLIKE MANY NOVELS, none of the characters or incidents in this book is imaginary. Any one not finding sufficient love interest is at liberty, while reading it, to insert whatever love interest he or she may have at the time. The writer has attempted to write an absolutely true book to see whether the shape of a country and the pattern of a month's action can, if truly presented, compete with a work of the imagination.[1]

Thus Hemingway wrote in his Foreword to *Green Hills of Africa* (1935). Perhaps he wanted to write "an absolutely true book" because he had written himself dry and was imaginatively bankrupt, as some of the critics who attacked the book or ignored it implied. Two of Hemingway's best short stories, "The Short Happy Life of Francis Macomber" and "The Snows of Kilimanjaro," came from the same African experience and immediately followed the publication of *Green Hills of Africa,* but in 1935 it might well have seemed that Hemingway was reduced to the travelogue. Hemingway had sold out. While the country struggled through the Depression and other authors were discovering Social Responsibility, he took a rich man's vacation to Africa, then had the temerity to write about it, capitalizing on his earlier successes but weakening his reputation. He seemed to be capitalizing too, on the vogue of true-life travel adventures. Following close on the heels of *Death in the Afternoon*—about bullfighting, of all things—the African book might almost seem an insult to the boys who stayed at home. One

[1] Ernest Hemingway, "Foreword," *Green Hills of Africa.* Subsequent reference in this chapter to this work will be in the text itself.

of Hemingway's reactions to the current criticism seemed to confirm his sensitivity. After seeing two favorable reviews of *Green Hills of Africa* in English newspapers, he said, "Over there you can write about the noncompetitive sports and they'll call it literature if that's what it is. Over here they see the subject matter and say, 'You can't write seriously about stuff like that.' Over here you have to write about strikes or social uplift movement or they don't even know if you can write."[2]

The book is well written, but it does lack esthetic depth as well as *current* social commentary. It cannot compete with works of the imagination, as Hemingway somewhat naively had hoped it could. From a lesser writer, *Green Hills of Africa* would probably have been treated more kindly, but from the author of *The Sun Also Rises* and *A Farewell to Arms* it seemed a presumptuous affair. Since the publication of *A Farewell to Arms* in 1929, Hemingway had published only two books: a collection of short stories and the equally controversial *Death in the Afternoon* (1932), which had also been something of a holiday book. But even on holiday, writing a book for his own pleasure about a passionate hobby of his, Hemingway capped the pattern of the first two novels with some random statements about or allusions to his master subject of love. As in the novels, the commentary is rather negativistic and bitter, and the book evoked such comments as Edmund Wilson's "neurotic" and "a little hysterical" and Max Eastman's "romantic nonsense and self-deception crying to heaven."[3] But in writing this book, Hemingway was suggesting a connection between love and death; certainly the book is not simply about bullfighting as a sport, and Hemingway says he was first drawn to the sport because the bull ring was "the only place where you could see life and death, i.e. violent death now that the wars were over . . . and I wanted very much to go to Spain where I could study it."[4]

Romantic love opposes death to life and denies eros. The bull, that great model of erotic strength, is ceremonially killed in the bull ring, and the *aficionado* is supposed to experience tragic sensations if all goes well. In contrast to this stylized drama, which is a mnemonic, religious

[2] Quoted by Leicester Hemingway, *My Brother, Ernest Hemingway*, p. 182.

[3] Edmund Wilson, "Hemingway: Gauge of Morale," *The Wound and the Bow*, p. 223; Max Eastman, "Bull in the Afternoon," *Art and the Life of Action*, p. 92.

[4] Ernest Hemingway, *Death in the Afternoon*, p. 2.

act, Hemingway says that the sensations of love cannot be recalled, yet when he is older he will write of his youth spent in fine whorehouses.[5]

That is, in one's youth one acts and is aimlessly erotic, compelled like the bull to savage acts with no rational defense but with instinctive dignity that may lead to tragedy. Hemingway tells a story of a brother and sister who enter the mythic life and death struggle: after their brother is killed by a bull, they follow it for two years and finally receive permission to kill the bull; then they ritualistically roast and eat his testicles, absorbing the bull's powers into themselves in a cyclical and redemptive act.[6] Hemingway later says that man enjoys killing when he is in rebellion against death; taking life is a godlike attribute that consoles the proud killer.[7]

The bullfighter whose profession is death becomes a proxy for the *aficionado* as well as a kind of priest who must not get "mixed up" with women. Marriage is good for the soul and the body, Hemingway says, but it is not good for the bullfighters "if they love their wives truly"; and thus the bullfighter must lead a casual love life, never permitting himself to become "involved" with women.[8] He enjoys erotic love and stimulates it to an unnatural degree among his women admirers (such as Brett in *The Sun Also Rises* and Pilar in *For Whom the Bell Tolls*) because he has, in the jargon, *cojones.* Like the bull he sacrifices, he is epitomized by his testicles, his power of life and immortality. Also like the bull, his species has a nine-months pregnancy, and the male can service up to fifty cows, though he is sometimes strangely inclined to monogamy. In order to be a good life-taker, the fighter exercises his lifegiving function without compromising himself to a woman, without, like those strange monogamous bulls, "falling in love"; he is a champion, a paragon, but even he can be devoured by the devourer woman if he is not aloof and like the normal bull in his lovemaking.

Admittedly, Hemingway is mythicizing the bull and the bullfight, but he is not sentimentalizing simple facts, as Eastman the literalist thought. In fact he continues to call sentimental distortions, such as bull-ring gestures that appeal to the uninitiated, "useless and romantic things."[9]

[5] *Ibid.*, pp. 138 and 173.

[6] *Ibid.*, pp. 24–25.

[7] *Ibid.*, p. 233.

[8] *Ibid.*, pp. 103–104.

[9] *Ibid.*, p. 12.

Another mythic metaphor concerns the loss of courage: after a wound a man can lose his courage, as he loses his seed into a bad woman, but perhaps he can find courage again in a different wound or woman.[10]

But if Hemingway is not sentimentalizing, he is simplifying the complicated problem of love. Love cannot be ignored, but perhaps he can treat it as the bullfighter does. Or at least he can envy the matador or the seed bull his uncomplicated life of having his cake and eating it too. (Not even the celibate priest does as well.) He concludes his description of the sad love life of the strange monogamous bull by telling his questioning lady companion that all stories end in death:

> Especially do all stories of monogamy end in death, and your man who is monogamous while he often lives most happily, dies in the most lonely fashion. . . . If two people love each other there can be no happy end to it.

Then he gives her his definition of love, and for the usually reticent Hemingway, the author who three years before had his hero Lieutenant Henry distrusting abstractions like honor and courage, the statement is a curious blend of sentiment and wisdom that he again protects with defensive irony; he tells the baffled lady that what he has just said has nothing at all to do with the topic of bulls.

> Sir, I do not know what you mean by love. It does not sound well as you say it.
>
> Madame, it is an old word and each one takes it new and wears it out himself. It is a word that fills with meaning as a bladder with air and the meaning goes out of it as quickly. It may be punctured as a bladder is punctured and patched and blown up again and if you have not had it it does not exist for you. All people talk of it, but those who have had it are all marked by it and I would not wish to speak of it further since of all things it is the most ridiculous to talk of and only fools go through it many times. I would sooner have the pox than to fall in love with another woman loving the one I have.
>
> What has this to do with the bulls, sir?
>
> Nothing, Madame, nothing at all, it is only conversation to give you your money's worth.[11]

Hemingway's irony is delightful, but it strongly suggests a defensive posture or a refusal to grapple with the subject of love that is obviously fascinating to him but that may be more than he can handle. In *Green*

[10] *Ibid.*, p. 222.
[11] *Ibid.*, p. 122.

*Hills of Africa* he fully accepted the challenge to write about agape rather than the appealingly simple love life of the bull and the matador, and that book can be viewed as dividing the early from the late Hemingway while it also connects the disillusioned, heavily ironic Hemingway and the agape Hemingway.

Certainly *Green Hills of Africa* is more than a big-game hunting narrative salted with assorted and more or less irrelevant reflections on American literature and life. The oft-cited opinion that "All American literature comes from one book by Mark Twain called *Huckleberry Finn*" is one of the best-known sentences in Hemingway, yet it comes from one of his least-read books and is part of an early conversation that has little to do with the central action of the narrative (22). More than a hunting story and repository for less-than-Olympian profundities, *Green Hills of Africa* is a story of Hemingway's maturation through a struggle within himself. In it he learns to love his fellow man and to be loved by him—to supplant envy, competition, and hate with affection and kinship. This meaning of the book is implicit, and properly so. To place his thoughts and feelings explicitly on the surface of the narrative would be the Boy Scout Manual way but not the artist's. Besides, Hemingway could not himself be sure of what he was getting at. His manner for the most part had been to let the stories tell themselves without his expository comments. This story was different only in that it happened exactly as he told it. What his foreword did not say, of course, was that Hemingway had the controlling choice of what incidents to report and how to report them. His "absolutely true book" is as subjective as any of his fiction. The book is not a journal, not a travelogue, but a parable that foreshadows two later comments: " 'No matter how a man alone ain't got no bloody fucking chance,' " which concluded *To Have and Have Not,* published the following year (1936), and the "No man is an island" meditation by John Donne, part of which was the epigraph of *For Whom the Bell Tolls,* published in 1940.

By parable I mean a method of narration that is deliberately veiled. Hemingway was not certain of the bridge he was on. To talk about love as such would be to spoil it. "No pleasure in anything if you mouth it up too much," the hunter Wilson comments in "The Short Happy Life of Francis Macomber,"[12] and "love" was a word, like "sacred," "glori-

[12] *The Short Stories of Ernest Hemingway,* p. 33.

ous," and "sacrifice," that had been spoiled.[13] To talk about love, then, it was necessary to dramatize it without using words like "love" and "brotherhood," words which could be corrupted, words whose meaning in all honesty Hemingway did not surely know. A remarkable clue is in the second sentence of the three-sentence Foreword: "Any one not finding sufficient love interest [in this book] is at liberty, while reading it, to insert whatever love interest he or she may have at the time."

But this flippant reference is to the "love" of his short stories and the first novels; is is the romantic love that is not real, not honest, and, therefore, not appropriate for an absolutely true book. It is the eros that he bitterly refers to as "the empty condoms of our great loves [that] float with no significance against one single, lasting thing—the [Gulf] stream" (150). It is the love *interest,* that added ingredient or embellishment of the plot that Hollywood and popular-magazine editors and readers look for in a story; it is not organic love, love that is intrinsic to the story, but a titillating, sugary flavoring. Clearly that sort of love is not present in *Green Hills of Africa.*

Then why does Hemingway bother to mention love at all? For one thing, he was painfully conscious of it, almost obsessed by it. For another, he was borrowing a literary irony he had seen Twain use in his admired *Huckleberry Finn*: "Persons attempting to find a motive in this narrative will be prosecuted; persons attempting to find a moral in it will be banished; persons attempting to find a plot in it will be shot."[14] Hemingway is alerting his readers to the presence of the topic of love that, like Twain's motive and moral, might otherwise be overlooked by the casual reader. The narrating Huck Finn does not moralize, but he detects morality and immorality. Hemingway does not talk about love, but he demonstrates his struggle to achieve it.

Eros is strangely subdued in *Green Hills of Africa.* Perhaps there were medical reasons. Hemingway had contracted a severe case of amoebic dysentery, a bleeding, debilitating disease (46). What remained of his abundant energy probably found sufficient outlet in the day-long hunts. Only late in the narrative are there any awakenings of the libidinous inclinations supposedly characteristic of Hemingway.

[13] Ernest Hemingway, *A Farewell to Arms*, p. 191.

[14] Mark Twain, "Notice," *Huckleberry Finn*, p. 5.

Hemingway is the only white man at a native farm; he asks his gun-bearer, M'Cola, if the farm boy has a sister—a farmer's daughter—and M'Cola says, " 'No. No,' to me very firmly and solemnly.

" 'Nothing tendacious, you understand. Curiosity.'

" 'M'Cola was firm. 'No,' he said and shook his head. . . .

"That disposed of the opportunities for social life," Hemingway concludes, and then turns his attention to another appetite, one for kidneys and liver (242).

The next day Hemingway meets another native with

> his wife, very pretty, very modest, very wifely. . . . I watched the most freshly brideful wife who stood a little in profile so that I saw her pretty pear-shaped breasts and the long, clean niggery legs and was studying her pleasant profile most profitably until her husband spoke to her suddenly and sharply, then in explanation and quiet command, and she moved around us, her eyes down, and went on along the trail that we had come, alone, we all watching her. He had seen the sable [antelope] that morning and, slightly suspicious, obviously displeased at leaving that now out-of-sight wife of wives that we had all taken with our eyes, he led us off and to the right along another trail. . . . (248–249)

On this same hunt one of his guides, "Garrick," tries to trade some "empty petrol boxes . . . for a piece of something." Hemingway has had little use for Garrick throughout the hunt, and finally he explodes and threatens to break the African's jaw. "I stood up and motioned to the women that they could have the petrol tins and the cases." And why is Hemingway the protector of women's virtue? "I was damned if I could not have anything to do with them if I would let Garrick make any passes" (277).

Hemingway is willing to submit to the respected M'Cola's admonitions, but he cannot resist being a bit hypocritical with the despised Garrick. Thus the struggle within Hemingway here ends in a rather tainted victory for the powers of agape, but the struggle is more extensively seen in his relations with his wife, Pauline, and his comments on American women in general.

Pauline, nicknamed "Poor Old Mama" and usually referred to by the abbreviation "P.O.M.," is almost maternally interested in Hemingway's health and his success in tracking down his various quarries. She worries —or at least Hemingway reports that she worries—when he returns from a hunt empty-handed (12).

Although Hemingway loves Africa and hunting, he is not entirely happy on this trip, through no fault of his wife. They are openly affectionate and get along remarkably well for man and wife (213). Hemingway says they have a thorough mutual understanding: "My wife knows now all I think, all I say, all I believe, all I can do, all that I cannot do and cannot be. I know also about my wife—completely" (18). Nevertheless, they quarrel, domestically and mundanely, over P.O.M.'s ill-fitting boots and over a malfunctioning camera. Each time Hemingway writes of himself as being more the wrongdoer than is his wife. With the boots she was stoic and enduring; he was righteous and a "four-letter man" and then almost immediately ashamed of himself (94–95). The same pattern of quick anger and remorse occurs later with the camera: "I was nervous now, irritable, righteous, pompous. . . . I was sorry I was such a bastard about the camera" (120).

Pauline, on the other hand, is quietly powerful:

> "I'm one of those quiet people."
>
> "By God if you're not," Pop said. "But you can puncture the old man [Hemingway] quick enough when he gets started."
>
> "That's what makes a woman a universal favorite," P.O.M. told him. (155)

She is "very desirable, cool, and neat-looking in her khaki and her boots, her Stetson on one side of her head . . ." (212).

In this context of happiness with his wife and self-anger when he does anything to disrupt their harmony, Hemingway comments on love in general. Good love is the supreme happiness:

> . . . I was happy as you are after you have been with a woman that you really love, when, empty, you feel it welling up again and there it is and you can never have it all and yet what there is, now, you can have, and you want more and more, to have, and be, and live in, to possess now again for always, for that long, sudden-ended always; making time stand still, sometimes so very still that afterwards you wait to hear it move, and it is slow in starting. But you are not alone, because if you have ever really loved her happy and untragic, she loves you always; no matter whom she loves or where she goes she loves you more. So if you have loved some woman and some country you are very fortunate and, if you die afterwards it makes no difference. (72–73)

With words like "empty," "welling," "possess," and "sudden-ended always" this good love is conveyed through eros, sexual love. It is not romantic love, for it is "happy and untragic," the reverse of the tragic, unhappy love of a Tristan and Iseult. In a different context Hemingway later equates romance with falseness, as he did in *Death in the Afternoon.* A stretch of plain "began to seem very impossible and romantic and untrue" (216). When his gun-bearer M'Cola dangerously and unethically carries a cocked rifle behind Hemingway's back, Pop excuses M'Cola to the angry Hemingway. A rhinoceros had been wounded, and M'Cola " 'was protecting Mama,' Pop said. 'That's why he had the gun cocked.' "

> "Can he shoot?"
> "No," Pop said. "But he would."
> "Shoot me in the pants," I said. "Romantic bastard." (79)

While good love is erotic and unromantic, bad love is bitter and peculiarly American, if not peculiar to America. The camp visitor Kandisky, Hemingway's friend Karl, and the white hunter Pop each combine goodness and intelligence with a feeling of bitterness about American women. Kandisky and Pop are "bitter about American women," and Karl thinks they are "terrible" (32, 184). Karl's wife is back home and Pauline pities him for being alone on the trip, but there is irony in Hemingway's agreement with his wife when he says, " 'Poor Karl' " (66). To be alone is to be unfettered.

To be fettered is to kill art. Through this rationale Hemingway arrives at some conclusions about women and their influence on a writer. Hemingway works these ideas into Chapter I through the less than subtle device of having Kandisky ask him questions about American writers. If one reads *Green Hills of Africa* as a drama about love, not simply as a true-adventure story, this opening discussion about American writing and love set on the high plains of East Africa is not so incongruous or gratuitous.

Hemingway wants to explain why " 'We do not have great writers. . . . Something happens to our good writers at a certain age' " (19). And that something is an arrested development of the power of love, a failure that may be personal or cultural. For eros, one must have a body, but " 'Emerson, Hawthorne, Whittier, and Company' " wrote as if they had only minds, " 'Nice, dry, clean minds.' " For art and agape, one must be a strong individual and not be like New York writers, " 'all angleworms in a bottle, trying to derive knowledge and nourishment from their own contact and from the bottle. . . . They are lonesome outside of the bottle. They do not want to be lonesome.' " For mature love one must not be afraid to be alone with one's beliefs or one's woman: " 'They [New York writers] are afraid to be alone in their beliefs and no woman would love any of them enough so that they could kill their lonesomeness in that woman, or make something with her that makes the rest unimportant' " (21–22).

Keeping up a wife is another way to destroy a talent (23). And some good writers are made "impotent" by the critics (24).

Hemingway concludes the conversation that "was becoming an interview" after Kandisky asks what things harm a writer: " 'Politics, women, drink, money, ambition. And a lack of politics, women, drink, money and ambition' " (28), an echo of the similar paradoxical remark about wounds and women in *Death in the Afternoon.*

In effect, what Hemingway is doing here is trying to make careful, crucial distinctions about eros and agape and their relation to the writer. He is not confused nor is he being cute. Love for the Hemingway of the early short stories and novels was personally ambivalent, or seemed to be. Here the confusion is on the point of working itself out. It was not that love was good and bad, but that there were two kinds of love—at least that many. The necessary isolation of the good writer, the writer who is true, is now seen as compatible with a kinship of men and love of a woman. Artistic isolation or originality is not separateness. Conventional marriages and acquaintanceships are not eros and agape.

Such a view helps one to see beneath the protective irony of the well-known passage in which the Gulf Stream image is used. It opens with a statement reminiscent of the "separate peace" theme of *A Farewell to Arms,* but it qualifies Lieutenant Henry's withdrawal from social involvement.

> If you serve time for society, democracy, and the other things quite young, and declining any further enlistment make yourself responsible only to yourself, you exchange the pleasant, comforting stench of comrades for something you can never feel in any other way than by yourself. That something I cannot yet define completely but the feeling comes when you write well and truly of something . . .

Sometimes at sea one may be alone with the feeling, and yet "this Gulf

Stream you are living with" can be an image of permanence, though it is paradoxically moving, and of human solidarity, though it is fluid, because it is eternal in its flow and it forever refreshes itself in spite of whatever human corruptions are in vogue, whoever may be in power. The rich and the poor, the venal and the cruel may infect or corrupt the Gulf Stream feeling with their "high-piled scow of garbage" of palm fronds, burned-out light bulbs, empty bottles, dead cats and rats, and occasional condoms, but in ten miles the stream has cleansed itself.

> and the palm fronds of our victories, the worn light bulbs of our discoveries and the empty condoms of our great loves float with no significance against one single, lasting thing—the stream. (148–150)

Truly *this* Hemingway has not declined "further enlistment" to withdraw into himself. His isolation is not literal or spiritual but artistic. "The pleasant comforting stench of comrades" is perhaps what the New York angleworm-writers have. The undefined "something" is simply love as the writer creates it, as all mature love is creative and active rather than passive. The Gulf Stream moves and the artist moves with it, living, knowing, learning, and loving.

Exactly contrary to the belletristic or esoteric are the extensions of the image. Here Hemingway is not typical of his earlier self who would have emphasized the present moment and the solitary heart. There is here a sense of time and community which the Stream provides in its agelessness and permanence. If the Stream can be read as a love metaphor, then, like love, the Stream flows for and around all times and peoples, all governments, and all good and evil. The love stream will swallow or absorb the blight of garbage—the garbage of all the false victories, discoveries, and loves. As he writes this passage, Hemingway has not yet written his novels of the Gulf Stream; he has written of the garbage mainly, and his early fiction offers little more than disillusionment and irony in answer to the question: If all is nada or garbage, why write a novel?

As noted above, Hemingway's reported quarrels with his wife are remarkable chiefly because of their rarity. They offer interesting contrasts to the enmity and bickering of the couples in the two African short stories, "The Snows of Kilimanjaro" and "The Short Happy Life of Francis Macomber." But with his hunting companion Karl (identified by Leicester Hemingway and others as Hemingway's Key West friend Charles Thompson) and some of the natives in their party, Hemingway has throughout the book a series of fights. In fact, the bitterness between Hemingway and Karl and the natives might almost be said to provide an organizational counterpoint to the main line of the story, which is simply the elemental one of the chase. Thematically, however, these quarrels are more than counterpoint, and compared to the comments on eros and American women, the problems of agape are more central to the theme of *Green Hills of Africa.*

Hemingway's enmity towards Karl centers about Karl's good luck as a hunter. Though Hemingway himself sees his attitude as childish, he cannot accept in good grace his friend's fortunate bags. For one thing, Karl succeeds, but only sloppily; he does not have great skill, only luck. For another, Hemingway's luck has been bad, and Hemingway envies and is jealous of Karl and his bigger and better trophies. At times, Karl is the one responsible for ill feeling between them, but the motivation of Karl's malaise seems to be inner moodiness rather than an object-fixed hatred. And when Karl is "bad," in spite of his better fortunes, his mood can only make Hemingway more bitter.

Yet Hemingway struggles within himself. He recognizes the conflict and thinks that his better self—the forces of agape—will win out. Here is the struggle as it takes place from the first chapter to the very last; Hemingway is complaining to the white hunter Pop:

> "Some [kudu bulls] are certainly spooked because Karl shot that one. If he'd only killed it clean instead of following it through the whole damn countryside. Christ, if he'd only kill any damn thing clean. Other new ones will come in. All we have to do is to wait them out, though. Of course they can't all know about it. But he's spooked this country to hell."
>
> "He gets so very excited," Pop said. "But he's a good lad. He made a beautiful shot on that leopard, you know. You don't want them killed any cleaner than that. Let it quiet down again."
>
> "Sure. I don't mean anything when I curse him." (14–15)

Later Hemingway has just made a fine shot and killed a rhinoceros. He is very pleased with his trophy, and on the way back to camp, he makes another "fancy" two-hundred yard shot of a reedbuck. As he is savoring his return to good form and good luck, he meets Karl who has been off on a separate hunt. Karl has killed a rhino twice the size of

Hemingway's, and although Hemingway consciously wants to congratulate Karl and be a good sport his Western competitiveness will not let him. Pop, P.O.M., and Hemingway "all spoke like people who were about to become seasick on a boat, or people who had suffered some heavy financial loss. We were ashamed and could do nothing about it." Hemingway tries to cover up his envy and to keep his sadness from making the sympathetic Karl sad, but he is not very successful. He does ruin Karl's pleasure. Pop echoes Hemingway's paradoxical feeling:

"I never felt more like a four-letter man," he said. "But it was like a kick in the stomach. I'm really delighted, of course."

"Me too," I said. "I'd rather have him beat me. You know that. Truly. But why couldn't he just get a good one, [a rhinoceros with horns only] two or three inches longer? . . .

"We were *awful*," P.O.M. said.

"I know it," I said. "And all the time I was trying to be jolly. You *know* I'm delighted he has it." (84–85)

The moral rationalizing is almost funny as the boyish man tries to grow up. Only the native skinner seems genuinely happy about Karl's kill, and Hemingway calls the skinner the only gentleman in the group.

We had tried, in all the shoot, never to be competitive. Karl and I had each tried to give the other the better chance on everything that came up. I was, truly, very fond of him and he was entirely unselfish and altogether self-sacrificing.

But while Karl is not nearly the athlete or shot Hemingway is, he is lucky, and the luck doesn't even out. Hemingway begins to press, and he begins to lose his confidence and treat Karl just a little shabbily: "we had not treated him too well, and still he had beaten me" (86).

As the safari goes on, the once-friendly rivalry becomes even more intense, in spite of Hemingway's conscious recognition of his selfishness. After having the edge taken off his great rhino kill, Karl becomes moody, and Hemingway cannot help him. Karl has a shot at a "marvellous" lion, but can't shoot because it is "in some sort of forest reserve." Hemingway says, " 'That's rotten,' " and tries to feel bad but can't (126).

The next day Hemingway, "deliberately selfish," takes the first shot at a herd of oryx and shoots "the very best of the lot," naturally "the one Karl had picked too" (126). On yet another oryx hunt Hemingway admits his selfishness and Karl's unselfishness (156).

On a zebra hunt on a hot, dusty plain, Hemingway and Karl have yet another row, instigated by Hemingway's smugness and righteousness. He goads Karl into shooting too fast too far, and then acts innocent to further irritate his friend: "The smug one, more righteous now than ever, refuses" to take his turn at shooting, a refusal that, supposedly motivated by magnanimity, only rubs in Karl's misses. But at the very height of his perversity, Hemingway is sorry. Writing of himself in the third person, perhaps in order to look on his actions more objectively, he says, "He knows he should not hurry him, that he should leave him alone, that he only upsets him by trying to speed him up, and that he has been a smugly righteous bastard again." On the ride back to camp, the bitterness leaves them, "and there is only the feeling of shortness of time again" (131–132). The sense of mortality, sharpened by their life-taking sport, also sharpens the sense of and need for love.

Thus on several occasions when Karl is in an ugly mood, Hemingway makes excuses for him and comforts him and tries to give him a better hunting location than he himself has (137–138, 151–152, 167–168). One moment Hemingway is bitter and sarcastic, the next he is truly generous and kind. No matter how selfish he is, at least he is honest with himself and his companions, and at least he struggles with his admitted weakness. He loves hunting, Hemingway says,

> "But I don't want that guy [Karl] to beat me. Pop, he's got the best buff, the best rhino, the best water-buck—"
>
> "You beat him on oryx," Pop said.
>
> "What's an oryx?"
>
> "He'll look damned handsome when you get him home."
>
> "I'm just kidding."
>
> "You beat him on impalla, on eland. You've got a first-rate bushbuck. Your leopard's as good as his. But he'll best you on anything where there's luck. He's got damned wonderful luck and he's a good lad. I think he's off his feed a little."
>
> "You know how fond I am of him. I like him as well as I like any one. But I want to see him have a good time. It's no fun to hunt if we get that way about it."
>
> "You'll see. He'll get a kudu at this next camp and he'll be on top of the wave."
>
> "I'm just a crabby bastard," I said. (153–154)

Karl admits that he has been lucky, and he senses Hemingway's bitterness, but "He was very gentle and he could tell what was in your mind, forgive you for it, and understand it."

"'Good old Karl,' I said, warmed with whiskey, understanding, and sentiment" (154).

That the story of Hemingway's relationship with Karl is not thematically incidental seems proved not only by its persistence but also by its presence in the last five pages of the book. The coming rainy season is drawing the safari to an end, and Hemingway has just returned to camp from his last hunt with a good kill. He is very happy and proud, but once more Karl is there already with a kudu trophy that dwarfs his. Hemingway is "cold in the pit of [his] stomach" at the sight of "the biggest, widest, darkest, longest curling, heaviest, most unbelievable pair of kudu horns in the world. Suddenly, poisoned with envy, I did not want to see mine again; never, never."

"'That's great,' I said, the words coming out as cheerfully as a croak. I tried it again, 'That's swell.'"

And while Karl describes his rather sloppy stalk, Hemingway tries, tries again, fighting the poison, intellectually opposing the "natural" reaction. Later Pop tries to console Hemingway, but he will have none of it: "'. . . why does he have to beat me so bloody badly?" (291–292).

The ecstasy and excitement and triumph of the last hunt has been ruined, and Hemingway is "bitter all night long. In the morning, though, it was gone. It was all gone and I have never had it again." Hemingway "accepts" Karl's better kudu trophy, and his two lesser ones—"strangely enough"—seem satisfactory to him. When Hemingway is, then, truly magnanimous, everyone feels better and the book ends happily, after Pop gives the final lesson:

> "We have very primitive emotions," he said. "It's impossible not to be competitive. Spoils everything, though."
>
> "I'm all through with that," I said. "I'm all right again. I had quite a trip, you know." (293)

They have been friends for a long time, but agape is a continuing, difficult process, perhaps better called "loving" than "love." That Hemingway is all through with competition is a sanguine estimate, but it is an appropriate note on which to end the book.

These struggles to love Karl parallel Hemingway's relations with the natives. In Chapter 1, P.O.M. asserts that the hunters are "interested in" the natives as well as game. Hemingway says that to understand the truth of a country, one must "get your good dope always from the people," and thus he studies Swahili (193). And when he meets a tribe of happy Masai, they become friends.

Seeing them running and so damned handsome and so happy made us all happy. I had never seen such quick disinterested friendliness, nor such fine looking people.

. . . They certainly were our friends . . . They had that attitude that makes brothers, that unexpressed but instant and complete acceptance that you must be Masai wherever it is you come from. That attitude you only get from the best of the English, the best of the Hungarians and the very best Spaniards; the thing that used to be the most clear distinction of nobility when there was nobility. It is an ignorant attitude and the people who have it do not survive, but very few pleasanter things ever happen to you than the encountering of it. (221)

Later Hemingway feels a universal kinship with some other natives: ". . . I was thinking all the country in the world is the same country and all hunters are the same people" (249).

Eventually even the appearance of the natives is not strange to him.

. . . all the words came to seem the proper and natural words and there was nothing odd or unseemly in the stretching of the ears, in the tribal scars, or in a man carrying a spear. The tribal marks and the tattooed places seemed natural and handsome adornments and I regretted not having any of my own. (52–53)

But though kinship between a man and a group or nation is possible, it is achieved only through agape between individuals, and Hemingway's achievement of love for the natives is really the most powerful element of agape in *Green Hills of Africa,* more powerful than the growth of his relationship with Karl, his wife, or Pop.

Carlos Baker suggests a parallel between Hemingway's gun-bearer M'Cola and Huckleberry Finn's Jim (a Bakerian rather than a Leslie A. Fiedlerian parallel).[15] Baker does not elaborate on his suggestion nor is the parallel a close one; in fact, the personalities of M'Cola and Jim are vastly different. But at least the parallel legitimately sets *Green Hills*

[15] Carlos Baker, *Hemingway: The Writer as Artist,* p. 172.

*of Africa* in an American tradition of character relationships, and it is a parallel thematically also. That is, both pairs of white and Negro men undergo a process of mutual learning and respect which ends in a kind of love for each other. But whereas Jim is a simple soul, M'Cola is fairly sophisticated. Hemingway has to earn M'Cola's friendship by demonstrating that his shooting is skillful, not lucky. As in *Huckleberry Finn,* however, the story is one of growing affection between the white man and the Negro. At first

In the early days, before we became good friends, he did not trust me at all. When anything came up he went into this blankness. I liked Charo much better then. We understood each other on the question of religion and Charo admired my shooting and always shook hands and smiled when we had killed anything particularly good. This was flattering and pleasing. M'Cola looked on all this early shooting as a series of lucky accidents. We were supposed to shoot. We had not yet shot anything that amounted to anything and he was not really my gun bearer. He was Mr. Jackson Phillip's gun bearer and he had been loaned to me. I meant nothing to him. He did not like me nor dislike me. He was politely contemptuous of Karl. Who he liked was Mama. (39–40)

After P.O.M. and Hemingway both shoot at a lion and Hemingway's bullet is the only one found in the body, ". . . M'Cola did not trust me for a long time." But then Mama's hunting license expires, and M'Cola is exclusively Hemingway's bearer. At the end of Part I "something had happened between us" (44).

That something had been tested in the heat of action. In the flashback to the rhino hunt, it is M'Cola who endangers Hemingway's life and infuriates him by carrying a cocked rifle behind him—in order to protect Mama from the possible charge of a wounded rhino, even though he can't shoot. But when the rhino is found dead, M'Cola is as pleased as Hemingway is.

"I believe he feels just the way you do about it," Pop said.
"He's my pal."
"I believe he is, you know," Pop said. (80)

After the long flashback of Part II—in which Hemingway by his skill and persistence earns the natives' respect—Part III begins as the safari is drawing to a close: "I knew there were only two more days to hunt before we must leave. M'Cola knew it too, and we were hunting together now, with no feeling of superiority on either side any more . . ." (176). But though they have gained each other's friendship, their human weaknesses pose a temporary threat to agape when M'Cola does not clean Hemingway's rifle.

> "The bastard never cleaned it last night after that rain," I thought and, very angry, I lifted the lug and slipped the bolt out. M'Cola was watching me with his head down. The other two were looking out through the blind. I held the rifle in one hand for him to look through the breech and then put the bolt back and shoved it forward softly, lowering it with my finger on the trigger so that it was ready to cock rather than keeping it on the safety.
>
> M'Cola had seen the rusty bore. His face had not changed and I had said nothing but I was full of contempt and there had been indictment, evidence, and condemnation without a word being spoken. So we sat there, he with his head bent so only the bald top showed, me leaning back and looking out through the slit, and we were no longer partners, no longer good friends; and nothing came to the salt. (203–204)

After the hunt, however, Hemingway forgets the grievous sin to his Springfield, then remembers it, forgives it, and doesn't tell on M'Cola. "I grinned at him and he shook his old bald head and it was understood that I had said nothing about the rifle" (213). They are friends again.

Through the third chapter Hemingway describes Droopy, his gun bearer before M'Cola. Droopy was younger than M'Cola and easier to get along with; Hemingway becomes fond of him too. And elsewhere throughout the safari Hemingway meets other natives whom he generally admires and befriends. One has such natural nobility that Hemingway names him the Roman, and when he has to leave his farm without saying goodbye to the Roman he feels very bad. "I liked the Roman very much and had a high regard for him" (276).

Only one member of the safari regularly angers Hemingway, and that guide is not popular with the other natives either. On the very last hunt, Hemingway is driven by the despised, lazy Garrick, so named because of his theatrical speech and actions, to the point of wanting to shoot him, but he settles for a pretended accident in which he pokes Garrick in the stomach with the handle of a shovel. Yet even with this graceless man Hemingway cannot be hard for long, and after striking him, he "began to feel sorry for the poor, bloody, useless, theatrical bastard" (279).

One other native, an old man who helps him on his last hunt, captures Hemingway's heart, as Hemingway apparently captures the old man's too. While the strong, proud Garrick wishes to give up the hunt for a wounded sable antelope, the old man perseveres with Hemingway. They work hard together, and, though they do not speak to each other, a bond grows between them. On the long ride back to camp, Hemingway shares his beer with the old man, and when the car is loaded for the final lap of the return journey, the old man refuses to leave Hemingway and holds onto his arm in the dark and talks quietly. Hemingway thinks he wants more money or a gift, but the native simply wants to go back with Hemingway. He begs and pleads to be taken along; he runs after the car screaming, "B'wana! I want to go with B'wana!" (289) in a cry not only touching in its intensity of devotion but also sad in the knowledge that men who love each other are continually being separated.

Finally when the safari is breaking up, Hemingway is given a sign of the success of his inner struggles.

> "Pop, what does it mean when they shake hands and get hold of your thumb and pull it?"
>
> "It's on the order of blood brotherhood but a little less formal. Who's been doing that to you?"
>
> "Everybody but Kamau." (293–294)

In his writing Hemingway has begun to enter into the brotherhood of man. His initiation was not easy. More likely brothers than the culturally remote African natives could be found, and their kinship was hard-earned; it passed through the fires of anger and the heat of hard work together. This "absolutely true book" reveals no glamorized, successful American novelist on an exotic vacation. Hemingway looks hard and steadily at himself among these few companions—wife, friend, guide, and natives—and this happy, real-life adventure is happy because he has learned something about love.

# 5 ~ ETERNAL TRIANGLE

An imagined kiss is more easily controlled, more thoroughly enjoyed, and less cluttery than an actual kiss.

—James Thurber and E. B. White,
*Is Sex Necessary?*

As soon as Hemingway finished *Green Hills of Africa,* he wrote two of his best short stories, "The Short Happy Life of Francis Macomber" and "The Snows of Kilimanjaro." Both were written and published in 1936. Like his "absolutely true" book, they were set in East Africa and involved characters who had some similarities to each other. The short stories, however, were not absolutely true but were imaginative embodiments of material that Hemingway had spun out of himself as much as drawn out of his African safari.

Obviously those critics who read this pair of short stories as autobiographical do so at their own considerable risk. Such exercises as Philip Young and Carlos Baker perform in drawing parallels are suggestive and stimulating but still hazardous. With this reservation clearly in mind, I should like to draw yet another parallel, which is even more dangerous but which may illuminate and at least provide a link between the short stories and *Green Hills of Africa.*

In "The Short Happy Life of Francis Macomber," Margot Macomber cuckolds her husband with the white hunter Wilson. That Pauline Hemingway did not commit adultery with Jackson Phillip ("Pop" of *Green Hills of Africa*) is assumed. There is not the slightest hint of such an incident in any biographical or autobiographical source, and Pauline Hemingway's personal morals appear to have been conventionally exemplary. Nevertheless, just as Hemingway's suffering with amoebic dysentery and retreat by airplane to a hospital in Nairobi were changed by the alchemy of artistic creation into the gangrenous wound and fantasy death-flight to the top of Mount Kilimanjaro of the fictitious Harry ("The Snows of Kilimanjaro"), so can the adultery of "The Short Happy Life of Francis Macomber" be found to have a less dramatic but still founded-in-reality counterpart.

The "Poor Old Mama" of *Green Hills of Africa* develops a strong affection for the white hunter. Their very nicknames, Mama and Pop, hint at an Oedipian relationship, created by Hemingway himself in so naming his wife and guide. To her, Pop was an ideal, and she did not hesitate to say so.

> . . . for Pop she had a complete, clear-seeing, absolutely trusting adoration. Pop was her ideal of how a man should be, brave, gentle, comic, never losing his temper, never bragging, never complaining except in a joke, tolerant, understanding, intelligent, drinking a little too much as a good man should, and, to her eyes, very handsome.

Hemingway himself is fond of Pop, but Mama is adulatory to the point of irritating Hemingway.

> "Let's talk about Mr. J. P. I don't like you to call him Pop. It's not dignified."
>
> "He and I aren't dignified together."
>
> "Yes, but I'm dignified with him. Don't you think he's wonderful?"[1]

In the month of the safari that *Green Hills of Africa* records, Mama's hunting license has expired and thus she spends much of her time in camp with Pop while Hemingway and Karl are out shooting. The arrangement itself is hardly remarkable except for the repeated statements of admiration for Pop that P.O.M. makes and the subsequent alteration of this situation into adultery in the Macomber story. The adultery is simply an extension for dramatic purposes of an actual passive triangle in *Green Hills of Africa.*

Pop and Mama—nonparticipants—take a parental interest in their "son's" somewhat adolescent sport. They are concerned when Hemingway's luck is running bad, and Pop is then even willing to bend his rule of "no killing on the side, no ornamental killing, no killing to kill . . ."[2] When Hemingway sets off on a two-day solo hunt, Mama maternally

[1] Ernest Hemingway, *Green Hills of Africa*, pp. 64–65.

[2] *Ibid.*, pp. 12–13, 16.

packs his kit and reminds him to take handkerchiefs, and Pop paternally gives him advice. Then as Hemingway drives off, he looks back to see "the two figures, the tall thick one and the small neat one, each wearing big Stetson hats, silhouetted on the road as they walked back toward camp, then I looked ahead at the dried-up, scrubby plain."[3] Whenever Hemingway returns to camp, the conversations are friendly but always with a gentle undercurrent of rivalry between Pop and Hemingway, with Pop usually being more aggressive and successful in little facetious remarks about Hemingway's ability as a shooter and as a writer.[4]

At last the safari ends and Hemingway closes with a passage about Pop. Somehow Pop is more important to the hunters than any other part of the safari. He has come to represent the upright and virtuous man, to epitomize the goodness of Africa, and to symbolize Hemingway's slowly evolving concept of agape, still limited by his competition with Karl, his little problems with the natives, and his quiet, almost Oedipian, rivalry with Pop.

> "You know," P.O.M. said, "I can't remember it. I can't remember Mr. J. P.'s face. And he's beautiful. I think about him and think about him and I can't see him. It's terrible. He isn't the way he looks in a photograph. In a little while I won't be able to remember him at all. Already I can't see him."
>
> "You must remember him," Karl said to her.
>
> "I can remember him," I said. "I'll write you a piece some time and put him in."[5]

Hemingway fulfilled his promise in the "Macomber" story.

Like all good stories, "Macomber" can bear rereading. It is complex enough to reveal itself slowly and piecemeal, like the good paintings which Hemingway has said he learned to write from.[6] And as in any good work of art, just as one thinks he has understood it he finds some other point of view, some other detail, some other nuance of meaning that tells of the ultimate futility of translating the original into anything else. But that "Macomber" is a story about love and that it belongs thematically in its chronological position, seems easily demonstrable. The problems arise when one begins to determine specific themes and their

[3] *Ibid.*, pp. 211–214.

[4] *Ibid.*, pp. 191–198, 294.

[5] *Ibid.*, p. 295.

[6] Lillian Ross, "How Do You Like It Now, Gentlemen?" *New Yorker* (May 13, 1950), pp. 57–60.

developments, for this story is rich and subtle. Certainly it is a misleading simplification to reduce "Macomber" to Harry Levin's statement that "the story is a plaintive modulation of two rather dissonant themes: *None but the brave deserves the fair* and *The female of the species is deadlier than the male.*"[7] If one had to choose a single Hemingway story that best reflects his concern with romance, eros, and agape, "Macomber" would be a good selection, especially since it was written during this pivotal period of Hemingway's career.

Here his destruction of one kind of love and romance is awful, for, in effect, Francis Macomber is a protagonist whose one change in the story is a rejection of passion. He is made to see the futility of "suffering" in love, of the "sweet agony" of romance. Obviously this theme is not explicit, but it is implied by the characters, the language, and the action.

At the beginning of the story there is neither eros nor agape to bind Margot and Francis Macomber together. Theirs is a marriage of convenience: Macomber has the pleasure and pride of a beautiful wife, Margot the money and prestige of a wealthy husband. They stay together also because Margot is beginning to age and feels she had better hold on to what she has. Macomber is too weak and cowardly even to possess his wife, much less love her, and he accepts the status quo. Macomber knew

> about his wife not leaving him. His wife had been a great beauty and she was still a great beauty in Africa, but she was not a great enough beauty any more at home to be able to leave him and better herself and she knew it and he knew it. She had missed the chance to leave him and he knew it. If he had been better with women she would probably have started to worry about him getting another new, beautiful wife; but she knew too much about him to worry about him either. Also, he had always had a great tolerance which seemed the nicest thing about him if it were not the most sinister.
>
> . . . They had a sound basis of union. Margot was too beautiful for Macomber to divorce her and Macomber had too much money for Margot ever to leave him.[8]

They apparently have sexual relations, but Margot must find them

[7] Harry Levin, "Observations on the Style of Ernest Hemingway," Carlos Baker, ed., *Hemingway and His Critics*, p. 114.

[8] "The Short Happy Life of Francis Macomber," *The Short Stories of Ernest Hemingway*, pp. 21–22. Subsequent references to this story in this chapter will be in the text itself.

unsatisfying, for she has had repeated affairs and in the story she cuckolds Macomber openly and almost before his eyes. He calls her a bitch, she calls him a coward (22–23). The marriage is sustained under the most degrading circumstances, based as it is on cowardice and bitchery, and it indicts the professional American wife, the feminine husband, and the materialistic standards that give their marriage its continued existence.

That Macomber is less than a whole man is suggested not only by his cowardice, but also by two names that Robert Wilson, the white hunter, innocently but pointedly uses to refer to him. Wilson thinks of him as a "beggar" and "sod," Britishisms for "bugger" and "sodomite" (26, 33). (Hemingway also permits himself a pun when, the morning after Wilson has slept with Margot, he has Wilson reply with the Britishism "topping" to Macomber's query as to how he has slept [23].) Macomber is not a homosexual, but he does not have the one distinguishing masculine trait that Wilson and our civilization most prize. Wilson indicates by the half-affectionate names by which he thinks of Macomber that Macomber's troubles with his wife are somehow sexual. Also, Macomber's first name, Francis, is both a masculine and feminine name, with the slightest alteration, and it was not uncommon in the thirties to regard Francis as a sissy's name. As Philip Young has pointed out, borrowing a phrase from D. H. Lawrence, Macomber has lost his "ithyphallic authority" over his wife.[9] What he knows of sex he has learned from "books, many books, too many books." And when he doesn't want to finish off the lion, Wilson looks at him and feels "as though he had opened the wrong door in a hotel and seen something shameful." Wilson to Macomber is a "naked" reproach (21, 17, 20).

Although Macomber is a good shot, on the safari he has only done well against the not dangerous game—for instance, the eland that Macomber ritualistically eats after funking on the lion hunt. Just as cannibals eat their victims to assimilate their powers, so Macomber eats the eland because it re-enforces the only powers Macomber has—both have good eyes, both are timid, both protect themselves by running from danger.

"That's eland he's offering you," Wilson said.
"They're the big cowy things that jump like hares, aren't they?"

[9] Philip Young, *Ernest Hemingway*, p. 42.

"I suppose that describes them," Wilson said.
"It's very good meat," Macomber said.
"Did you shoot it, Francis?" she asked.
"Yes."
"They're not dangerous, are they?"
"Only if they fall on you," Wilson told her.
"I'm so glad" (9).

Macomber has become "cowy" like the male eland he eats in that he has been psychically unsexed. The thought that Margot might have to worry about Macomber leaving her if he were "better with women," suggests a degree of psychical impotence in Macomber which might be cured by just such a catharsis that the climactic buffalo hunt provides.

This animal symbolism is further complemented in the story. From Biblical times through the Middle Ages, two symbols of eros and agape had been a lion and a unicorn (or a hart, hind, etc. "Eland" is cognate with "elk," "stag," "hart," and "hind.") Macomber is capable of the unicorn—agape—but the lion—eros—frightens and eludes him. Not so Mr. Wilson. Margot says, " 'What importance is there to whether Francis is any good at killing lions? That's not his trade. That's Mr. Wilson's trade. Mr. Wilson is very impressive killing anything. You do kill anything, don't you?' " (8). And that night Margot cuckolds Macomber once more. The powers of agape which Macomber does possess are underrated by Margot. She appreciates only the hunter who can bring down the lion, and Wilson, being well capable of lion, lets Macomber be hind. Wilson gives grudging admiration to Macomber even though he has done the one thing which Wilson most despises—run in fear of his life. In other words, Wilson recognizes the value of agape which Macomber possesses, even though his wife can see no virtue in his actions. Wilson wants Macomber to be good according to his code, and the white hunter is very happy when Macomber becomes a whole man and redeems the lion business by doing well on the buffalo hunt. (The buffalo he shoots are, of course, all bulls, traditional symbols of virility and fertility.)

The dualism of hate and love is neatly re-enforced throughout the story. Whereas the impala, another deerlike animal that Macomber shoots, flees in fear, bounding wildly "in long, leg-drawn-up leaps as unbelievable and as floating as those one makes sometimes in dreams," the lion he stalks hugs the earth and charges full of hate. There is hate in eros. The lion, like Wilson, is cool and has no fear, even of man. After he is wounded, he lies in the grass, his eyes "narrowed with hate," gathering up "all of him, pain, sickness, hatred, and all of his remaining strength" for the attack on the object of his hate (19).

To Wilson's way of thinking, all Macomber needed to be a man was to become a killer, a hater, and that is what happens, ironically, when Wilson sleeps with Margot after the lion fiasco. Macomber, who had been so tolerant, now hates Wilson worse than he had hated any of his wife's other lovers, and as he begins firing at the buffalo, his only feeling is hatred of Wilson (28). The irony of Wilson's role is intensified later when Macomber's hatred results in physical courage:

> Look at the beggar now, Wilson thought. It's that some of them stay little boys so long, Wilson thought. Sometimes all their lives. Their figures stay boyish when they're fifty. The great American boy-men. Damned strange people. But he liked this Macomber now. Damned strange fellow. Probably meant the end of cuckoldry too. Well, that would be a damned good thing. Damned good thing. Beggar had probably been afraid all his life. Don't know what started it. But over now. Hadn't had time to be afraid with the buff. That and being angry too. Motor car too. Motor cars made it familiar. Be a damn fire eater now. He'd seen it in the war work the same way. More of a change than any loss of virginity. Fear gone like an operation. Something else grew in its place. Main thing a man had. Made him into a man. Women knew it too. No bloody fear. (33)

Previously Wilson had said that stalking the wounded lion was not a job for "boys," referring to African servants (17), but now the word has an added implication. The motor car, like the rifle, is a sign of Macomber's recovered masculine authority, and now that he has demonstrated the eros-hate triggered by Wilson, Wilson can justify his regard for Macomber and his agape. But Wilson's victory is a pyrrhic one.

Margot recognizes Wilson's authority but not Macomber's because of the eros-hate potential of the white hunter. She questions Macomber's order to stay in the car during the lion hunt, but she stays when he says that the order was Wilson's. Afterwards she sarcastically excuses Macomber's cowardice: " 'What importance is there to whether Francis is any good at killing lions?' " (16, 8).

Although Macomber had been afraid of the lion—eros—his wife is drawn toward the lion and rather sad at its death; she would have loved to hear its deep-throated roaring at night. (Incidentally we also learn that Wilson had a "throaty" voice [13, 23]). And while Macomber becomes a "ruddy fire eater" on the buffalo hunt, Margot develops a hatred of the bulls and a real illness, just as Macomber had become ill when hunting the lion. She thinks the chase by car unfair and a downed bull "hateful looking." Although Margot had facetiously told Macomber how "marvellous" the lion hunt was, it is now Macomber's turn to ask Margot if the buffalo hunt wasn't marvellous.

> "I hated it."
> "Why?"
> "I hated it," she said bitterly. "I loathed it."
> "You know I don't think I'd ever be afraid of anything again," Macomber said to Wilson. (32)

The Macombers have pivoted around the unchanging center of Wilson, and Margot has lost her sexual initiative. Their hateful balance has been upset by this other force of love. But the majestic, cool lion has become a "wicked"-eyed buffalo with a "thinly-haired belly crawling with ticks" (36). The heroic and noble qualities of the lion are missing in the raw, virile power and beastliness of the latter erotic animal.

Following the pattern of other Hemingway heroes who undergo an initiation or learning experience, Macomber changes at this point. He had been obsessed with learning to do things right, and Wilson is the man of the code, the man who does things right. From the very first page this is clear. After the lion hunt, when the triangle returns to camp for lunch:

> "Will you have lime juice or lemon squash?" Macomber asked.
> "I'll have a gimlet," Robert Wilson told him.
> "I'll have a gimlet too. I need something," Macomber's wife said.
> "I suppose it's the thing to do," Macomber agreed. "Tell him to make three gimlets." (3)

Ironically, it is the pair who have not failed who need the alcoholic drinks. Margot follows the admired Wilson's lead in ordering the drink, as does Macomber after he thinks that it is "the thing to do."

But Macomber is teaching Wilson something too. Wilson had "rather liked him" until he bolted from the wounded lion. Not only has Macomber shown himself a coward, but "a bloody four-letter man as well.

. . . how is one to know about an American?" Wilson asks himself. He insults Macomber in an attempt to break off with him, but Macomber knows so little about Wilson's "code" that he simply accepts the insults as just criticisms. Unconsciously, he turns the other cheek to Wilson, and his evidence of moral courage gives Wilson the impression that perhaps after all Macomber is teachable, redeemable, if not already learned about the code. When Macomber loses his physical fear the next day on the buffalo hunt, Wilson's belief that "You most certainly could not tell a damned thing about an American" has been confirmed (7–8).

Wilson even anticipates this change before the buffalo hunt begins. Margot cannot perceive it, and she looks forward to Macomber's further humiliation as an "impotent" hunter—one who can't shoot—and to Wilson's further glorification as a "potent" hunter. There are fundamental parallels between eros and the war or killer instinct which is transferred in peaceful times to sports. By deeds of derring-do, the medieval knight, the swashbuckler, and the big-game hunter pursue a similar goal, courting danger for its own sake, experiencing sensual thrill from their encounters. Unlike the Tristan-type lover, however, Macomber is the husband, not the third side of the triangle, and whereas the Tristan lover has the dangers and unhappiness of unrequited or forbidden love, Macomber has the security and unhappiness of lawful marriage. In displaying his physical courage on the buffalo hunt, Macomber symbolically rejects the suffering of his corrupted romance with Margot and accepts a type of eros untouched by the longing for passion. (". . . as the society columnist put it, they were adding more than a spice of *adventure* to their much envied and ever-enduring *Romance* by a *Safari* in what was known as *Darkest Africa* . . ." [22].) He consummates that ever-thirsting passion in action, the antithesis of the passive Tristan love. As John Killinger points out, Macomber is reborn on the buffalo hunt; he loses his fear, a loss expressed in the Freudian symbol of a dam bursting.[10] " 'Something happened in me after we first saw the buff and started after him. Like a dam bursting. It was pure excitement' " (32).

The important link is seen in Wilson's statement to Margot after Macomber's death. He assumes that she killed Macomber for fear of losing him! Macomber's new-found courage-eros will enable him to leave his wife—to end his enslavement to her—and to find some degree

[10] John Killinger, *Hemingway and the Dead Gods*, p. 45.

of happiness in a nonromantic life. Although Margot had not been proud of her husband's display of cowardice with the lion, she definitely is unhappy about his discovery of courage. She sees that she is about to lose control of her vassal.

Wilson considers American women "the hardest in the world; the hardest, the cruelest, the most predatory and the most attractive and their men have softened or gone to pieces nervously as they have hardened" (8). The reversal of sexual analogies ("softened" and "hardened") is at least subconsciously pertinent and intended here. The American woman has tried to assume the male's sexual role, and the American man has lost his "ithyphallic authority" over the American woman.

"She's damn cruel but they're all cruel. They govern, of course, and to govern one has to be cruel sometimes. Still, I've seen enough of their damn terrorism," Wilson thinks (10).

Later, Macomber would " 'like to clear away that lion business. . . . It's not very pleasant to have your wife see you do something like that' " (11). If Macomber can redeem himself, it will end his ambiguous relationship with his wife.

After Macomber had bolted, Margot looked like "an extremely handsome and well-kept woman of the beauty and social position which had, five years before, commanded five thousand dollars as the price of endorsing, with photographs, a beauty product which she had never used" (4). Although she is middle-aged, after sleeping with Wilson—the real man, the eros man whom she can admire and give herself to—"She looked younger . . . more innocent and fresher and not so professionally beautiful" (27). Finally when Macomber displays courage on the buffalo hunt, she is white-faced, gets a headache, and looks "ill" (29–31). She changes physically with her changing position of dominance, and when Macomber becomes dominant—or perhaps only assumes his masculine role—of course this real man cannot be her husband; when Macomber begins to prove himself the very sort of man who supposedly could please her, ironically she kills him, nicely enough, with her Mannlicher (cf. the German "manly") rifle. Now an important question is, did she intend to kill Macomber or to save him from the charging buffalo? The Tristan myth demands that love exist only outside of marriage. As Macomber regains his manhood, represented in his act of physical courage, the eternal hypotenuse of the triangle, Wilson, unimaginatively imagines that the now-potent man and the desirable woman must break up. Wilson has had no evidence other than the common bickering between the Macombers to support his assumption that Macomber will leave Margot now that he has "come of age." But the Tristan myth runs so deep that even the fairly simple, often perplexed Wilson (and most of Hemingway's critics, including Carlos Baker and Philip Young) assume its operation in circumstances that do not completely fit the mythic pattern.

Wilson is in the Tristan position of the triangle, yet it is Macomber who is more the victim of love than Wilson is. Wilson takes his eros where he finds it; he is unattached; his double cot will accommodate any windfall, and he gives no hint of romantic idealization of Margot—in fact, his thoughts about American women and Margot are quite brutally realistic, perhaps even exaggerated. Yet it is interesting to note the effect of this strange American couple on his love ethic. In spite of Margot's physical attractiveness to him and her pliancy and readiness—she kisses him on the mouth in front of her husband and goes to Wilson's tent at night—Wilson does not wish to sleep with her a second time, ostensibly to save Macomber's feelings further injury. Yet Wilson is inconsistent; at one moment he despises both of them; at the next he admires one, then the other. Macomber's cowardice is somewhat mitigated by his sincerity and naivety. Margot's bitchiness is compensated for by her great charm.

Wilson is perplexed, but his decision to leave Margot alone (26) is a rather funny one, for this red-faced Tristan, like all the others before him, will have little to say about it. It is Margot who took and may again take the initiative. Further, there is the possibility that there is no "romance" on this safari: there is no point in sleeping with Iseult if King Mark is there and can't do anything about it. Just as there is no thrill in hunting without danger, there is no romantic love without some danger. For a Tristan, there is no "sport" in sleeping with one's wife, or even with another's wife if the husband is not a source of possible danger.[11] The dam-bursting feeling of excitement and happiness that Macomber feels on the buffalo hunt is sexually suggestive, and Wilson also equates

[11] Cf. Sigmund Freud's "Contributions to the Psychology of Love," *On Creativity and the Unconscious.*

the hunt with sex: "More of a change than any loss of virginity. Fear gone like an operation. Something else grew in its place. Main thing a man had. Made him into a man. Women knew it too. No bloody fear" (33). I have already suggested the linguistic similarity of the phallus to guns and of Macomber's initiation to eros through hunting: he has been able to "shoot" before, but now he knows more than simply the technical operation.

The ending of the story is ironic and pathetic. Wilson has assumed, as do most critics, that Margot has shot Macomber because she could not stand to lose him. The fact is that all evidence points to a truly accidental death at the very time when the Tristan syndrome is about to suffer defeat. "Mrs. Macomber, in the car, had shot at the buffalo with the 6.5 Mannlicher *as it seemed about to gore Macomber* . . ." (36; my emphasis).

As Warren Beck points out, if Margot wanted Macomber dead, she might have waited to see what kind of job the onrushing buffalo could do.[12] Further, given the distance from which Margot shoots, her unmentioned degree of skill with rifles, the nearness of Macomber to her target (the buffalo drops dead within two yards of Macomber's body), and the lowering of the buffalo's head as it prepares to gore Macomber, it is easy to see how Margot, in drawing a bead on the buffalo, could lower and swing her rifle from the higher level and safer distance of the buffalo's head to Macomber's head, the point of attack of the buffalo.

Clearly Margot's feelings are mixed about Macomber's new-found virility. It means the loss of her dominance over him, but it does not necessarily mean her unhappiness. She was not happy when Macomber proved himself a coward with the lion (5). And their eleven-year marriage of convenience has been convenient but not happy. She wonders if his new-found bravery will be permanent, or will it be an interlude before another crisis?

"You've gotten awfully brave, awfully suddenly," his wife said contemptuously, but her contempt was not secure. She was very afraid of something.

Macomber laughed, a very natural hearty laugh. "You know I *have*," he said. "I really have."

[12] Warren Beck, "The Shorter Happy Life of Mrs. Macomber," *Modern Fiction Studies*, 1 (November 1955), 28–37. I am also indebted to Beck's essay for its careful assessment of characterization in the story.

"Isn't it sort of late?" Margot said bitterly. Because she had done the best she could for many years back and the way they were together now was no one person's fault.

"Not for me," said Macomber.

Margot said nothing but sat back in the corner of the seat. (34)

Another curious detail that doesn't seem casual is the odor of verbena that comes to Wilson at the beginning of the hunt (26). Mircea Eliade notes that verbena is mystically supposed to have first grown on Calvary; thus its peculiar healing qualities.[13] While Wilson is thinking what a good morning it is, hoping for Macomber's good luck, Macomber is hating Wilson. The professional hunter, who lives by a code, is tolerant of Macomber even though he has broken the code. On the other hand, the usually tolerant Macomber is full of hate. Though Hemingway's use of verbena may have an easier explanation, the irony is highlighted by Eliade's information. On the fatal hunt it is hatred of Wilson that seems to trigger Macomber's courage-eros. As Macomber shoots he has "no fear, only hatred of Wilson . . ." (28). Metaphorically these last actions represent sexual initiation which culminates in death, just as Eros and Death from the time of the Greeks and perhaps even before have been seen to have similar features. The sensual excitement of the hunt is repeatedly suggested in the "long heaviness" of the buffalo galloping "stiff-necked, stiff-bodied" with "upswept wide black horns," "steady plunging gait," and "plunging hugeness" (27). Sexual imagery may be suggested even by the description of the place where Macomber meets the charging bull and his death.

As the car moved slowly across the open space toward the island of brushy trees that ran in a tongue of foliage along a dry water course that cut the open swale, Macomber felt his heart pounding and his mouth was dry again, but it was excitement, not fear.

"Here's where he went in," Wilson said. Then to the gun-bearer in Swahili, "Take the blood spoor." (35)

The bull buffalo, the epitome of virility, has disappeared in the vaginal landscape. When Macomber follows him, literally and figuratively, he too is swallowed up, though quite ironically and pitifully by the con-

[13] Mircea Eliade, *Cosmos and History*, p. 30.

suming female who kills her mate at the moment when he symbolically gratifies her.[14]

What would have been the aftermath had the buffalo not charged or had Margot aimed a foot higher? The loveless Macomber of the beginning of the story has only a great, *sinister* "tolerance" (22). Through the parallel of sport he learns eros. The dam of his psychical impotence bursts. There is further suggestion that Macomber will move to agape after his initiation. Although he is stimulated to erotism by his hatred of Wilson, after the bursting of the dam there is a budding friendship of equals that binds them in their hunt and warm conversation. Wilson goes so far as to reveal his simple code of life to Macomber.

"You know, I'd like to try another lion," Macomber said. "I'm really not afraid of them now. After all, what can they do to you?"

"That's it," said Wilson. "Worst one can do is kill you. How does it go? Shakespeare. Damned good. See if I can remember. Oh, damned good. Used to quote it to myself at one time. Let's see. 'By my troth, I care not; a man can die but once; we owe God a death and let it go which way it will he that dies this year is quit for the next.' Damned fine, eh?"

Wilson is then embarrassed, "having brought out this thing he had lived by, but he had seen men come of age before and it always moved him. It was not a matter of their twenty-first birthday.

". . . he liked this Macomber now" (32–33).

Wilson himself has not changed; his great talent is simply for eros alone. Brotherly love would be possible for him with a code-educated Macomber, but not with women. "Women *are* a nuisance on safari," he thinks (25).

From the far corner of the seat Margaret Macomber looked at the two of them. There was no change in Wilson. She saw Wilson as she had seen him the day before when she had first realized what his great talent was. But she saw the change in Francis Macomber now. (33)

[14] See Maurice Maeterlinck's *The Life of the Bee* (Alfred Sutro, tr.), and Remy de Gourmont's *The Natural Philosophy of Love* (Ezra Pound, tr.), Chapter 17. The strong queen bee on her mating flight flies higher and higher with the males in pursuit, until only one enduring male remains. They copulate in the air, the strongest male with the stronger queen—selective breeding with a vengeance. Then the male drops to his death, his sex organs and entrails pulled from him as he falls away from the love clutch.

For Wilson, with his cold, flat, blue, machine-gunner's eyes, regards the subtle and difficult relations of men and women simply as "emotional trash," dirty garbage to be avoided even at the cost of insulting his employer (7).

The really difficult question of change concerns Margot. Had Macomber lived, would she have been the lady or the tiger? These things seem clear: at the beginning she is capable of eros, and, like Brett Ashley, she is a bitch with class and a kind of barren fertility goddess. It is not clear if she is motivated by the Tristan myth as Wilson seems to be. She suffers, but not because of her love for a Tristan. All too sharply she seems to see the limitations of her current hypotenuse, Wilson. He has but one great talent, and in spite of their rocky marriage, Macomber is a King Mark whom she has gone through crises with. Together they have, at least, endured. Finally, there is an ambiguity and mystery about Margot Macomber. Perhaps the difficulty is mainly a male one limited to Wilson, Macomber, the author Hemingway, and the male reader. It may stem from a primordial fear of the female and her physical differences; Freud suggests that much of the whole problem of sex may stem from that source of "mere" physical difference, the very female use of sex as a tool for achieving nonsexual ends, and the "effect of coitus in discharging tensions and inducing flaccidity" that "may be a prototype of what these fears represent."[15] In any case, the mythic dimension of the story is apparent, and no discursive analysis is ultimately the story itself nor a substitute for the wisdom of the myth.

[15] Freud, "The Taboo of Virginity," *On Creativity and the Unconscious*, pp. 193–194.

# 6 ~ WOMAN OR WIFE?

Love bade me welcome: yet my soul drew back,
  Guiltie of dust and sinne.

—George Herbert, "Love"

All beings we love are vessels full of gall, which we drink eyes closed.

—Charles Baudelaire

THE SNOWS OF KILIMANJARO is in some ways similar to "The Short Happy Life of Francis Macomber." It was published a month before the Macomber story, and both are set in East Africa while an American couple is on safari. On the surface, "The Snows" seems to have as its theme the corruption of the American writer, but although this approach to the story is a profitable one, the fact that Harry is a writer is not of great consequence. Harry's role transcends his particular profession, and his story may also be read as one of the corruption of love. As Carlos Baker has said about the Macomber and Kilimanjaro stories:

> Both deal . . . with the achievement and loss of moral manhood. Both look further into the now familiar men-without-women theme. The focal point in each is the corrupting power of women and money, two of the forces aggressively mentioned in *Green Hills of Africa* as impediments to American writing men.[1]

Aside from the obvious differences in the action of the two stories, "The Snows" differs from "Macomber" chiefly in the variations of the men and women's characterizations. Both Margot Macomber and Helen of "The Snows" are dominating women who are good at and enjoy love-making, but Helen's dominance is passive—it does not take the form of the active bitchery of Margot. Harry has willingly submitted to the protection and power of wealthy Helen, while it was Margot Macomber

[1] Carlos Baker, *Hemingway: The Writer as Artist*, p. 186. Cf. Chapter I, *Green Hills of Africa.*

who stayed with Francis because he had money. Helen is "tolerant" of Harry's male bitchery, while it was Francis Macomber who was tolerant of Margot. Helen reads "enormously" and is overly influenced by books, while Francis was the bookworm of the Macombers. And finally, if one applies the Tristan myth to "The Snows," a different role is seen for the Hemingway woman. Helen can be read as a type of Iseult of the White Hand, while Margot, if anything, was the other, first Iseult, Iseult the Fair. (Iseult of the White Hand was Tristan's unsatisfactory substitute for Iseult the Fair; he married Iseult of the White Hand but never loved her, and in revenge she finally betrays him. The name Helen may justifiably suggest the Trojan Paris' wife.)

These variations on a theme suggest several things: Hemingway was intent upon following through with some of the ideas suggested to him by *Green Hills of Africa.* But he was not sure what the best embodiment of his ideas would be, or, perhaps, he did not know until he wrote both stories what he wanted to say. He had recognized a fertile situation for good fiction in his exotic African setting, and, in the manner of some of his earlier fiction, he chose to write more than one story about the material, as if approaching it in two ways would get more out of it or guarantee that he had missed nothing of importance in the imaginative situation. See the uses of the Italian wound, for instance, in *The Sun Also Rises, A Farewell to Arms, Across the River and into the Trees,* and several short stories.

"The Snows" is not, therefore, a simple preface to or a superfluous variation of "Macomber." It is a very good story that embodies ideas of its own. My point here is simply that it is a better story when read in the light of comparison with and contrast to *Green Hills of Africa* and "Macomber." And like those two works, "The Snows" is largely concerned with a romantic vision of life and love.

Like the Macombers, Harry and Helen would seem to be an ideal couple with "everything to live for." But Harry is a morally sick man; his physical wound is symbolic of his inner illness. The wound to his leg epitomizes his sickness, for it is a type of castration wound and had been subconsciously self-inflicted. (Harry had neglected a thorn scratch and then treated it improperly.) Like Francis Macomber he has been partially responsible for the loss of his manhood, and he has, or imagines he has, a devouring mate eager to seize any sexual advantage.

Harry himself regards his life as a failure. He has prostituted his art: "each day of not writing, of comfort, of being that which he despised, dulled his ability and softened his will to work so that, finally, he did no work at all."[2] The months and years of idleness slip by. He never acts, he never loves, he never carries out his plans. He returns to Africa simply because he had once been happy there, and he thinks perhaps there he can "work the fat off his soul" (60). Scorning the challenge of real life all around him, he postpones writing the stories he knows, and he postpones loving an eminently lovable woman simply because she is his and is available at the present moment.

His is the sickness of Tristan; his end is the obscene, filthy, diseased product of a romantic dream in which the present is bitter and only the past contains any happiness. Thus the flashbacks and the action in them and in the fantasy death-flight at the end of the story. Present time in the story is static, passive. Yet in his sickness, bitterness, and remorse, where is Harry? Irony of ironies, he, like Melville in *Typee*, is in the Garden of Eden. He had returned to Africa because "Africa was where he had been happiest in the good time of his life, so he had come out here to start again" (59). But the myth of the eternal return, the recapturing of the "good times," is destroyed by the gangrenous wound that attracts vultures and hyenas. Here on the beautiful, teeming plain near Mt. Kilimanjaro and its western summit, called the House of God, Harry is to die with his dreams unfulfilled.

"This was a pleasant camp under big trees against a hill, with good water, and close by, a nearly dry water hole where sand grouse flighted in the mornings" (53). And here too are Adam and Eve back in the Garden, trying desperately to pretend they are something else, and Harry feeling very sorry that the only way to the House of God is death.

The epigraph to the story has caused some uneasiness, but as soon as one accepts the possibility of a mythic dimension in the story, it seems rather obviously a device to alert the reader to a point contained within the story, a point which follows Harry's death but which is to be kept in mind throughout the story. Kilimanjaro is a sacred mountain, a type of the sacred mountains widely used in ancient myths and familiar to

[2] Ernest Hemingway, 'The Snows of Kilimanjaro," *The Short Stories of Ernest Hemingway*, p. 59. Subsequent references to this story in this chapter will be in the text itself.

our culture through Biblical mountains, Dante's Mount Purgatory, Bunyan's Delectable Mountains, and others. It is the meeting point of heaven, earth, and hell from which the universe spreads out. At its base the earthly Paradise is traditionally located, and the road to the center of the universe and this sacred mountain is always a difficult one.[3]

That Kilimanjaro "is said to be the highest mountain in Africa," that a leopard's body lies near the western summit, the House of God, and that "no one has explained what the leopard was seeking at that altitude" (52), all indicate the sacred nature of the mountain and the religious or mythic nature of Harry's fantasy at the end of the story. In addition to having a Sacred Mountain, Dante's *Commedia* also has a leopard, a symbol of worldly pleasure and lechery, the values that Harry has traded his art for.[4] Thus the appropriateness of Harry's flight to join the leopard in death at the top of the mountain. Clearly, what both the leopard and Harry were seeking is the House of God, the summit to which the leopard has irrationally climbed and to which Harry flies at his death, finally achieving in his longed-for death that happiness which he never permitted himself in life: "There, ahead, all he could see, as wide as all the world, great, high, and unbelievably white in the sun, was the square top of Kilimanjaro. And then he knew that there was where he was going" (76).

The day before his death Harry had resolved that "because no thing could hurt him if he did not care . . . he would not care for death" (72). Thus he would conquer death; it would have no dominion. The death that had obsessed him all his life would die. In five flashbacks Harry returns to his past, and each time his thoughts turn to scenes of death or love. The combination is significant.

It has been noted before that death and eros are somehow related.

[3] Mircea Eliade, *Cosmos and History*, pp. 12–18, suggests this parallel but does not mention Hemingway's story. That Hemingway was aware of the possibility of "racial knowledge" or archetypes in his work is borne out by an interview (see George Plimpton, "Ernest Hemingway," *Writers at Work*, second series, p. 237).

[4] Cf. Alfred G. Engstrom, "Dante, Flaubert, and 'The Snows of Kilimanjaro'," *Modern Language Notes*, 65 (1950), 203–205. In order to show how Hemingway ties in the art theme, Engstrom cites a passage from Flaubert that has parallels to the Hemingway story. The mountain for Dante is Righteousness; for Flaubert, Perfect Art; and for Hemingway, Death. It should be noted, however, that Engstrom cites no evidence to the effect that Hemingway knew either of the two "sources."

The Greek sculptor modeling Eros and Death with similar features and the metaphysical poet punning with "die" to mean sexual intercourse are followed by the popular song and the popular novel that sentimentalize death. The first of Hemingway's flashbacks tells of death and suffering that Harry has seen. All the scenes are of winter, and snow is instrumental in the death of the fleeing Greek refugees, though it covers the tracks of the deserter. Harry remembers too the skiing he enjoyed so much. These random thoughts, reminding us of the title and the epigraph, prepare for the denouement, because snow is a death symbol and skiing is both a type of the death flight (which is explicit at the end of the story) and a type of the sexual act.

In the second flashback the combination of eros and death or violence is elaborated. Here Harry clarifies what the earlier loves of his life were, those loves that he can never find in Helen. The Tristan syndrome is at work again: Harry has had a succession of lovers, but it is only his first love, his unrequited love, that is real for him. The flashback begins with Harry alone and lonely in Constantinople, apparently covering the Greco-Turk War, as Hemingway did in the fall of 1922. Harry had left Paris after a quarrel with his wife (not his lover), "whored the whole time" in a futile attempt to "kill his loneliness, but only made it worse," and then "had written her, the first one, the one who left him, a letter telling her how he had never been able to kill it" (64). He writes to her that he thought he once saw her in Paris, and followed the woman, and felt "faint and sick inside," and all the women he had slept with since knowing her only made him miss her more, and "he knew he could not cure himself of loving her" (64–65).

After sending the letter, asking her to write, "and that night missing her so much it made him feel hollow sick inside," he takes a hot Armenian belly-scalding slut away from a British subaltern after a fist fight and sleeps with the "smooth, rose-petal, syrupy, smooth-bellied, big-breasted" woman who "needed no pillow under her buttocks . . ." (65).

The next day he accompanies a Greek attack that is horribly botched —the new officers are incompetent, the artillery fires into its own troops, the Greeks run and are shot by their officers, and there follows things that are "much worse." In contrast to this elemental struggle, he returns to Paris and finds a stupid-looking, potato-faced American poet talking about Dada to the affected Roumanian Tristan Tzara, founder of the Dada movement.

Harry is in love again with his wife, their quarrel is over, the madness all over, but the "first one," the one he gets sick over, answers his letter, and his wife finds out about his "sickness," and "that was the end of the beginning of that" (66).

Harry concludes his reverie by remembering all his numerous quarrels with women, quarrels that always took place when he was feeling best. He had seen the world change and a "subtler change" that it was his duty to write of, but now he never would.

In this flashback are revealed Harry's real problem and the concepts of eros, agape, and romantic love. Contrary to the popular image of the Hemingway hero as a free lover, we see here sexual indulgence with an important qualification or reservation. Eros, Harry finds, is no remedy for romantic love. It is hard to overemphasize the importance of Harry's thinking he could not cure himself of love.

The irony of longing for a woman in the past who rejected him is beyond Harry's grasp, but at least he recognizes it as a sickness, and he also returns un-Tristan-like to a wife whom he also loves. When the flashback ends, we can see Harry repeating himself. In Africa he quarrels with another woman whom he thinks he does not love. But what might he have thought of Helen had he lived another ten years and found himself with another woman? He would have thought of Helen as a woman he once loved; he would remember with longing those "good breasts" and "useful thighs" that he looks on rather academically now.

A further irony which Hemingway must consciously intend is his use of the real name of the affected Roumanian in Paris. Tristan Tzara is obviously too sophisticated to have an Iseult.

The flashback has another interest in its biographical parallels. Not only was Hemingway a war correspondent in the Greco-Turk War, but he was also caught in a compromising situation much as Harry was. Hemingway's "first one"—Iseult—was Agnes H. von Kurowsky, the real-life counterpart of Catherine Barkley of *A Farewell to Arms.* When he was married to Hadley Richardson, his first wife, he reportedly wrote a "fond letter" to Agnes, and incompatibility eventually led to his divorce from Hadley.[5] One biographer, Milt Machlin, even assumes that Hadley, like Helen in "The Snows," knew of a reply from Agnes, but there is no evidence for assuming the historicity of every event in the story.[6] From Hemingway's "true" account of the African safari, *Green Hills of Africa*, we may read of his warm, happy relationship with P.O.M., Pauline Pfeiffer, his second wife. Hemingway later said that he, like Harry, had been happiest in Africa, but, unlike Harry, he said that Pauline was the best wife he ever had. Thus the changes in the Macomber and Kilimanjaro stories must be considered major. Is the legal relationship of man and woman also changed?

Both Carlos Baker and Philip Young tacitly assume that Harry and Helen are man and wife; both critics refer to Helen, in passing, as "wife."[7] And, indeed, if one reads the story casually, there is little reason to suppose that they are not married. Engstrom, however, refers to Helen as Harry's mistress: "His wealthy mistress is with him."[8] Although Engstrom is writing about the mountain and leopard symbolism, he goes on to quote a passage from the story which contains the hints "this rich bitch" and "she kept him well."

If Harry and Helen are not married, a further variation on the situation common to *Green Hills of Africa* and "Macomber" would be established and would be of importance to a consideration of Hemingway's love ethic. The evidence is this: at the outset of "Macomber" it is clearly established that the Macombers are man and wife. In "The Snows" Helen is never directly referred to as Harry's wife, and there is only one allusion to her as a wife. That allusion, significantly, comes from Helen's own lips. After the first flashback Harry asks Helen where they stayed in Paris.

> "At the Crillon. . . .
>
> "There and at the Pavillion Henri-Quatre in St. Germain. You said you loved it there."
>
> "Love is a dunghill," said Harry. "And I'm the cock that gets on it to crow."

[5] Leicester Hemingway, *My Brother, Ernest Hemingway*, p. 52.

[6] Milt Machlin, *The Private Hell of Hemingway*, pp. 53–54.

[7] Carlos Baker, *Hemingway: The Writer as Artist*, pp. 191–196, and Philip Young, *Ernest Hemingway*, pp. 46–50.

[8] Alfred G. Engstrom, "Dante, Flaubert, and 'The Snows of Kilimanjaro'," *Modern Language Notes*, 65 (1950), 203–205.

"If you have to go away," she said, "is it absolutely necessary to kill off everything you leave behind? I mean do you have to take away everything? Do you have to kill your horse, and your wife and burn your saddle and your armour?"

"Yes," he said. "Your damned money was my armour. My Swift and my Armour." (57–58)

The soft woman uses the euphemism "go away" for "die" and sentimentalizes his death to produce an ironic effect for the reader and for Harry, one which he seizes upon in his pun. She seriously envisions Harry as a medieval knight, but her history is not accurate if she thinks of him as a Tristan and of herself as his legal wife. It was Iseult the Fair, the adulteress, who died at Tristan's death, not his wife, Iseult of the White Hand. But if Helen thinks metaphorically of her relation with her Tristan Harry, then indeed they are man and wife, married in spirit and undying devotion if not in fact. Harry's bitterness toward her and the corrupting influence on his art of her wealth is thus capsuled in his pun. While she romanticizes, he plays to the groundlings, and the pun has a nice appropriateness as it links the names of two large meat-packing houses, in which Helen might possibly have had a financial interest, with Harry, another piece of meat, no longer much of a man, decaying and dying in the pre-eminent land of carnivores, with hyenas and vultures waiting for their Treet.

At least Helen's remark establishes the possibility that Harry and she are married. Contrary evidence would include Harry's remark, " 'If you hadn't left your own people . . . to take me on—' " (55) and the previously cited "she kept him well" (60). In other places "he went to her" (59), and "she had acquired him" (62). Never is it "married me" or "married him." In indirect discourse Harry usually thinks of her as "the woman," "the rich bitch," or simply "she." The other characters, the servants and the pilot, Compton, use the indeterminate "Memsahib." In speaking or thinking of him, Helen uses "dear," "darling," and "Harry," but never "husband."

When one notices the ambiguity of the relationship, as indicated by these names and phrases, the contrast with "Macomber" is striking. In that story the marriage of the pair was painful, emphatic, and clear. The conclusion that might be drawn is that if Harry and Helen are married, as probably most critics and readers assume, phrases like "take me on," "kept him," and "acquired him" connote the cheapness and shallowness of their marriage, which is in fact more like a prolonged affair than a marriage. (Such a view is sensible and would gain some support from Hemingway's position as a defender of marriage in his own life. The state of marriage apparently had value for Hemingway, and he respected it through four marriages.)[9] Perhaps the reader who assumes that marriage binds Harry and Helen believes so because Harry is so manifestly unhappy, and no such couple would stay together except for moral and legal sanctions. Such reasoning would have greater merit if Harry and Helen were pictured as creatures of traditional Anglo-Saxon morality, but they are not. Such reasoning also underestimates both the power of money, the armour that Helen supplies so abundantly, and the weakness of Harry. Harry is poor but dishonest, willing to let Helen believe he loves her for the sake of his security.

"It was strange that when he did not love her at all and was lying, that he should be able to give her more for her money than when he had really loved" (60–61). If he were married to her, he would perhaps have no reason to sham his love to keep his material position except for the reason of common decency that would not allow him to hurt the naive woman who had bounced about from man to man and now thinks she has found her true love. On the other hand, she tells him once that the money " 'was always yours as much as mine' " (55).

In any event, the ambiguity of their relationship indicates the relative unimportance to them of the technical state of marriage and the breakdown, by extension, of the institution of marriage. For the Macombers and for Harry and Helen it is hard to see where adultery leaves off and marriage begins, where hate leaves off and love begins.

Harry's feelings for Helen are violently mixed. Although he had "sold vitality" in exchange for security and comfort, he had received a bonus along with his regular dividends.

> She was still a good-looking woman, he thought, and she had a pleasant body. She had a great talent and appreciation for the bed, she was not pretty, but

[9] See Leicester Hemingway, *My Brother, Ernest Hemingway.* His is probably the most reliable biography to date, but it has been challenged on some points. Carlos Baker is at work on the official biography of Hemingway, and one hopes it will settle the numerous myths that pass for fact in so many essays and books.

he liked her face, she read enormously, liked to ride and shoot and, certainly, she drank too much. . . .

She was a damned nice woman too. He would as soon be in bed with her as any one; rather with her, because she was richer, because she was very pleasant and appreciative and because she never made scenes. (61–62)

She looked at him with her well-known, well-loved face from *Spur* and *Town and Country*, only a little the worse for drink, only a little the worse for bed, but *Town and Country* never showed those good breasts and those useful thighs and those lightly small-of-back-caressing hands, and as he looked and saw her well-known pleasant smile, he felt death come again. (67)

Quite fittingly he feels death at the same moment that he feels eros.

Yet he hates Helen for another reason than that he fears death and associates love for her with it. He has a deep-seated malaise that prevents him from enjoying this kind, somewhat groping and distressed woman who waits only on him, who seems in fact to have an obsessive regard for him, who possesses him just as she possesses her money. The night Harry dies, Helen has a dream about her daughter and her very rude father. That night Harry has been rude to Helen too, and a likely excuse for the presence of the dream in the story is that Helen has an Electra complex.

Like the Macombers, they are repeatedly quarreling, or rather Harry is, since Helen tries her best to avoid disputes. Harry insists on being brutally realistic about his gangrenous wound, but Helen would rather not recognize the odor and pain and the hyenas and the vultures, signs of Harry's death and her loneliness. His resignation bewilders her. Her hopefulness is only bitter irony for him who has already felt death and knows its closeness. He hates Helen for being rich, for putting him in an inferior role, being dominated by her money; but of course it is himself he must ultimately hate for succumbing to her temptations. And he must hate, too, the example of her selflessness which she thrusts upon him, even if he knows it stems from her fear of being left alone.

Although he cannot see it, this romancer who thinks he is being cruelly realistic is destroying Helen's love for him, just as his quarrels destroyed his previous loves.

"Why, I loved you," Helen protests. "I love you now. I'll always love you. Don't you love me?"

"No," said the man. "I don't think so. I never have." (55)

His love is the "first one," or the last one, but always a phantom.

He thinks to himself:

> He had never quarreled much with this woman, while with the women that he loved he had quarrelled so much they had finally, always, with the corrosion of the quarrelling, killed what they had together. He had loved too much, demanded too much, and he wore it all out. (64)

What a commentary on true love! Since Harry doesn't love Helen, they don't quarrel much. She is "a fine woman, marvellous really." "He had been cruel and unjust," but he doesn't love her!

Both Helen and Harry affect the Tristan-Iseult pose, but in different ways. It has been noted that Harry has been bitterly realistic about his imminent death that started with an innocent-seeming thorn scratch. That bitterness, however, is not the opposite of romance. He says he loved Paris and Africa and all the places where he had been happy, but most of his flashbacks to the scenes he has never written about are to scenes of death, violence, and destruction; fire, suicide, poverty, murder, and an agonizing wounding. His only remedy for these calamities that marked his life and spirit was romance, which was for him a necessary illusion.

At his death, when the world of pain and suffering seems dominant to him, he thinks that romance has somehow cheated him or escaped him. "So this was the way it ended in a bickering over a drink" (54). When Helen reminds him that he loved Paris, there is a saving recognition when Harry says, "Love is a dunghill." What has he known of the mutual need and help that Helen thinks he is scorning? Harry is referring instead to that emotion of his that he feels cheated him. It is not eros at all, for the Armenian slut and Helen herself did very nicely for that. But Harry is still lonely and empty after that lovemaking which he does almost compulsively. Harry is a Tristan reacting against his sick vision which ends in memories of death and violence and obscene vultures and hermaphroditic hyenas waiting for him to die.

It is Helen who makes the chivalric allusion to Harry as a dying knight, but she is essentially criticizing his romantic disillusionment by her tacit preservation and use of the "necessary illusion," if it is that. She clings to love, she clutches love to her in the person of Harry, giving him everything she has—her wealth, her body, her devotion. Can she help it if Harry resents the first, recognizes the second as universally available, and grudgingly, dog-in-the-manger accepts the third? Being a Tristan, he wants nothing that can be his. He wants none of this Iseult of the White Hand, this "rich bitch." He has used her money for his armour, to protect his emotions, to keep himself from becoming truly involved with another person.

The repulsion that he rightly feels is due to her dominance over him. Everything that she gives him increases her power over him. Unlike Margot Macomber, Helen does not complain; she endures, forgives—even in his death fantasy Harry puts her in a kindly role—and so she dominates him as she loves him and sucks off the energy that he would have channeled into his art. Harry has been, like Francis Macomber, a coward, though not in the physical way that Macomber was. Harry wants death to come and get it over with, but he has not the moral courage to obtain his freedom by loving Helen. He had made himself nothing more than a gigolo.

His concern for himself distinguishes Harry from Helen and is also the cause of his failure to write. Helen says,

> "You can't die if you don't give up."
> "Where did you read that? You're such a bloody fool."
> "You might think about some one else."
> "For Christ's sake," he said, "That's been my trade." (53)

Harry tries to make a Robert Cohn-like figure out of Helen by attributing her idealism to too much reading. Later Harry thinks, "She was always thoughtful. . . . On anything she knew about, or had read, or that she had ever heard" (59). And later, "she read enormously. . . ." (61). But the burden of their problem rests with him, and because he no longer cares for others, he is no longer a writer. In flashback three we learn that he used to be kind—when he was poor and unknown. Fame nourished his self-esteem and killed his friendships. "No, he thought, when everything you do, you do too long, and do too late, you can't expect to find the people still there. The people all are gone. The party's over and you are with your hostess now" (73).

But Helen is kind in many little things, is thoughtful, and wants desperately to be loved and loving because, a little like Robert Jordan's Maria, she has had a bad time—not the hell of war, violence, and slow death that Harry remembers, but the equally crippling agony of a struggle with oneself, a struggle that Harry has postponed until the infected scratch makes it too late, except to regret having avoided the battle for the sake of his security and comfort.

Her struggle had started when her comfortable, tranquil world was, like Harry's, touched by death, the death of her husband when she was still "comparatively young." As in Hemingway's earlier story "The Gambler, the Nun, and the Radio," her history was a search for opiates, first, devotion to her children, then horses (phallic totems), then books, then bottles, then lovers. But none of these, and least of all the lovers, who bored her, was a permanent deadener. She was still alive, a raw nerve, and "acutely frightened of being alone" (61).

Because she admired Harry's writing and envied him his independent life, she "acquired him" and then, second step, fell in love with him, thus regaining some semblance of the human solidarity she had had with her husband. The cost for Harry was a trade of freedom for security and comfort. Ironically, the very qualities Helen values and acquires are also security and comfort, but she has seen into a void during *her* freedom. She wants none of it and no doubt is puzzled at Harry's esteem for independence, which he obviously regrets having lost.

Helen asks Harry not to quarrel with her anymore. She places an overpaid value on his affection and is willing to settle for simple toleration because she is neurotically afraid of being alone.

> "You don't have to destroy me. Do you? I'm only a middle-aged woman who loves you and wants to do what you want to do. I've been destroyed two or three times already. You wouldn't want to destroy me again, would you?"
>
> "I'd like to destroy you a few times in bed," he said.
>
> "Yes. That's the good destruction. That's the way we're made to be destroyed." (63)

She has known the agony of loneliness and the destruction that is worse than loneliness, the discovery of hate or indifference in the men she thought loved her but who were, alas, only lovers. But even here at Helen's moment of high seriousness, Harry can think of destruction only as eros.

"Macomber" had ended with Margot exhorting Wilson to stop his accusations. She succeeded when she used the word "please." "The Snows" begins with Helen exhorting Harry to "Please don't" refer so casually to the odor of his gangrenous leg, and it ends with Helen crying, "Harry! Please, oh Harry!" Please, Harry, she means, don't leave me, for I will be alone. Both women are left alone, but Helen is crying her "please" to her dead man.

Harry is flying to the House of God. It is a trip that crosses many hazards, just as every journey to a Sacred Mountain traditionally does. The "old cock" Harry is put in the Puss Moth, where there is, naturally, room for only one. The pilot says, " 'I'll be back for the Mem'," as indeed he may (75). Getting Harry in the plane is difficult; he has not made things easy for such a momentous flight. There are wart-hog holes and a bumpy field on take-off, a heavy forest, high hills, columns of rising heat that bump the plane, a blizzard of locusts, and a heavy rainstorm, but having met and passed these hazards of life, Harry bursts through the storm to see "as wide as all the world, great, high, and unbelievably white in the sun . . . the square top of Kilimanjaro. And then he knew that there was where he was going" (76).

In these terms his death must be considered a victory—as senseless as the leopard's perhaps, but a victory. Death, the "stinking bastard," the hyena that lay upon his chest, is done with (74). The leopard's frozen carcass on top of Kilimanjaro, the Sacred Mountain, knows no decay or violation by the scavengers of the plains. The hyena makes "a strange, human, almost crying sound" (76). Helen wakes and Harry is gone.

# 7 ~ HOLLOW AND SICK

All the sweetness of love is steeped in bitter gall and deadly venom.

—Maurice Scève

It remains that man has for centuries nibbled at the idea of connection, intimate connection between his sperm and his cerebration.

—Ezra Pound, "Translator's Postscript" to *The Natural Philosophy of Love* by Remy de Gourmont

IN 1937 Hemingway shifted his setting from Africa, the scene of his last book and of two of his best short stories, to Key West, Florida. The character types changed too, but of greatest significance were a decided emphasis on and clarification of those ideas of agape which had begun to influence his work. He told his brother Leicester that *To Have and Have Not* was "in many ways the most important story he had ever written. Before it, he hadn't cared how life went as long as he could create productively. From this point on, he really gave a damn about other peoples' lives."[1]

While giving a damn is not exactly an affirmation of life and love, it is a beginning, and the critics are in general agreement that *To Have and Have Not* is, in one critic's words, "a crisis novel."[2] Carlos Baker and Philip Young disagree on the effectiveness of the novel, but they also read it as a turning point in Hemingway's career and similarly interpret its theme. Baker sees the theme as "the decline of the individual. . . . The novel . . . contains Hemingway's notes towards the definition of a decaying culture, and his disgust with the smell of death to come." Hemingway realized the difficulty of contrasting the Harry Morgan parts with the Richard and Helen Gordon parts, and he wanted to revise the manuscript, but under pressure of reporting the Spanish Civil War, he didn't find the time or energy to change it. Nevertheless, Baker

[1] Leicester Hemingway, *My Brother, Ernest Hemingway*, p. 204.

[2] Maxwell Geismar, *Writers in Crisis*, p. 67.

continues, *To Have and Have Not* really embodies Hemingway's theme; it is neither sermon nor propaganda, and thus it is better than most proletarian fiction of the thirties.[3]

Young sees the theme as the repudiation of Hemingway's previous isolation. Although the theme is the most important contribution of the novel, it "does not grow very inevitably out of the action." The conclusion is "not skillfully transacted." Thus *To Have and Have Not* is "more significant for the way it marks this revolution in the course of the author's thinking than for anything else."[4]

No doubt it is a "problem" novel, as the conflicting opinions of Baker and Young would indicate, but just because it is generally judged as a lesser creation is reason enough to inquire why. Is it possible that we today can also hail it as "good" thematically—as Marxists did—and "bad," or less than completely successful, artistically? From a certain point of view one's judgment cannot be so divided, and it would seem that the supposed revolution in Hemingway's thinking, as expressed in *To Have and Have Not,* was not so sudden or violent as has been generally held. Not only had the revolution been a slow one—really an evolution—but, also, the novel itself was not the complete declaration of dependence that has sometimes been assumed. Had not *For Whom the Bell Tolls* followed it, *To Have and Have Not* would, no doubt, have been regarded as a rather strange literary sport, and possible three hundred years from now, literary historians in Australia would be arguing that the novel was really a youthful Herman Wouk's first book.

*To Have and Have Not* is not a bad novel, but it is less than good because Hemingway is not convincing. Surely, the characters and action are individually vivid and believable, but when Harry dies saying, " 'No matter how a man alone ain't got no bloody fucking chance'," we can ascribe that statement to Harry without feeling that Hemingway the author is also committed to that message of universal dependency.[5] Hemingway's previous ideas on love had seemed complicated, and his conscious thinking about man in society had perhaps even changed. But he had not converted himself body and soul, and the novel reflects his

[3] Carlos Baker, *Hemingway: The Writer as Artist*, pp. 204–206.

[4] Philip Young, *Ernest Hemingway*, pp. 71–73.

[5] Ernest Hemingway, *To Have and Have Not*, p. 225. Subsequent references to this novel in this chapter will be in the text itself.

uncertainty. Thus the novel more clearly evolves and states ideas on love than his previous work had, but the ideas are not entirely assimilated to the form. *To Have and Have Not* is a less than successful novel but an important one because of the emerging ideas which were to take root and grow but also to be pruned in his subsequent work.

An inevitable misreading of the theme of the novel centers around its title, perhaps the least appropriate of Hemingway's usually good titles. Not only Marxists would take the title as a guide to a proletarian theme; the opposition of the destitute Harry Morgan to the comparatively wealthy Richard Gordon and the millionaire yachtsmen would convince most readers that the novel had to do with a contrast between the wealthy and the poor, the haves and the have-nots. Such is not the case. Material goods or money is an easy and common symbol of wealth that Hemingway also uses, but in themselves, goods and money are only symbols; they stand for something else and mean little to Hemingway. In this novel, the haves are wealthy, the have-nots poor, but not in the usual pecuniary sense. In fact, Hemingway effects an irony by creating the materially wealthy people as have-nots.

To have what? To have not what? How are the haves separated from the have-nots? Who are which? To answer these questions is to find more complexity and rewarding thought in the novel than is usually conceded. The characters *can* be divided according to economics, but such a division is insignificant as well as overlapping and frustrating. They are not neatly divided into two classes, but range through the whole economic spectrum. At one end are the veterans doomed to a twentieth-century serfdom and the family man Albert, an honest Florida conch who is slowly starving because he can find no work. At the other end are the double-crossing Mr. Johnson, Tommy and Helene Bradley, and the yachtsmen the reader briefly meets in Chapter 24. Interesting and important as these minor characters are, the central figures belong near the middle of the spectrum: Harry and Marie Morgan (a little on the minus side of the middle) and Richard and Helen Gordon (a little on the plus side). Significant minor characters who are also neither poor nor rich are Bee-lips the lawyer, Professor MacWalsey, fishing-boat captain Willie, Freddy the bartender, and the bank-robbing Cuban revolutionists. There can be no doubt that there is a wide economic range and that money is a prime motivation in the lives of the characters, but the novel is not about money or about the Depression. It *uses* money, and it is *set* in the Depression.

Nor is a social or political division of the characters any more sensible or worthwhile than an economic one. Birth, position, and prior condition of servitude are background factors. Political implications are minor and more often than not ambiguous, if not outright irrelevant. The "committed" critics and authors of the thirties who hailed *To Have and Have Not* as a signal of Hemingway's commitment to society could not possibly have found any positive political ideas in the book. True, Hemingway looks at the power of wealth, the excesses of revolutions, the degradation of poverty, the proposed remedies of socialism, the dangers of political power, and the corruption of bureaucracy, but the novel is no more about these problems than it is about deep-sea fishing and smuggling.

Hemingway is saying that his have–have-not distinction crosses social, economic, and political lines. The good guys are really the haves, and what they have is love, agape. (Something else they have is *cojones*, Harry Morgan's quaint and seemingly sole criterion for "having," until his deathbed re-evaluation of his life.) The have-nots lack agape; they are lonely, hollow, sick; they haven't a chance, as Harry would say. Harry Morgan takes up the ways of the have-nots; he is not driven simply by economic necessity into a life of violence, though he rationalizes it that way. His disintegration and destruction are paralleled by Richard Gordon's, the writer's, self-discovery and consequent shame. Harry's problems are not simply contrasted to those of Gordon and the other minor characters; all of the action, including the vignettes, parallels, reflects, and re-enforces the message of Harry's life.

Harry has moments of doubt about his lawlessness and the horrors it leads him into, and at the end of his life he repudiates his actions. He was proud. He valued his *cojones* and self too highly. His final change of heart is foreshadowed throughout the novel, and whatever the judgment is of the realism of his conversion to agape, it is not sudden or unprepared for.

In theme, then, *To Have and Have Not* states simply that man alone, the loveless man, has no chance, and further that eros, the love of a woman, is not enough. Man is redeemed through constructive work, but that work, though not necessarily communal, must be social and nonpredatory (Hemingway frequently alludes to the animality of Harry and others [53, 86, 113, 121, 128, and 163]). That is, though a man may work alone, he must work "for" his fellow man. Harry, a loner, works for himself, and he believes that the end of self-preservation justifies any means, no matter how destructive, no matter who may suffer. Harry's defense that he smuggles and murders for the sake of his wife and children is not very convincing, as we shall see.

On the basis of this philosophy of rugged individualism and of the ends justifying the means, all men will perish—the tough Harry Morgans, the deceitful and deceived Richard Gordons, the idealistic yet brutal revolutionaries, and the fraudulent captains of industry. For some the recognition comes late, for some not at all—they only sense their illness and know not its cause. But all their hollow ships will crash on the rocks of loneliness. When a society is characterized and dominated by excessive concern for the isolated individual (the self), the society too will crash and disintegrate. Thus the form of the novel is a complementary series of degenerations and of episodes of growing violence.

The five chapters of Part One are written in the first person with Harry Morgan as the narrator. The point of view is manipulated radically throughout the novel, and the fact that at the beginning Harry himself reports is dramatically indicative of the pretty pass his world has come to. The brutal slayings that Harry witnesses in the Havana street are told very coolly, very disinterestedly. That is not to say that Harry was not excited or the reader unmoved. Quite the contrary. But the violent death of the three refugees does not involve Harry. He is an "innocent bystander," an onlooker, a man isolated from this accident of fate which, though it made him feel "pretty bad," is thrust from his consciousness by a "quick one out of the first bottle I saw open" (8). Harry returns to his boat, tells his charterboat client what has happened, and then seems to forget it. Huck Finn had nightmares over the meaningless violence he saw, but this grown-up wanderer never mentions it again.

The three murdered Cubans were revolutionaries who had wanted Harry to take them to Florida, and he had refused, not because it was illegal, but because people talk and he could not afford to lose his boat to the officials who might seize it. "They were nice-looking fellows all right and I would have liked to have done them the favor" (3)—for $3,000. But why stick your neck out? Minutes later, the three are murdered.

Eddy, Harry's alcoholic helper, had also seen the killings, and when he rejoins Harry on the boat, he asks the fisherman Mr. Johnson not to talk about the killings: " 'It makes me sick to even think about it.' " So Eddy too had " 'better have a drink' " (9).

Still in his first chapter, Hemingway quickly drops the opening scene of violence and takes up Mr. Johnson, a wealthy American of obscure background and occupation to whom Harry has chartered his boat for three weeks. Johnson knows little of fishing, and Harry merely tolerates him because of the large fee he anticipates. After losing a good marlin and subsequently carelessly losing another along with Harry's expensive rod and reel, Johnson doublecrosses Harry and leaves Cuba owing a broke Harry $825. Frankie, a loyal friend, then offers to find some illegal cargo for Harry's return trip to Florida. On this note, the first chapter ends, and Hemingway has already presented most of the ideas which he will use throughout the book. First, drink is both a corruption and a necessary medicine. Eddy used to be "a good man on a boat once, before he got to be a rummy" (18); and Harry drinks after the murders and after Johnson doublecrosses him. Second, the loss of love is revealed through two modes, the one open, direct, and violent—the murders—the other cowardly, indirect, and passive—the doublecross. The murders and doublecross head a list of violent and passive crimes against men and mankind that mounts throughout the novel. Third, mental sickness accompanies losses. To see what causes a sickness is to see what the sick man cares for. Eddy gets sick thinking about the murders (9). Harry gets sick thinking about his lost tackle (22). And fourth, hope is born from friendship. The deaf, down-and-out Frankie is Harry's loyal and goodhearted friend who comforts him in his loss and undertakes to help him.

Later in the novel these four ideas will be modified or extended. Perverted sex, compulsive sex, and drugs like sleeping pills can later be connected with drink as a sign of a disintegrated individual who is grasping at something, instead of someone, outside himself for his stability. The active and passive forms of violence become more personal as the novel progresses. Nothing more violent than murder will occur, but the violence is more horrible as it draws nearer the central figure from the peripheral characters and as it comes to hurt the innocent as well as the involved. As the exterior violence increases, the interior sickness and hollowness also magnifies, as if violence and deceit were a spreading cancer destined to corrupt the entire society. The faint note of caring at the end of Chapter 1 becomes an overwhelming diapason of commitment at the end of the novel. Not only do the Harry Morgans need Frankies, they need all men to care for them; and the Harry Morgans need to care for all of them, including the Bee-lipses, the Eddys, the Richard Gordons, and the Cuban bank robbers and murderers.

Like Chapter 1, Chapter 2 primarily develops the feeling of quiet, cold cruelty that engulfs the characters so easily that they seem to take it for granted. Mr. Sing, who smuggles Chinese into the United States from Cuba, makes an alliance with the hard-up Harry. Harry distrusts Sing and guards against a doublecross by him, but it is Harry who later doublecrosses Sing. The double standard of immorality never seems to occur to Harry. The only thing he feels bad about is his momentary anger at Eddy who accuses Harry of not treating him "square."

> "Who did you ever treat square, you rummy? . . . You'd doublecross your own mother."
>
> That was true, too. But I felt bad about hitting him. You know how you feel when you hit a drunk. (38)

Harry also has some appreciation for his other accomplice, Frankie, but it is hardly friendship that he feels for the emotional Cuban.

> "You not worry any more?"
>
> "Hell no," I said. "Plenty big business. Much obliged."
>
> "Good," said Frankie and patted me on the back. "Make me happier than nothing. All I want is you happy. Chinamen good business, eh?"
>
> "Wonderful."
>
> "Make me happy," said Frankie. I saw he was about ready to cry because he was so pleased everything was all right, so I patted him on the back. Some Frankie. (36)

Chapter 3 is an interlude that lets us see another latent side of Harry's nature. He is an observer of man and nature. He passes a British freighter "loaded deep with sugar and her plates were rusty. A limey in an old blue sweater looked down at me from her stern as I went by her" (41). "It was a fine sunset and there was a nice light breeze"(45). Such details hint that Harry is capable of going outside himself, and when he discovers that Eddy has stowed away, Harry is not so much angry as sorry for Eddy, for he thinks that he will have to kill Eddy to keep him from accidentally telling of the smuggling. Eddy, however, causes Harry to revise his thinking. Perhaps the drunk has touched a sensitive spot when he says, " 'Us conchs ought to stick together when we're in trouble' " (43).

The fourth chapter of Part One is another episode of dramatized violence. Harry and Eddy pick up the twelve Chinese wetbacks, and Harry, the boat Pilate, coolly and deliberately breaks the arm of Mr. Sing, the would-be Savior of the Chinese. Then Harry breaks Mr. Sing's neck, after first breaking one of his arms, and he compares the dying man to a fish on a gaff, flopping, flailing, making funny little noises. Smoothly, quietly, not unlike the pleasure of fishing, Harry murders the polite Mr. Sing, drops him into the Gulf Stream to bait up fish, and scrubs the blood off the stern deck.

> "What did you have against him?" Eddy asked me.
>
> "Nothing," I said. "He was the easiest man to do business with I ever met. I thought there must be something wrong all the time."
>
> "What did you kill him for?" [Eddy asks Pilate.]
>
> "To keep from killing twelve other Chinks," I told him.
>
> "Harry," he said, "you've got to give me one because I can feel them coming on. It made me sick to see his head all loose like that."
>
> So I gave him one. (55)

Harry's standards are comparative. It is all right to doublecross a man who might doublecross you. It is proper to murder one man to keep from murdering twelve. He would have killed the twelve Chinese somewhere at sea rather than run the risk of actually landing them in Florida. Now he can simply turn his boat back to the Cuban shore and at gunpoint force the Chinese to wade ashore.

"Now I tell you it would take a hell of a mean man to butcher a bunch of Chinks like that and I'll bet there would be plenty of trouble, too, let alone mess" (57).

On the cruise back to Key West (Chapter 5), Harry suffers no remorse. Eddy gets sick, but not tough Harry. The only thing that perplexes him is Mr. Sing's naive trust in him. The Chinese had been so easy to do business with. "He certainly wasn't much of a business man.

Maybe he was. Maybe he just trusted me. I tell you I couldn't figure him" (60).

Harry plans to "do away" with Eddy before they reach Florida. (At least Harry has to use a euphemism when he thinks of murdering his long-time companion!) Can a greater loss of kinship be imagined than his rationalizing of the murder of his helper? Eddy would get drunk and talk, Eddy was better off dead anyway, Eddy wasn't on his crew list and Harry would have to pay a fine if he had him aboard. On the other hand, he didn't want to do away with Eddy and later be sorry for it, and his mind is made up for him when he discovers that, unknown to him, Eddy has had his name added to the crew list. Harry lets him off with a warning.

> "If you ever open your mouth about last night I'll hear of it and I'll do away with you."
>
> "You know I'm no squealer, Harry."
>
> "You're a rummy. But no matter how rum dumb you get, if you ever talk about that, I promise you."
>
> "I'm a good man," he said. "You oughtn't to talk to me like that." (62)

And Harry shares a bottle with Eddy as they near Key West.

The trip had been a "good" one after all. The last scene of Part One is of domestic tranquility: Harry drinks his whiskey in his living room, smokes a cigar, and listens to Gracie Allen. He sends his wife to the door to chase away the drunken Eddy, who comes to see him, probably for a handout.

The amoral Harry tells his wife that Eddy is a lucky rummy. Marie, not Mary the mother of Mr. Sing, but maybe Mary Magdalene, says, " 'There ain't any lucky rummies—' " (physical dissolution is the outward sign of an inward disgrace).

" 'No,' " says Harry. " 'I guess there aren't' " (64).

The short—twenty-page—Part Two is the "Fall" which follows the "Spring" of Part One. The last part is "Winter." The hope of spring is gone. Summer is past. Violence and hate were sown in the spring, at the beginning of things, and the harvest is one of more violence and hate, of increasing hollowness and sickness for Harry, with only flashes of the hope and spiritual sustenance of agape.

Harry and a Negro helper, Wesley, are both wounded as they leave Cuba with smuggled liquor. The narrative is no longer in the first person, although Harry is the focus throughout the next three chapters. The shift in point of view may be felt to complement the growing impersonality of the inevitably corrupting forces of nonlove. As Harry and Wesley struggle to get home they quarrel and feel pain and sickness. When they are discovered by another fishing boat, captained by Harry's friend Willie, they think they are saved, but Captain Willie has chartered his boat to two Washington government men who want to capture Harry and turn him in. Although Willie thwarts their plan, Harry and Wesley are left alone to suffer and make their way to port as best they can.

When Harry tells Wesley that one must have confidence while steering, the Negro's reply strikes a chord (that will later re-echo in Harry's mind); he says, " 'I got confidence. . . . But the way this trip gone I ain't got confidence no more' " (67). Man has turned against man. The once-reliable Cubans, who did not previously hinder smuggling, had opened fire on them. The tanker Harry and Wesley spot seems to look like the silhouette of Miami, which is far off their course. What is certain any more?

Harry and Wesley quarrel.

> "I hurt," the nigger said. "I hurt worse all the time."
>
> "I'm sorry, Wesley," the man said. "But I got to steer."
>
> "You treat a man no better than a dog," the nigger said. He was getting ugly now. But the man was still sorry for him.
>
> "I'm going to make you comfortable, Wesley," he said. "You just lay quiet now."
>
> "You don't care what happens to a man," the nigger said. "You ain't hardly human."
>
> "I'm going to fix you up good," the man said. "You just lay quiet."
>
> "You ain't going to fix me up," the nigger said. The man whose name was Harry Morgan, said nothing then because he liked the nigger and there was nothing to do now but hit him, and he couldn't hit him. (69)

Men must quarrel, and men must hate and be evil. When Wesley belatedly asks Harry why they were smuggling liquor even though Prohibition was over, Harry rhetorically asks, " 'Why don't people be honest and decent and make a decent honest living?' " (70).

Wesley becomes "religious," Harry thinks, only because he is hurt. Harry is too tough and too proud to cry or complain, but he is learning the lesson that he will speak when he knows he is safely dying and no one can accuse him, as he accuses Wesley, of being, "out of his head" or "becoming religious." The great irony is, of course, that Harry's dying warning is attributed to his own wound-induced madness.

The worst thing Harry feels is "the smell of the booze," the symbol of decay and weakness. The bullet-broken bottles have spread the liquor all over the boat, and the smell makes Harry sick. He feels "hollow and unsteady" (73). "He was thinking that he had never really felt pain before" (74). Literally Harry is sick from his bullet-riddled arm, that will eventually be amputated. Symbolically he is sick of what the liquor and the wound to his arm represent—another wound, like that other Harry's of "The Snows of Kilimanjaro," which is castrative in type and representative of a loss of both eros and life.

The two vacationing government men who want to capture Harry and Wesley are caricatures of officialdom, who, though not very believable, contract with Captain Willie, who is Harry's "brother."

> "Fishing is nonsense," said Frederick Harrison. "If you catch a sailfish what do you do with it? You can't eat it. This is really interesting. I'm glad to see this at first hand. Wounded as he is that man cannot escape. It's too rough at sea. We know his boat."
> "You're really capturing him single-handed," said the secretary admiringly.
> "And unarmed, too," said Frederick Harrison.
> "With no G men nonsense," said the secretary.
> "Edgar Hoover exaggerates his publicity," said Frederick Harrison. (82)

But Willie refuses to steer his boat alongside Harry's; instead he warns Harry and then cruises away.

> "Thanks, brother," came the voice of Harry.
> "That chap your brother?" asked Frederick Harrison, his face very red but his love for information still unappeased.
> "No, sir," said Captain Willie. "Most everybody goes in boats calls each other brother." (83)

A fraternity exists among the boatmen, the disciples who are fishers of fish; and Harrison, who has said, "Fishing is nonsense," is excluded from it. Having *cojones* is another mark of the brotherhood. Willie tells his passengers that Harry has them (78). But the government men do not: they desire to "capture" Harry and Wesley only when they know the bootleggers are helpless. But bravery is not necessary, for Wesley lacks it and is still, in Harry's words, "a all right nigger" (87).

This brotherhood is no proof against the rages of life, but it offers some hope. Wesley can be "all right," even though he curses Harry and says, " 'You ain't human' "; Captain Willie is a "good skate" (86). And now that Harry is near home, he feels "a strange, hollow singing in his heart. He always felt this way coming home at the end of a trip" (87). He is over being "sicklike" in the boat, and he is heading for his peaceful, happy home just as he did at the end of spring. The difference is that Harry will be cut. His arm must be amputated. The wound of hate cannot be healed this time.

With its rapidly shifting points of view "Winter," the third, last and longest part, suggests the confusion and chaos, the disintegration of life. Unstable form follows unstable content, which is a reflection of a segment of modern life. The point of view shifts and the characters shift. No longer does Harry dominate the action. In Part Two he lost the first-person point of view; in Part Three he is upstaged by the characters of a story within his story. Many minor characters are introduced, and the Gordons, being central to much of the action, are more than minor characters. Here also a third element is developed that further complicates the relatively simple opposition of hate and agape in the first two parts. Part Three concerns eros and romance (absent in Parts One and Two) as well as hate and agape, and Hemingway loses no time introducing the lion of eros and the snake of romance.

While the violence will continue in the form of Harry's contract to carry four bank robbers off to Cuba, the Northern tourists are introduced as foils to Harry and Marie and the other Key West natives. The roles played by the tourists are completely isolated from the main action of Harry's escape and death, although the characters occasionally see each other. The "action" that the tourists are involved in is almost completely erotic or romantic. Thus three sections in Part Three stand out as developments of the eros and romance themes. The first, Chapter 12, concerns Harry and Marie and their lovemaking. The second, Chapter 21, concerns Richard and Helen Gordon and their falling out of love. The third, Chapter 24, concerns the four sets of isolated, otherwise untreated yachtsmen and their various perversions of love.

Throughout these sections Hemingway has a lamentable tendency to caricature and stereotype. He hacks away until the point is unmistakably but somewhat unrealistically clear. For example, a foreshadowing of Helen Gordon's important denunciation of the love that is " 'just another dirty lie' " (185) occurs at the beginning of Part Three where "the old man with the long gray hair over the back of his collar who sells rubber goods specialties" (91) gratuitously—or perhaps simply awkwardly, since he does have a foreshadowing function—moves on and off scene. Here also the good-whore stereotype is used to set up the reader for a tacit comparison of the professional, good-hearted, but downtrodden whore with the amateur, wealthy, corrupting bitches on the yachts and in the mansions who charge more but charge indirectly. The city government has taken to arresting and fining streetwalkers. " 'That's all they pick on now,' says Big Lucie's daughter. 'Any kind of sporting people. Anybody with any sort of a cheerful outlook' " (93). Albert, Harry's friend, reports that he has known the minor character Miss Richards "ever since she used to be in jungle town, but two or three of the hardest working married women in town used to be sporting women and this was a hard working woman, I tell you that" (99). Harry's wife Marie was also once "a sporting woman" who is now desperately faithful to Harry and, presumably as a result of her experience, a wonderful piece.

The night before Harry is to carry off the Cuban bankrobbing revolutionaries, he goes home to his bedded wife. She awakes and takes the initiative in a remarkably vocal lovemaking scene. For a man who is usually reticent and is sometimes described as an animal, sometimes as a baby, he and Marie do a lot of talking. The burden of their intercourse is that Marie is greatly excited by Harry and his wonderful build. "I'd like to do it and never sleep,' " she says (115). She is fascinated by his castrative wound too. Harry asks:

> "Listen, do you mind the arm? Don't it make you feel funny?"
> "You're silly. I like it. Any that's you I like. Put it across there. Put it along there. Go on. I like it, true."
> "It's like a flipper on a loggerhead."
> "You ain't no loggerhead. Do they really do it three days? Coot for three days?"
> "Sure." (113)

But Marie is glad that his amputation was of an arm and not a leg (114). This ambiguity is further defined by her bleached blonde hair. She has begun to let it grow out, but Harry insists that she keep it bleached, suggesting an allusion that Leslie A. Fiedler describes as the opposition of the Blonde Angel and the Dark Lady. The irony is that Marie is anything but the "Pale Protestant Virgin." Fiedler explains:

As late as Theda Bara, the old myth still holds, however stereotyped and debased; but with Jean Harlow we enter another phase. From her to Marilyn Monroe, we have lived through an uninterrupted series of sexually potent "dyed blondes"—the very term, and the dull jokes about peroxide bottles which surround it, betray our growing sense that there is no genuine Fair Lady, only brunettes wearing false colours.[6]

The success of the Morgans' marriage is a bit ridiculous in its " 'Ah, Harry. That's it. Ah, you honey' " (113), but the point is that Harry has a wife—more houri than whore—who is his match sexually. Hemingway's heroes have not had hot wives with the exception of the chronologically close Margot Macomber and possibly Helen of "The Snows of Kilimanjaro," if, in fact, the couple in that story is married. And the one certain exception up to *To Have and Have Not,* Margot Macomber, is hot for other men, not for good old Francis. The Hemingway bachelor, of course, has always made a fine, erotic match for himself, but here Harry has a wife who seems even more eager for bed than any Hemingway male ever was. Harry has had other sexual experience, but the implications are that it was all premarital, like Marie's, rather than extramarital. Harry is faithful, but while they are having sexual intercourse, Marie asks Harry if he ever "did it" with a Negress and what it was like. Harry answers,

"Like nurse shark."

"You're funny. Harry, I wish you didn't have to go. I wish you didn't ever have to go. Who's the best you ever did it with?"

"You." [Who else? the faithful husband answers.]

"You lie. You always lie to me. [One hopes no pun is intended.] There. There. There."

"No. You're the best."

"I'm old."

"You'll never be old."

"I've had that thing."

"That don't make no difference when a woman's any good."

"Go ahead. Go ahead now. Put the stump there. Hold it there. Hold it. Hold it now. Hold it."

[6] Leslie A. Fielder, "From Clarissa to Temple Drake: Women and Love in the Classic American Novel," *The Griffin* (July 1957), p. 23.

"We're making too much noise."
"We're whispering."
"I got to get out before it's daylight." (113–114)

Harry's admonition and Marie's weak reply are anticlimactic in more ways than one.

What clinches the certainty of Hemingway's change is his granting the hero and heroine children—three daughters no less. Jake Barnes had been sexless, and Frederic Henry had lost his despised, mother-lover–killing child at its birth. But the shock that reportedly came to Hemingway with the arrival of the unexpected, unwanted son to him and Hadley Hemingway in 1923, was, perhaps, wearing off. And after two more sons, by his second wife, he realized that the presence of children in a home had not the disastrous implications of responsibility and restriction that he had once imagined. Nevertheless, Harry Morgan's children are remote from the story. They afford some justification for Harry's rationalization of his smuggling and helping the Cubans escape, and in the bedroom scene Harry tells Marie to be more quiet so as not to wake them. The killer doesn't want his children corrupted by the knowledge of sex. When Harry is getting ready for the trip to Cuba, he says, " 'Shit'," a word that annoys Marie.

"Aw, Harry, don't talk like that in the house."
"You talk worse than that in bed sometimes."
"That's different. I don't like to hear shit at my own table." (126)

Harry has a certain reservation about sex that approaches prudishness. Whereas Marie enjoys eros for eros' sake, Harry takes a more functional view of sex; he wants sons. His daughters seem unsatisfactory to him, and he wonders why he and Marie couldn't have boys. " 'That's because you're such a man. That way it always comes out girls.'

" 'I ain't no hell of a man,' Harry said" (126).

Again later he wonders why they didn't have sons, and he speculates that perhaps "the boys in her went out before I knew her" (127)—as indeed they did.

This domestic aspect of Harry extends to his home itself, which he owns. As he contemplates the danger of his trip, he surveys his home and its treasures. What he sees and values reveals Harry's bourgeois tastes and romantic susceptibility.

He sat at the table and looked at the piano, the sideboard and the radio, the picture of September Morn, and the pictures of the cupids holding bows behind their heads, the shiny real-oak table and the shiny real-oak chairs and the curtains on the windows and he thought, What chance have I to enjoy my home? (127)

Then the mate of the domestic panther fetches his Tommy gun, he pats her on the back with the stump of his arm, and he goes off to his death, still a boy. The night before, after they "did it," Harry had fallen asleep, and Marie, the mother, the peroxide-blonde Virgin Mary lay awake to glory in her having him.

I've been a lucky woman. Him saying like a loggerhead [turtle]. I'm glad it was a arm and not a leg. I wouldn't like him to have lost a leg. . . . Do you suppose those turtles feel like we do? Do you suppose all that time they feel like that? Or do you suppose it hurts the she? I think of the damnedest things. Look at him, sleeping just like a baby. . . . Christ, I could do that all night if a man was built that way. I'd like to do it and never sleep. Never, never, no never. No, never, never, never. . . . Look at him sleep. Look at him sleep there like a kid. (114–115)

The innocent American Adam and Christ-in-Harry go off to be martyred for the Haves who preach the gospel of love. Back home his wife yearns to lose herself in an endless reptilian copulation, to find in eros an everlasting sensual gratification.

The second section that importantly treats eros and romance and the loss of agape is Chapter 21. The chapters between 12 and 21 have dealt with Harry's plans to seize his impounded boat and, failing that, to rent a friend's boat for the escape to Cuba. Chapter 18 is the dramatic climax of the escape in which Harry, about to be double-crossed, double-crosses the Cubans, slays all four of them, but is himself fatally wounded in the belly. As he lies slowly dying in the drifting boat amid the money stolen from the bank, the blood from the dead, and the surge of the Gulf Stream, the action shifts to Richard Gordon, a moderately successful writer, and to his point of view.

The morning after the bank robbery, Gordon sees Marie coming home from the sheriff's office. To Gordon's eyes, Marie is "appalling," "a battleship," "terrific," a sloppy and unattractive woman whom Gordon erroneously assumes must arouse disgust and hatred in her husband; she must find the sexual act repugnant. After seeing her for just a moment, knowing nothing specifically about her, he makes his ironic misinterpretations and rushes home to record his "observations" for the novel he is writing, "a novel about a strike in a textile factory" (176) with a "love interest." He would contrast Marie to a "young, firm-breasted, full-lipped little Jewess" (177) who had a real interest in the labor-organizer–hero's work—and presumably a real interest in sex.

Yet this writer who wants to know all about life and love treats his love-hungry wife, Helen, cruelly. To her polite inquiry about the bank robbery, he replies, " 'Don't talk to me. . . . I'm going to work. I have it all in my head.'

" 'That's fine,' she said. 'I'll leave you alone' " (176).

What an awful foreshadowing! The writer has ideas in his head but no knowledge in his heart. His wife, Helen, finally exhausted by her own loneliness, will leave him.

The lovely, clear-skinned Helen is not *seen* by her husband, who chases after the "famous beautiful" Helene Bradley, another Helen of Troy, everybody's mistress, who interests him " 'both as a woman and as a social phenomenon.' "

> "A writer has to know about everything," Richard Gordon said. "He can't restrict his experience to conform to Bourgeois standards."
>
> "Oh," said Helen Gordon. "And what does a writer's wife do?" (140)

Richard Gordon does not even understand the warning inherent in her question.

Immediately before the scene in which Helen and Richard break up, comes the brief, camera-eye Chapter 20, which describes Harry's drifting boat with its gruesome cargo. The shifting back and forth between the Gordons and Harry, their paths never crossing, is an ironic, possibly too obvious contrast of the complete sexual adjustment of Harry and Marie with the completely unsatisfactory adjustment of Richard and Helen. Less obvious and more important is the comparison of Harry's physical destruction with Richard Gordon's psychic collapse. Both men choose nonloving lines of action to obtain what they feel are justifiable ends: survival for Harry and his family, "art" for Gordon. A difference is that Harry has some stature in his quest; Gordon is merely pitiful.

He returns home to his wife after an abortive liaison with Helene

Bradley. Still smarting from the slaps she has given him, he receives another kind of slap from his wife, whom he surprises sitting on a couch in the dark with John MacWalsey, a heavy-drinking but kindly professor of economics vacationing in Key West. The Gordons exchange recriminations. Richard is covered with lipstick; Helen has permitted MacWalsey to kiss her. Richard calls Helen a bitch; she threatens to leave him. He has acted like a conceited rooster, yet he has not wanted children, only the indulgence of his own pleasures. He left her alone too much, and she turned to the sympathetic and also lonely MacWalsey for companionship. Though she is not even sure how to spell his name, she may marry him; and she is through with Richard. She no longer even hates him. She simply dislikes him.

"Richard Gordon said nothing. A hollow had come in him where his heart had been, and everything he heard, or said, seemed to be overheard" (185).

Helen is "not really" married to Richard, for Richard had refused to be married in her Roman Catholic Church, a refusal that hurt not only Helen but also her mother. But Helen had agreed to Richard's terms, for she was in love.

> "Everything I believed in and everything I cared about I left for you because you were so wonderful and you loved me so much that love was all that mattered. Love was the greatest thing, wasn't it? Love was what we had that no one else had or could ever have. And you were a genius and I was your whole life. I was your partner and your little black flower. Slop. Love is just another dirty lie. Love is ergoapiol pills to make me come around because you were afraid to have a baby. Love is quinine and quinine and quinine until I'm deaf with it. Love is that dirty, aborting horror that you took me to. Love is my insides all messed up. It's half catheters and half whirling douches. I know about love. Love always hangs up behind the bathroom door. It smells like lysol. To hell with love. Love is you making me happy and then going off to sleep with your mouth open while I lie awake all night afraid to say my prayers even because I know I have no right to any more. Love is all the dirty little tricks you taught me that you probably got out of some book. All right. I'm through with you and I'm through with love. Your kind of picknose love. You writer." (185–186)

You hypocritical writer who shifted with the winds of doctrine, "'changing your politics to suit the fashion,'" exploding with "'your rages and jealousies and your meannesses'" (186–187). This dirty ugly mess is at once the end of the dream of romantic love and the failure of eros when used as a tool of romantic love. Only an Iseult could react so bitterly to the Grail that had turned into a mess of ordure in her hands. Some instinct perhaps had kept the original Tristan and Iseult from consummating their love, but the American dreamer was not so content. He sought life for the dream and found it a nightmare.

Helen will turn to MacWalsey as to her father, of whom he reminds her: a man who drank and fought, who was simple and perhaps slept with other women but never hurt his wife—a man who was, above all, kind.

Richard Gordon can take all this acrimony until Helen bitterly asks how Helene Bradley liked him in bed. " 'Did she think you were wonderful?' " (188). His self-esteem is crushed. Not only does he discover that his wife does not love him, but she touches upon the sorest spot of all, his masculinity. That afternoon in the very midst of his lovemaking with Helene Bradley, she looking up at "the white ceiling with its cake-frosting modeling of cupids, doves and scroll work" (188–189), Helene's husband had entered the room.

" '*Please don't stop,*' " she had pleaded, for after all her husband knows of her tastes (and he himself has, apparently, the taste of a voyeur). But Richard Gordon had not the savoir faire to continue, and Helene, insulted and, worse, sexually frustrated, slapped him twice and ordered him to leave (189–190). His manhood has been impugned twice.

Because he had been slapped, he slaps Helen—illogically, desperately —for he only now realizes something of this wife with the "sad, angry face, pretty with crying, the lips swollen freshly like something after rain, her curly dark hair wild about her face . . ." (188). This chapter, written from Gordon's point of view, shows Gordon seeing his wife for the first time as a person separate from himself and capable of an individuality that could, paradoxically, have been happily joined with his. She can know nothing of his destruction at the Bradleys'. If she did, perhaps she would not simply feel sorry for him, but also have sympathy for him, this pitiful barnyard rooster without balls: "Richard Gordon could hear the clock ticking and he felt as hollow as the room was quiet" (190). The sick Harry, now the hollow Gordon.

Their apologies are empty, last bitter exchanges, and Helen's pity only wounds Gordon more, and he retaliates by impugning *her* sexual capacities, thus bringing her to tears. The double shock has awakened Gordon to his selfish vanity. He sees the loveliness and charm and sexuality of his wife's face and body, and he sees his own inadequacy that has been sexual only in a symbolic way. Of course the knowledge comes too late as they say goodbye.

This modern Tristan has not died for love. Love itself is dead. Tristan now simply pursues eros, the "experience" that will help him be a better writer. When his wife speaks of the necessary illusion of love, he is amazed. And of all people to want to revive love—a wife! His amazement and shock are understandable. Maxwell Geismar says of the "Love-is-a-dirty-lie" passage: ". . . it is doubtful whether anywhere else in his work Hemingway's conception of a human passion is quite as frightful as this, so mechanical and sterile, detached from all human feeling."[7]

Like the walls of Jericho, Gordon's defenses against the vital demanding commitment of love come tumbling down. What follows his separation from Helen has not even the saving grace of sorrow, much less a sense of tragedy. At the same hour that Harry Morgan's body is dying and his mind is trying to formulate the meaning of his exemplary experience, Gordon is trying to lose his recently discovered and distasteful individuality. He drinks. Images of romance crowd him. He drinks more. He fights, striking out at something he cannot hit but which he tried to objectify. He tries to find companionship, but all he finds is a homosexual and the beer-bought, drunken, coarse acquaintance of near-derelicts.

He goes to "Conch town, where all was starched, well-shuttered, virtue, failure, grits and boiled grunts, undernourishment, prejudice, righteousness, interbreeding and the comforts of religion; the open-doored, lighted Cuban bolito houses, shacks whose only romance was their names" (193). He visits one bolito house, the Lilac Time, and discovers "that drinking was never going to do any good to him now" (195). He meets Herbert Spellman, an admirer of his novels who, like Gordon, is a " 'sucker for anything on the social conflict' " (197) and a social parasite who is in love with the movie star Sylvia Sydney. His

[7] Geismar, *Writers in Crisis*, p. 73.

cliché-ridden mind guesses the cliché of Gordon's next book—the love "interest" in the textile factory story.

Gordon leaves and goes to Freddy's bar. The phonograph plays "Isle of Capri" and the swarming mass of veterans in town from their government work camp drink and fight. The scene is like something out of Dante's Hell. Society is adrift. Society has disintegrated. All is chaos:

> . . . a man came hurtling out of the open door, another man on top of him. They fell and rolled on the sidewalk, and the man on top, holding the other's hair in both hands, banged his head up and down on the cement, making a sickening noise. No one at the bar was paying any attention. (200–201)

When the sheriff arrives and tries to stop the fight, the fighters object; the sheriff just wants to spoil their fun. After all, isn't the victim his brother's kicker? And can't he "take it" as well as anyone?

The world is turned upside down. Friends fight. The most admirable achievement of man is his ability to "take it." Man is born to "take it." The punchy fighter tells Gordon his secret: not only do the blows not hurt, sometimes they feel good.

The friendly fighters adopt Gordon as a source of drinking money. Because another man at the bar has saved part of his meager pay, he too has to "take it," is hit and kicked until he falls down; his assailant is happily victorious, and again no one cares about the victim.

Hemingway admits an ironic Virgil in the form of a relatively sober Communist to comment on this hellish scene, and Gordon is his audience:

> "Aren't they fine boys?" said the tall man. "War is a purifying and ennobling force. . . ."
>
> "These [veterans] are the elite. The very top cream of the scum. . . .
>
> ". . . we are the desperate ones," the man said. "The ones with nothing to lose. We are the completely brutalized ones. . . . We have been beaten so far that the only solace is booze and the only pride is in being able to take it." (205–206)

The decay of the majority of these have nots—men with neither love nor money—is often related to sexual decay. One of the punchy drunks has the "old rale"—syphilis. "Red" had been a clean-living, good fighter once, but an opponent with syphilis had given it to Red in the ring during clinches. And Red's wonderful wife had left him, yet he pitifully talks as though she were still "nuts" about him, working "like a slave" for him. He is so "beat" and trodden that he too must believe a romantic dream of love. He has no idea where his dream girl is.

> "He don't even know what country she's in."
> "But listen, buddy," said the red-headed one. "Wherever she is, that little girl is faithful." (211)

Sometimes he thinks maybe she is Ginger Rogers and has gone into motion pictures. The veteran, like Gordon, is now alone and degenerating faster and faster. Yet even at the edge of desperation, romance lives. Even with the "old rale," man goes on, for what difference does disease to the body make when the social body and its mind are incurably ill?

A knowing slip occurs when Gordon sees Professor MacWalsey at the bar and tells his veteran friends that MacWalsey has ruined his life. The veterans offer to beat MacWalsey to death, but Gordon tells them to leave him alone. They protest:

> "You said that rat ruined your wife."
> "My life. Not my wife."
> "Jesse! Pardon me. I'm sorry, pal." (214)

Since everyone has had or will have his *life* ruined, there is no point in making a fuss over it (or over an accident like the rale). But to ruin a man's *wife* is a specific, comprehensible, punishable act; man can retaliate there. A rule of love has been broken. Yet these same men make Gordon sick when they tell him the story about the sailors who " 'go ashore there in the evening up under Riverside Drive there's old guys with long beards come down and you can piss in their beards for a dollar' " (206–207).

Gordon is directly caught up in the swirl of meaningless violence when he sees MacWalsey. As the story of the sailors made him feel sick, so does the sight of the man who "ruined his life." Furthermore, the Communist tells him that his social protest books were "shit." His ego bared to its pitiful weakness, himself alone and defenseless, he joins in the physical violence symbolic of his psychic disintegration. When he sees MacWalsey, Gordon feels a sickness in his chest (212), and finally he lashes out at him, only to be "cooled" in turn by one of the bar's bouncers.

The end of the chapter of violence is a quiet foreshadowing of the theme of brotherly care and responsibility that Harry Morgan will soon utter. Though Gordon attacked him, MacWalsey helps the writer into a cab and starts to take him home, not knowing that Gordon and his wife have separated. But when Gordon comes to, he is still angry and leaves the cab. MacWalsey tells the cab driver that he is worried about Gordon, and the driver asks, "'Is he your brother?'" "'In a way,'" MacWalsey answers, in the way that we are all brothers to anyone whose lives we ruin simply by having lives of our own. He reflects on this paradox of involvement, and he is Hemingway's spokesman in his realization of the cruel payments in fear, loneliness, and hate for whatever pleasure another man would enjoy. "... why must all the operations in life be performed without an anesthetic?" MacWalsey asks himself as he watches Gordon's lurching retreat (221). To complete his own life, to lose his own loneliness and find love, MacWalsey operates on Gordon, cuts him off from his identity, which may be pitiful but is nonetheless a tie that, once loosed, sets him, like the veterans, adrift. MacWalsey knows Gordon is stupid, but Gordon's very incapacity makes MacWalsey's responsibility greater. He is ashamed and disgusted with himself and the surgery that may, after all, not succeed. To fulfill, he wrongs. To love, he generates hate. Even to return to the world of the loving requires some pain, but the Professor will inflict it on Gordon because loving is a necessary operation that justifies the pain.

Chapter 23, which follows, is the one in which Harry finally gets out the statement he has been learning all his life. He is dying and he is delirious, or at least so thinks the Coast Guard captain from whose point of view the action is seen. Harry is desperate to get out the message that has cost him so dearly and perhaps will save other men. At first he tells the captain that there is "no exit":

> "A man," said Harry Morgan, very slowly. "Ain't got no hasn't got any can't really isn't any way out. . . ."
>
> "Four men," said the captain helpfully. . . . [The captain pumps Harry for information, thinking that Harry is trying to tell him who the murderers were.]
>
> "A man," corrected Harry; then stopped.
>
> "All right. A man," the captain said.
>
> [A man, any man, everyman. One's luck may hold for a time, but eventu-

ally for all men, whether they are fools like Gordon or pirates like Harry Morgan,] "No matter how a man alone ain't got no bloody fucking chance."

He shut his eyes. It had taken him a long time to get it out and it had taken him all of his life to learn it.

He lay there his eyes open again.

"Come on," said the captain to the mate. "You sure you don't want anything, Harry?"

Harry Morgan looked at him but he did not answer. He had told them, but they had not heard. (224–225)

Harry's priceless lesson is, ironically, attributed to the opposite of great wisdom. No one at all will profit from Harry's death. As if to underscore the irony indelibly, the next chapter—the third and last key chapter of Part Three—is a roving camera-eye view of five new sets of characters, mostly the economic haves, but really all have-nots. They are on their yachts in the yacht basin where Harry and his boat are being towed. Whatever its structural appropriateness, the chapter is an excellent summary of the hollowness and sickness of have-not lives.

The first scene shows the wealthy Wallace Johnston and his not so wealthy "friend" Henry Carpenter, who does what the bachelor Johnston wants him to do, and thus Johnston doesn't have to pay blackmail to bus boys and sailors. Johnston is rude and abrupt with his steward, and he cannot bear Tommy Bradley, whom he suspects of being impotent, and his whore of a wife, Helene. Johnston and Carpenter quibble about the virtues of the Bradleys. Carpenter has, "of course," slept with Helene and found it "marvellous," but the homosexual Johnston is revolted by the idea. They finally part for the night. Carpenter's opposition to Johnston is like the coquette's who is merely playing hard to get and thus making herself seem more attractive. Johnston will "keep" Carpenter to satisfy his "rather special" sexual pleasures for a while longer, but when he lets Carpenter go, the man will be an "inevitable suicide" (227–233).

On one of the largest yachts in the basin, another perversion of eros is represented by a sexually vigorous sixty-year-old grain broker who has pushed his luck too far. The Internal Revenue Bureau is investigating his illegal activities, and his doctor has ordered him to forgo liquor, the "chemical courage that had soothed his mind and warmed his heart for so many years" (234). As fate closes in on him, he finally realizes that he is alone. He had had a wife whom he had married only for her money and who had divorced him after twenty years of "keeping up appearances, and he had never missed her nor had he ever loved her" (235). His sexual vigor had been channeled into a special use: high finance gambling. His sexual vitality "gave him the confidence to gamble well," and he also had innate abilities, "skepticism" and "lack of morals." He deceived people into thinking he wanted to help and befriend them, but he really only wanted to use them as "accomplices." When he had achieved his end, they were discarded, for he had no "remorse or pity." But time has caught up to him, and his corrupted erotic power has diminished, as flesh must. His chest shrunken, his belly bloated, "his now useless and disproportionately large equipment that had once been his pride" inert, he finally feels remorse (235–236).

The grain broker has gone it alone, and he is brought to the end of the American dream just as he has driven so many erstwhile friends, partners, and competitors to their American nightmares—maybe only a financial fall, but maybe "the leaning drop . . . from forty-two floors up, with no rush of plumes as when an eagle falls" or maybe "a step forward onto the third rail in front of the Aurora-Elgin train" with "unsaleable combination eggbeaters and fruit juice extractors" in your overcoat pockets. To cure their physical or spiritual ills, ". . . some used the native tradition of the Colt or Smith and Wesson . . . those admirable American instruments so easily carried, so sure of effect, so well designed to end the American dream when it becomes a nightmare . . ." (237–238).

On the first two yachts are men who have openly misused their bodies and spirits in what the pious world readily recognizes as perversions, but the third yacht contains a pious family that, for all its clarity of conscience, is just as corrupt as those men who are driven to self-destruction by the heaviness of their guilt and loneliness. This "pleasant, dull and upright family" has not hated, has not won its wealth through violence or cheating, but it has marketed a product that costs three cents a quart to make and sells for a dollar a pint. The implication is clear that hating your fellowman can take on an innocent-seeming guise. Their guilt may not be criminal, but it is antisocial and a denial of the community of man. In their ignorance, neither can they love. Their emotions are conventional and shallow, and Hemingway writes of them ironically when he says, "They are a happy family and all love each other."

The father is a paragon of virtue, admired by all. His daughter is lovely, and her fiancé is the All-American boy, which means he is a bit on the emasculated side, but never mind; "with a lovely girl like Frances intention counts as much as performance" (239). Here the conclusion re-enforces the use of eros or sexual skill as a necessary sign of agape. In another context, one could hardly imagine its connection to agape, but no longer does Hemingway restrict love to eros alone. Love encompasses eros and agape. The insipid fiancé has not even the erotic instinct to sense the deficiency of his shallow relationships in which the easy, unlearned, unfought for, loveless loving marks him as a man like the grain broker and the homosexual's boyfriend who will end up alone. The fiancé may be different in not having enough sense to know the pathos of his fate. Because he is so conventional, so much the right thing in the world in which he moves, he may forever assume his own happiness.

Following a paragraph about twenty-four Esthonian yachtsmen is the final, the female, the most horrible of the scenes that contrast with Harry's death. Dorothy Hollis, the wife of an alcoholic Hollywood director, is the narcissistic mistress of "a professional son-in-law of the very rich," who has just fallen asleep after making love to her. She has three crutches: the first, not the alcohol that the sick men use, but luminol, for she cannot sleep; the second, her own image, for, blessed with beauty, fame, riches, youth, she is alone and turns to her mirror for companionship; and the third, sex, for her lover is sweet and, unlike the fiancé of the nice family's daughter, an excellent lover—if he could only keep from getting drunk and falling asleep. But like all Tristans, this one would not be any good for her if she married him. He would be after someone new, or younger, or blonde, or "Chinese or Lesbian or goodness knows what" (244).

Dorothy Hollis wonders if she is becoming a bitch—stupid, well-intentioned, and really selfish. She wonders why men can't be more stable and stay awake long enough to satisfy her. She wonders if she ought to masturbate, and she does, and eros has gone from a tool of perversion (with the homosexual and the grain broker) to an edgeless tool (a non-tool of the nonloving, nice people), to a tool of inversion (the masturbation of the loveless, lonely beautiful bitch). Masturbation, the final surrender of the eros that must live in two bodies or not at all, the demise of the eros that led to agape and pulled the likes of Dorothy Hollis up to the achievement of a Marie Morgan, who found a one-armed panther to lavish her love upon.

The narrative is stream of consciousness as she decides whether or not to masturbate, whether her lover is sweet or not. He isn't, but she is—lovely, lovely, lovely; here, here, here. Her conscience is not quite clear on her decisions, but finally her guide is her own pleasure, her own relief from care, and she goes to sleep with a final thought that she must not lie on her face and crush out her loveliness (245–246).

As these yachtsmen and their loves fall asleep, Harry Morgan's boat is towed into the yacht basin. The irony is complete except for a few more touches: the farcical scene in which the dead Albert's wife falls into the water and loses her dental plate, emerges, and hysterically screams in lisps, to the immense enjoyment of the crowd gathered to see the unfolding of the last act of the "tragedy"—the tragedy with no catharsis for them or anyone else because everyone knew Harry was delirious when he whispered his message.

Perhaps Marie knew it all along, but she had only Harry. In her isolation at Harry's death, it is now her turn to feel "hate and a hollow feeling. I'm empty like a empty house" (257).

Her grief is real. She remembers her first happiness with Harry. She remembers when she first dyed her hair blonde—"just like gold"—and how much Harry liked it.

Harry may not have learned the lesson of agape until too late, but his symbolic goodness in the art of eros was something, at least, and Marie valued it in itself and for what it signified. "Good men are scarce," she thinks (261). And now she is old and not so desirable, "and there ain't nothing now but take it every day the way it comes and just get started doing something right away. That's what I got to do. But Jesus Christ, what do you do at nights is what I want to know" (261).

The closing description is magnificent in its sexual imagery and ironic suggestiveness in contrast to the bloody mess and loneliness of the town of Key West that night.

> Outside it was a lovely, cool, sub-tropical winter day and the palm branches were sawing in the light north wind. Some winter people rode by the house on bicycles. They were laughing. In the big yard of the house across the street a peacock squawked.

Through the window you could see the sea looking hard and new and blue in the winter light.

A large white yacht was coming into the harbor and seven miles out on the horizon you could see a tanker, small and neat in profile against the blue sea, hugging the reef as she made to the westward to keep from wasting fuel against the stream. (261–262)

The peacock—the beautiful symbol of sex and vanity, the two irreconcilables—squawks, an ugly sound from an ugly, beautiful bird. Eros must be mated with something other than the self and self-interest before the good sound will come forth. Meanwhile, endure. As Marie returns to her house to look out on the everlasting, everflowing Gulf Stream which will help her to endure, so Hemingway will return to the image of the Stream in *The Old Man and the Sea.* By then he has an answer to the squawk of the peacock.

# 8 ~ ONE ± ONE = ONE

*To Lucasta, Going to the Warres*

Tell me not (Sweet) I am unkinde,
  That from the Nunnerie
Of thy chaste breast, and quiet minde,
  To Warre and Armes I flie.

True; a new Mistresse now I chase,
  The first Foe in the Field;
And with a stronger Faith imbrace
  A Sword, a Horse, a Shield.

Yet this Inconstancy is such,
  As you too shall adore;
I could not love thee (Deare) so much,
  Lov'd I not Honour more.

—Richard Lovelace

There are three most mysticall unions; Two natures in one person; three persons in one nature; one soule in two bodies. For though indeed they bee really divided, yet are they so united, as they seeme but one, and make rather a duality then two distinct soules.

—Sir Thomas Browne, *Religio Medici*

For Whom the Bell Tolls (1940) is the last novel in what may be called Hemingway's middle, transitional period. It appeared at the end of a decade of writing which was marred by a cooling off of the critics' praise—perhaps in terms of craftsmanship a justified critical change. The Spanish novel was itself, however, highly successful and generally well received by the critics. It preceded a decade of silence; Hemingway was not to publish anything save journalistic dispatches and several introductions until *Across the River and into the Trees* in 1950.

Thus, though the beginning of this period is difficult to set precisely, the end of it is conveniently marked chronologically and thematically. To simplify and illustrate the marking of the periods, one might say that before the middle period Hemingway wrote ironically of Robert Cohn's devotion to W. H. Hudson's *The Purple Land* and its romantic vision. It would be hard to imagine Hemingway writing ironically about a Robert Cohn at the end of this period. In *For Whom the Bell Tolls* his latter-day Robert, also with a good Hebraic allusion in his last name (Jordan), has ideals and an ideal love, both of which are tested in action and proved to be sound.

That Hemingway had a conscious theme of agape in mind is indicated by the title and the epigraph. Yet the question remains whether or not the novel is a successful demonstration of that theme. Furthermore, what happens to the ideas of eros and the Tristan myth of romantic love? Has Hemingway resurrected romantic love? Restored the "necessary illusion" of love that Joseph Wood Krutch wrote of in 1929 in *The Modern Temper?* Or merely begun to go soft? One might answer each of these last questions positively, but there is a reading of the novel which transcends these questions and which sees the novel as a fairly consistent argument for a blend of eros and agape set in a mode that might be described as mythic realism, a phrase that could, after all, also describe the earlier *The Sun Also Rises* and *A Farewell to Arms.*

An important difference is that of characterization. Although the Spanish novel has so-called romantic elements, the hero Robert Jordan is no Tristan—no Jake Barnes and no Lieutenant Henry. Nor is Maria a Brett Ashley or even a Catherine Barkley. Instead of the expatriates of Paris or the soldiers of World War I, Hemingway writes of Spanish guerrillas who are for the most part unlettered and unsophisticated. It is true that the love story of Jordan and Maria bears a strong resemblance to that of Lieutenant Henry and Catherine of *A Farewell to Arms,* but the differences at least indicate a strong shift in purpose, a conscious attempt to see love in a different way and to reinterpret its values. The difference is crystallized in the endings: not the heroine, but the hero, Robert Jordan, dies, and he dies for a reason, a cause; but Catherine Barkley of the earlier novel dies, as Lieutenant Henry believes, for no reason at all; she has simply been caught in a biological trap.

The opening of Bédier's *Tristan* ("My lords, if you would hear a high tale of love and death . . .") could preface *For Whom the Bell Tolls,* just as it could *A Farewell to Arms.* With acute ironic effect it could preface *The Sun Also Rises* and *To Have and Have Not* also; the death in the former novel is merely the death of romantic love; the love in the latter novel between Harry Morgan and his wife is singularly unromantic, in the traditional way of courtly love. But there are profound differences between Lieutenant Henry and Robert Jordan. Perhaps neither Hemingway the author nor his hero has yet understood what he is about—"All we know is that we do not know"[1]—but they demonstrate an important shift toward agape. Their attitudes toward love will never be the same.

*The Fifth Column* (1938) serves as a preface for the Spanish novel. Written in Madrid while Hemingway was reporting on the Civil War,

[1] Ernest Hemingway, *For Whom the Bell Tolls,* p. 175. Subsequent references to this novel in this chapter will be in the text itself.

this first and only full-length play shows him working out some of his feelings and ideas about the Spanish and their problems. The play reads well but it has dead lines and forced humor and a melodramatic plot. It is easy to see why, in a prefatory note to its publication, Hemingway should have had some doubts about its merit. In contrasting *The Fifth Column* to the *First Forty-Nine Stories,* with which it was first published, Lionel Trilling observed that the play was the work of a man, the short stories the work of an artist; he also said that the play was Hemingway's poor effort to prove his social consciousness, a comment that is partly accurate since the play is in part about social consciousness.[2]

If for no merit of its own, it is interesting as a preface to *For Whom the Bell Tolls,* for its theme has many parallels to that of the novel. The play would seem to have been a testing ground for the more generous and ambitious treatment of the novel. As Alfred Kazin said of the play and the previous novel, *To Have and Have Not,* Hemingway was "reaching for something in these two productions that he could not identify satisfactorily or project with confidence." Philip Rawlings and Harry Morgan are tormented individuals looking for human fellowship but yet are contemptuous of it.[3]

The brief first scene in the play which shows a soldier and a prostitute looking for an empty room in a hotel sets the tone and theme: war and loveless sex are handmaidens, and no true love can flourish in the hateful environment of war, in which brutality, hypocrisy, and ignorance seem to have crushed and driven out kindness, sincerity, and truth. The protagonist Philip Rawlings has, like Robert Jordan, committed himself to a cause which he admires, but the idea of brotherhood and freedom and its achievement through hatred and fear pose a dilemma for Philip.

Dorothy Bridges is "a tall handsome blonde" with "a very cultivated voice," but she is also "a bored Vassar bitch" who doesn't understand the war or want to.[4] She has set her sights on marrying and reforming

[2] Lionel Trilling, "Hemingway and His Critics," *Hemingway and His Critics,* Carlos Baker, ed., pp. 61–70.

[3] Alfred Kazin, *On Native Grounds,* p. 262.

[4] Ernest Hemingway, *The Fifth Column,* pp. 4–5. Subsequent references to this play in this chapter will be in the text itself.

the supposedly carefree, debauched Philip, not knowing that he is really a dedicated secret agent of the Spanish Republic fighting the fifth column within Madrid. (How did Hollywood overlook this story?) Philip recognizes Dorothy's shortcomings. She is lazy, spoiled, "rather stupid, and enormously on the make" (51). But he loves her for her beauty, friendliness, charm, innocence, and bravery. She has had "men, affairs, abortions, ambitions," but somehow, we are asked to believe, she is still "rather innocent" and love-hungry for Philip alone (77).

His love for her is immediate, and the painful joy of it contrasts sharply with the chaste butchery of his bloody job. His love has made him bitter about war and his self-denying role in it; he would like to run away from it, but the "cause," the abstract love of all mankind (except for those dirty fifth columnists and other fascists), makes him finally scorn the weakness of his private love. Dorothy is, after all, only "a very handsome commodity," "a commodity you shouldn't pay too high a price for" (99).

Thus Philip, with Hemingway, reluctantly rejects romance. "And romantic love, the nineteenth century dream, *égoisme à deux,* the love of Catherine and Henry that was an ivory tower against the world, is crumbling away."[5] Eros, naturally, may remain. It is a phallic pillar of strength that endures. Philip scorns Dorothy not because she is erotically unsatisfactory but precisely because she is so satisfactory that he may be tempted to sacrifice his agape. "You—you—you don't want the commodity?" Dorothy stammers. "I can't afford it," Philip replies (100). Then he trots off to his room where the voluptuous Anita (the Dark Lady) and Max (the good comrade) wait for him.

What a joke! What has the self-denying hero lost? Nothing but the chains of romance. He can now be free in his male world of danger and adventure and still have the "commodity" on the side without any of the threats of stability (boredom) and marriage (slavery) that the Fair Lady entails. Our latter-day Tristan must rub his hands in merriment at his own cleverness. He has improved vastly on the solution of *A Farewell to Arms.* The heroine is disposed of without all that mess, and all in the name of a good and noble cause.

In *For Whom the Bell Tolls* the variations on the theme continue. The

[5] Edgar Johnson, "Farewell the Separate Peace," *Ernest Hemingway: The Man and His Work,* John K. M. McCaffery, ed., p. 141.

self-sacrificing hero finds love in the midst of the hatreds of war, but instead of rejecting love—a love, by the way, which is not so easy to classify or ridicule as is Philip's for Dorothy—Robert Jordan transcends hate through the love of an individual, and it is the hero who dies then instead of the heroine. This theme of agape has been recognized in one way or another by a number of readers. For instance, Malcolm Cowley observes that Hemingway symbolically returned to society with *For Whom the Bell Tolls* "after a spiritual exile that had begun in 1918, when he was wounded on the Italian front."[6] Alfred Kazin says that Hemingway "found the thwarted ideal clear and radiant again through the martyrdom of the Spanish masses" and the "profound romanticist . . . had at last come to terms with the ideal," had destroyed his nihilism in "this study in epic courage and compassion."[7] Pier Francesco Paolini expresses the view that *For Whom the Bell Tolls* is theoretically a triumph over the self and nihilism and a victory for commitment to society[8] (the antiself); and Carlos Baker says that the novel "is partisan in a larger way than the modern use of the term suggests. Its partisanship is in the cause of humanity."[9]

Yet given these similar thematic interpretations, Baker calls the novel Hemingway's best, Kazin and Paolini regard it as an artistic failure.

It is a hopeless and needless task to decide which is the "best" of any group of novels unless one has clearly set forth the criteria for his judgment. For the purposes of this analysis, concerned with love and its forms, *For Whom the Bell Tolls* is a climax. If it does not have the artistic unity and grace of *The Sun Also Rises*, or the subtle correspondence of form and meaning of *A Farewell to Arms*, the earlier novels are less ambitious in their conceptions, one might argue, and the themes and tones of them were, in a sense, ready at hand. Robert E. Knoll has described *The Sun Also Rises*, presumably without any pejorative intention of calling it a travel guide, as the best picture of the expatriates in the Paris of the twenties.[10] That is, Hemingway was holding up a mirror in the earlier novel; in *For Whom the Bell Tolls* he was creating his

6 Malcolm Cowley, *Exile's Return*, p. 292.

7 Kazin, *On Native Grounds*, pp. 263–266.

8 Pier Francesco Paolini, "The Hemingway of the Major Works," *Hemingway and His Critics*, Carlos Baker, ed., pp. 132–133.

9 Carlos Baker, *Hemingway: The Writer as Artist*, pp. 237 n., 241.

10 Robert E. Knoll, ed., *McAlmon and the Lost Generation*, p. 374.

subject and materials, and they were not directly concerned with a political battle in Spain or an American teacher of Spanish turned bridge-blower for a cause.

The obvious material of the Spanish novel is the ancient epic material of a story of love imposed upon a story of war. It is the pattern of the *Iliad* and the *Aeneid* as well as *A Farewell to Arms*, and, less directly, of *Across the River and into the Trees.*[11] Important differences, of course, lie in the kinds of love Homer, Virgil, and Hemingway depict. Agape and eros existed for the Greek and Roman, but romantic love was, if anything, merely an aberration of a sick mind. Nor is it likely that the earlier epic writers consciously used war as a sin or evil that diametrically opposed love as hate opposes agape. For Hemingway, the concept of love unifies the stories of war and love. The tragedy of war is not so much its death and destruction, for these are man's lot in many forms other than war. War is horrible because it is a type of complete hatred, the total, irrational negation of love. Thus civil war is the worst sort of war, for it is fought between compatriots and kinsmen who have had the opportunity to love each other. That they have turned from love and that they are most cruel and savage to each other is the bitterest of ironies.

A central dilemma for Robert Jordan is that he has come to Spain because he loves the Spanish people and their country, but he is very clearly not committed to communism or anarchism; his politics stop at a belief in liberty, equality, and fraternity. He feels he is justified in fighting against forces which seem opposed to these principles in Spain. That the fascists are being backed by non-Spanish powers (Italy and Germany) makes Jordan's decision initially simple. And his later realization that International Communism is using the Spanish people for equally materialistic ends is an unfortunate but reconcilable discovery. In the narration of the last three days of Jordan's enlistment in the cause—the period of time which the novel covers—Jordan comes to see the futility of his sacrifice, even though he heroically makes that sacrifice without tears or regret. He has, however, modified his cause. He dies *after* he has obtained the love of a woman and the respect and affection of the guerrillas, for whom he makes a final effort of will (to

[11] See Baker, *Hemingway: The Writer as Artist*, pp. 247–250.

insure their safe escape). Without the personal love of Maria and the guerrillas, he would have died badly and futilely and bitterly.

His death, however, is not completely satisfactory. His struggle to remain conscious and to keep from destroying himself is symbolically understandable when, victorious in this struggle, he aligns the sights of his machine gun on Lieutenant Berrendo, the fascist officer who, in an earlier episode, had shown himself to be a good man. In his last act, Jordan will destroy, for the love of his friends, another soldier with virtues similar to his own. War cannot offer any satisfactory black-white, good-evil solutions. The means being destructive, the result will be destructive. The Loyalist attack which justified Jordan's blowing of the bridge and which led to his death is a debacle that was foredoomed because of treachery. The messenger who could have had the attack and the blowing of the bridge postponed is held up by the Loyalists themselves and is almost killed as a spy.

Comrade André Marty, chief commissar of the International Brigades, epitomizes the irony of justifying evil means. "His face looked as though it were modelled from the waste material you find under the claws of a very old lion" (417). While men like Jordan and the guerrillas fight the fascists, Comrade Marty " 'kills more than the bubonic plague . . . He kills rare things. Trotzkyites. Divagationers' " (418). He plays at being a general, he interferes, and he is inexplicable to Andrés, the simple guerrilla who is delayed by him in his important mission. Comrade Marty is a man without love; he is hated by his own people, and he himself trusts no one: "He knew that you could trust no one. No one. Ever. Not your wife. Not your brother. Not your oldest comrade. No one. Ever" (421). In this vacuum of love he hypocritically feels "genuinely sorry" for his victims "as human beings" (422), but, as supposed deviationists from his particular cause, they must die.

Before the blowing of the bridge, it is Pablo, the leader of the guerrilla band, who causes Jordan the most trouble and anxiety. At the bridge, the Christian Anselmo must kill a young boy, a fascist guard, who is from his own village. In fact, throughout the novel it is the Loyalists who get much the worst of it in comparison with the fascists and their activities. In 1953, Deming Brown could write that "*For Whom the Bell Tolls* has never been published in the Soviet Union," perhaps because "there are serious ideological deficiencies in the book, in Soviet eyes"[12]—as indeed there are. This deliberate reversal of the ideal situation of the hero fighting for an ideal—a who-are-the-bad-guys quandary—is heavily emphasized in the characterization of Lieutenant Berrendo, the enemy, and Pablo, the guerrilla leader, and in the long flashback in Chapter 10 that describes how Pablo led the peasants and laborers in seizing control of a village held by the fascists early in the war. At Jordan's insistence, Pilar tells the bloody story of the assault on the barracks of the *guardia civil,* the shooting of the surviving guards, and the brutal, drawn-out deaths of the fascist townspeople. Even the dedicated Pilar does not like to remember the taking of the town. Much happened, she says, " 'And all of it ugly' " (99). It was stuff that bad dreams are made of, yet the horror had a fascination for Pilar, and she admired the strength and leadership that Pablo showed that day as he executed the surviving *guardias civiles* and organized the flailing of the fascists.

Pilar comments, " 'If you have not seen the day of revolution in a small town where all know all in the town and always have known all, you have seen nothing' " (106). Though at first the common people have little taste for the flailings, they are soon worked up to savagery. First, a man who has a personal grudge against the mayor begins the flailing when the other peasants are reluctant. Second, a fascist goes proudly and defiantly to his death, his control and pride angering the people and convincing them that " 'these who came out were truly enemies and should be killed' " (111). The cowardly behavior of a third victim serves to arouse the people further and finally to turn them into a mob led by drunkards thirsting for the blood of their compatriots. A fourth victim was, ironically, a fascist only because of his love for his wife.

The irony of fighting for any cause is most sharply focused on Pablo's disappointment at the way the priest died at the hands of the mob. The priest had behaved with dignity until the very end when the mob was upon him chopping with its sickles and reaping hooks. A priest should set an example, Pablo had told Pilar.

" 'I thought you hated priests.'

" 'Yes,' said Pablo. . . . 'But a *Spanish* priest. A *Spanish* priest should die very well' " (128).

[12] Deming Brown, "Hemingway in Russia," *Hemingway and His Critics*, Carlos Baker, ed., p. 157.

Pablo recognizes the priest as his compatriot at the same time that he condemns him to death.

The negation of life, the violent deaths and the hate, is also the negation of love. Thus, correspondingly, Pilar reports what to her was the significant aftermath: Pablo could not make love to her that night. His hatred, though not directed at Pilar, had made him impotent.

" 'Pilar, tonight we will do nothing.'

" 'Good,' I told him. 'That pleases me' " (128).

While Pablo sleeps like a baby, Pilar remains awake. She hears the weeping of the widow of the man who had become a fascist to please his religious wife. Pilar knows that the revolution has begun badly.

The association of eros with death is further heightened in that Don Faustino, one of the fascists, has been a girl chaser, and when Pilar is nearly crushed against a barred window by one of the drunken mob, she protects herself by striking the drunken Loyalist's testicles.

It is true that there is one worse day to come in Pilar's life, and that is in the same village when the fascists retake the town three days later. But of that horror Pilar does not wish to speak, and the listening Maria too has had enough. The war had begun badly for Pilar, and it would continue thus, one kinsman outdoing the other in violence and hate.

Robert Jordan is fascinated by the story and wants to hear of the fascists retaking the town. His appetite for violence had been whetted, and perhaps he has succumbed to a cause. The same Pablo who was responsible for the atrocities in the village now resists Jordan's intention of blowing up the bridge. Jordan cannot fight for people but only for a cause, the abstraction of freedom, one of the kind of words that always embarrassed Frederic Henry and that he found obscene. Thus Jordan's dilemma is highlighted by Hemingway's choice of treating the incident of the Loyalists' atrocities rather than the fascists'. The fascists are men too, strong or weak, good or bad, after their fashion. But they are not devils, no more than this Pablo with whom Jordan is now in a strange alliance. The fascists, in fact, achieve a kind of martyrdom and respect. It is the mob that is the devil, Pilar says (122), and even when Maria tells Jordan of her parents' deaths and her rape, the story is anticlimactic, neither as vivid nor as horrible as Pilar's tale, for the raping fascists have, at least, a common physical pleasure in their brutality, and they are Moors, not Spaniards but outlanders, barbarians. The

Loyalists had to be artificially aroused by drink and Pablo's commands and talk of the "obscene" abstraction liberty.

In a sense then, the stories of Jordan and Lieutenant Henry are similar, but there is this important difference: Jordan never withdraws from his involvement even when the futility and absurdity of it becomes clear to him. He is self-educated to see the irony of using hate and violence as a means to an abstract good, but act he must. After he shoots a fascist scout, a man he had never seen before (265) and thus would have no apparent reason to hate and kill, Jordan examines the soldier's papers, learns his identity, and reflects on who he was and what he had done.

> I've probably seen him run through the streets ahead of the bulls at the Feria in Pamplona, Robert Jordan thought. You never kill any one that you want to kill in a war, he said to himself. Well, hardly ever, he amended and went on reading the letters. (302)

In one letter from the dead soldier's sister there are two other ironies:

> There was quite a lot of religion in the letter and she prayed to Saint Anthony, to the Blessed Virgin of Pilar, and to other Virgins to protect him and she wanted him never to forget that he was also protected by the Sacred Heart of Jesus that he wore still, she trusted, at all times over his own heart where it had been proven innumerable—this was underlined—times to have the power of stopping bullets. (30)

That Sacred Heart of Jesus was the red device that the soldier wore on his uniform and that had served as an aiming point for the shot of Jordan, who belongs to a congregation of a different Pilar.

> I guess I've done my good deed for today, he said to himself. I guess you have all right, he repeated. . . .
>
> All right, he said to himself. I'm sorry, if that does any good.
>
> It doesn't, he said to himself.
>
> All right then, drop it, he said to himself.
>
> All right, it's dropped.
>
> But it would not drop that easily. How many is that you have killed? he asked himself. I don't know. Do you think you have a right to kill any one? No. But I have to. How many of those you have killed have been real fascists? Very few. But they are all the enemy to whose force we are opposing force. But you like the people of Navarra better than those of any other part of Spain. Yes. And you kill them. Yes. If you don't believe it go down there to

the camp. Don't you know it is wrong to kill? Yes. But you do it? Yes. And you still believe absolutely that your cause is right? Yes.

It is right, he told himself, not reassuringly, but proudly. I believe in the people and their right to govern themselves as they wish. But you mustn't believe in killing, he told himself. You must do it as a necessity but you must not believe in it. If you believe in it the whole thing is wrong. (303–304)[13]

Another of the enemy, Lieutenant Paco Berrendo, is also treated sympathetically. His close friend and fellow officer is killed in the assault of El Sordo's last stand (Chapter 27). After the fascist planes come and blast the guerrillas, Lieutenant Berrendo "quickly and . . . gently" shoots Joaquin, the one guerrilla not yet dead. Then Berrendo orders the heads of the guerrillas to be cut off. And he says to himself, in his rage at the death of his friend and his own brutality, "What a bad thing war is." He walks down from the hill praying for his dead comrade and not wishing to see his orders carried out (322).

At the same moment on a distant hill, Jordan interprets the sounds of the fighting and knows that El Sordo's band is lost. "Then as the quiet kept on a hollow feeling came in his chest" (323). The same feeling of hollowness affects Lieutenant Berrendo (326). He thinks of his dead friend, of his own barbarity, and of his God as he prays both for his friend and for El Sordo and his men. "It was the first time he had prayed since the start of the movement [the war]" (327).

In one single scene we see the hero and his chief adversary, and they are both good men, the enemy being ironically better than many of the hero's supposed allies, such as Comrade Marty and Pablo. This crucial parallelism is repeated at the end of the novel where the wounded Jordan lies in wait to shoot at and delay the fascist cavalry pursuing Maria and the guerrillas. The fascist leader is, of course, Lieutenant Berrendo. Jordan prepares to kill him and then be killed by some other one of the "enemy"—perhaps a Lieutenant Berrendo or perhaps a Pablo. The book ends on that bitter yet heroic note.

It is significant that Jordan's eminent death is a solitary one. Whatever the justification for hate and destruction is, the man who gives himself to those forces of death will suffer isolation, loneliness, and despair. Before he volunteered for duty in Spain and for the particular as-

[13] See also Robert Penn Warren's comments on the irony of *For Whom the Bell Tolls*, in "Introduction," *A Farewell to Arms*, pp. xxv–xxvi.

signment of blowing up the bridge, Jordan had been, it would seem, an unattached man. He has a family, of whom he thinks only briefly, but no wife. In the guerrilla's cave he finds both a wife and a family. For their safety, he resists unconsciousness and the urge to commit suicide as easy ways out. Yet he is still lonely.

Earlier, at the bridge, he had felt the loneliness of hate and destruction. "He would like to have had the squirrel with him in his pocket. He would have liked to have had anything that he could touch. He rubbed his elbows against the pine needles but it was not the same. Nobody knows how lonely you can be when you do this" (433).

And after the bridge, the elation of action is gone.

> The anger and the emptiness and the hate that had come with the let-down after the bridge, when he had looked up from where he had lain and crouching, seen Anselmo dead, were still all through him. In him, too, was despair from the sorrow that soldiers turn to hatred in order that they may continue to be soldiers. Now it was over he was lonely, detached and unelated and he hated every one he saw. (447)

Jordan conquers this hatred when he remembers that he must rid himself of egotism and that then the hate will ebb. But at his sacrificial death the loneliness returns, because, whatever its merits, it is a death of hate and more destruction. The alcohol that would have helped is gone—"the flask was not there when he felt for it. Then he felt that much more alone because he knew there was not going to be even that. I guess I'd counted on that, he said" (467)—and so Jordan must argue with himself to steel his body and mind against the pain of his broken leg (another castrative wound) and the physical and moral fear that eats at his resolution. The love of Maria makes the difference, for while she lives and loves the memory of Jordan, he had explained, some part of Jordan will be with her.

> "As long as there is one of us there is both of us. . . . What I do now I do alone. I could not do it well with thee. If thou goest then I go, too. Do you not see how it is? Whichever one there is, is both."
>
> "I will stay with thee."
>
> "Nay, rabbit. Listen. That people cannot do together. Each one must do it alone. But if thou goest then I go with thee. It is in the way that I go too. Thou wilt go now, I know. For thou art good and kind. Thou wilt go now for us both." (463)

The function or "use" of Maria as an antidote for loneliness is known to Jordan much before his death, of course. During their second night together ". . . he felt the long light body, warm against him, comforting against him, abolishing loneliness against him, magically, by a simple touching of flanks, of shoulders and of feet, making an alliance against death with him . . ." (264).

In general, Pablo is a foil for Jordan, but in respect to the idea of loneliness they are much alike. Both of them turn to alcohol as a solace for their isolation that was born in them by their barbarity. In the early days of the war, Pablo says, " 'I was very barbarous. . . .

> "I am drunk on wine and and would be happy except for those people I have killed. All of them fill me with sorrow. . . ."
>
> "I would restore them all to life."
>
> "And then you would walk on the water," Pilar said. (208–209)

Whiskey, Anselmo says, " '*That* is what kills the worm that haunts us' " (205).

When Jordan first arrives at Pablo's camp, Pilar tells the American that Pablo has " 'taken a leather wine bottle to drink alone in the woods' " (31). Jordan drinks wine with all the guerrillas, but he tries to save the anesthetic absinthe for himself alone (48, 50–51, 57). The "real" absinthe that Jordan drinks has wormwood in it and is as bitter as gall.

In his loneliness, Pablo looks for consolation in the bottom of the cup and then seeks it in conversation with his beloved horses. After the guerrillas have deposed him as their leader, he talks to his bay stallion as if the horse were a sympathetic human, as if the horse could receive and reciprocate the love Pablo cannot find with the other guerrillas and the interloper Jordan.

> "Thou my big good little pony," Pablo was saying to the horse in the dark; it was the big bay stallion he was speaking to. "Thou lovely white-faced big beauty. Thou with the big neck arching like the viaduct of my pueblo," he stopped. "But arching more and much finer." The horse was snatching grass, swinging his head sideways as he pulled, annoyed by the man and his talking. "Thou art no woman, nor a fool," Pablo told the bay horse. "Thou, oh, thou, thee, thee, my big little pony. Thou art no woman like a rock that is burning. Thou art no colt of a girl with cropped head and the movement of a foal still wet from its mother. Thou dost not insult nor lie nor not understand. Thou, oh, thee, oh my good big little pony." (63–64)

But the horse is merely annoyed by Pablo. He is not human; he cannot love.

Later Pilar tells Jordan:

> "Every one needs to talk to some one," the woman said. "Before we had religion and other nonsense. Now for every one there should be some one to whom one can speak frankly, for all the valor that one could have one becomes very alone."
>
> "We are not alone. We are all together [Jordan answers]." (89)

But Pablo hangs on the fringe of the group, mocking it and its suicidal plan to blow the bridge, but still being unable to run away from the group that he needs. Even within the cave, Pablo "sat by himself" (206), and refused to have anything to do with Jordan's plans (178). He is entirely alone and even antisocial, in a profound way, when he steals Jordan's dynamite exploders and threatens to ruin the plan entirely.

Now gone from the group physically as well as spiritually, Pablo can stand the sickness and hollowness no longer. He had irretrievably thrown away the exploders, but had then found himself "too lonely." He still hates Jordan for having brought a difficult mission to his people, but he realizes " 'if we must finish we must finish together.' " Having run off, Pablo has found " 'a loneliness that cannot be borne. . . . I do not like to be alone. *Sabes?* Yesterday all day alone working for the good of all I was not lonely. But last night. *Hombre! Qué mal lo pasé!*' " (390–391).

Even the goodly Anselmo tastes the bad kind of loneliness when he spends a day by himself watching the bridge and the road. His loneliness comes from the killing he has done. When he is alone, he thinks of his violence, which he is sorry for but which he thinks was necessary because of the war. ". . . he felt so lonely that there was a hollowness in him as of hunger," a hunger that is partly assuaged when he reasons that he has at least worked hard for the Republic and "the good that we will all share later" (197).

Thus the problem that Pablo poses: he has in the past been needlessly brutal. Now in his sorrow and remorse he is a real danger to the others in their plans to kill and destroy in order to have a good future without death and hate. Yet when the other guerrillas agree to kill Pablo, he shrewdly plays the role of an innocent, and he thinks that no one has the *cojones* to murder him (213–214). Jordan will kill him if he has to, but he does not hate Pablo (221). The guerrillas vacillate too long, and Pablo lives, first to betray them by stealing the exploders, second to aid them by returning to bring more guerrillas and horses, and third to guarantee their safe escape from the bridge by more brutality—he machine-guns the new guerrillas without any qualms, for his friends' lives are at stake. The bigger cause of the Republic does not matter, and Pablo does not know that "every man is a piece of the *Continent.*" " 'They were not of our band,' " he explains (456). The cruel wheel of fortune revolves once more (225–227). The murdered guerrillas remain in the shadows, except for one, a "good shepherd" whom Pilar knows and who feels "gravity" within him (395). This other good shepherd will also die futilely, and Pablo, saving his people, will again come to know their ingratitude and horror for a heinous crime committed in the name of love (454–456). W. M. Frohock uses *For Whom the Bell Tolls* as an example of the novel of violence or, in Jean Pouillon's phrase, the novel of destiny:

> The hero finds himself in a predicament such that the only possible exit is through inflicting physical harm on some other human. In the infliction of harm he also finds the way to his own destruction. But still he accepts the way of violence because life, as he sees life, is like that: violence is man's fate.[14]

Jordan's final sacrifice is ironically illuminated when it is compared with Pablo's sacrifice and crucifixion of the good shepherd and his band, for Jordan too will be, though unwittingly, killing a good man, Lieutenant Berrendo. Jordan is horrified by Pablo's deed and in ignorance of one aspect of his own, yet Jordan is conscious of the reasons for his need of, first, alcohol and then Maria. Both have powers to assuage the loneliness of hate. The significant difference between Pablo and Jordan is the difference of recognition. Pablo can only feel his loneliness and act, paradoxically and brutally, to remedy it. Jordan both feels and understands, and when he acts, his knowledge gives a nobility and sense of tragedy to his actions. He senses his moral dilemma, even if he does not specifically know who Lieutenant Berrendo, his final adversary, is. In the words of the Talmud, "Whosoever saves a single life is as if he had saved the whole world; whosoever destroys a single life is as if he had destroyed the whole world."

[14] W. M. Frohock, *The Novel of Violence in America*, 2d ed., pp. 6–7.

The moral predicament of a war for love is widely demonstrated in passages about the necessity of forgetting violence (138); reconciling the "cause" with murder (165); the inhuman rigidity of military orders (191); the brutalizing effect of war (196); the disillusionment of a "just" war (228 ff); the necessity of lies in war (230); the ecstasy and purging of battle, followed by disillusionment (236–239); killing of fine people on both sides (248); deserting the few for the good of the many (273); allowing El Sordo's band to die unaided, so that the mission may be carried out (294–296); the Republican generals who hate each other and cannot believe in the people (359); determination of sides in the war by circumstantial facts and fate (367); Andrés' speeding through enemy territory but being fatally delayed by suspicion, fear, ignorance, and red tape in friendly territory (396–401); failure of Loyalist attack because of treachery (429); and the irony that soldiers must hate in order to live (447).

Certain images and episodes combine the ideas of war, hate, and death with eros, and thus they provide a link between two of the three controlling motifs of the novel: war (a kind of antilove), eros, and agape. In addition to the above-mentioned sexual allusions in Pilar's story of the Republican seizure of the village and particularly of Pablo's impotence on that night after the brutal victory, we learn that the hardened fighter Pilar had been the mistress of a bullfighter who had died of tuberculosis (182–190).

> She was with him thus five years and never was unfaithful to him, that is almost never, and then after the funeral, she took up with Pablo who led picador horses in the ring and was like all the bulls that Finito had spent his life killing. But neither bull force nor bull courage lasted, she knew now, and what did last? I last, she thought. Yes, I have lasted. But for what? (190)

For all her loving of these two men, Pilar has never conceived. She is that rarity, a barren gypsy (255). Maria, too, may be a barren lover. Pilar says that when she was raped by the fascists, if she could she would have then conceived (354). But rape is hardly even eros; it is divorced from productivity; it is death, a form of extreme violence. While lying in his sleeping bag with Maria, Jordan kills the fascist scout:

> "Thou," she said. "I saw all."
>
> "Thou saw nothing. One man. One man from a horse. *Vete.* Get thee back."

"Say that you love me."

"No. Not now."

"Not love me now? . . ."

"One does not do that and love all in the same moment."

"I want to go to hold the legs of the gun and while it speaks love thee all in the same moment."

"Thou art crazy. Get thee back now."

"I am not crazy," she said. "I love thee."

"Then get thee back."

"Good. I go. And if thou dost not love me, I love thee enough for both." (269–270)

Maria's love that can combine love with death, that can unconsciously link the phallus and the machine gun, is to Jordan an insanity. She has "no place in his life now," he thinks (267). Perhaps he is also thinking of Pilar's morbidly fascinating description of the odor of death as being compounded of the smell of a brass porthole on a rolling ship, the smell of the mouth of an old woman who has just drunk the blood of slaughtered beasts, the smell of dead chrysanthemums, the odor of the slops and refuse of whorehouses—the "odor of love's labor lost"—and the mixed smell of dead flowers, dead earth, and the sexual doings of worn-out whores. This smell of lovemaking in such a context is no longer the smell of life, but of death. Eros corrupted is death, and Jordan fears it and will not smell Pilar's wonderful concoction (256).

Perhaps Jordan is also thinking of the death-through-love that was the fate of his father who was driven to suicide by a bullying wife (338–339).

In both cases the love is eros alone, and Maria feels and represents something beyond that. War is a whore—" '*Qué puta es la guerra* . . . War is a bitchery' " (465). Eros alone is foul, is death and the smell of death, the smell of the whorehouse. But love is not eros alone.

Eros alone is allied to anger and fear and, through its association with romantic love, it is also allied to death, paradoxical as that may be, since it is also the source of life. Perhaps the best approach to an understanding of the ambivalence of eros is through the dominant symbol of it that Hemingway uses: the horse. From the first chapter to the last, repeated references to horses focus the reader's attention upon them even when they seemingly appear as mere background shadows. It would seem more than coincidence that in *The Fifth Column* the names of the hero and heroine foreshadow aspects of the novel. Jordan is a bridge destroyer, and Philip Rawlings of the play sexually "destroys" Dorothy Bridges. ("Destroy" is used in this sexual sense in "The Snows of Kilimanjaro" [p. 63], published two years before the play and also containing a bitch as heroine.) More pertinent here, though also more tenuous, is the literal meaning of Philip—"lover of horses."

When Jordan arrives at the guerrillas' camp, the first things he notices are cropped grass, signs of picketing, a horse trail, and fresh manure. Then he sees the horses in their corral (12). From Jordan's first arrival, the guerrillas' camp is consciously and strongly associated with these funerary and erotic symbols. The ancient use of the horse as a funerary beast is combined with his use as a symbol of maleness and virility to suggest a link with the concept of death as a desirable end to romantic love.[15]

Pablo is a sad, isolated man, but he has some spirit and joy with his horses, of which he is very proud and loving. When he learns that Jordan too is a "man of horses," a rapport is established between them. For Pablo, stealing and capturing horses has become an end in itself; the killing of the enemy who rode the horses is almost incidental (13–14). The only glory of his life is his horses. Anselmo rebukes Pablo for his selfishness and his excessive love of his horses (a meaningful combination):

> "Thyself now since a long time. Thyself and thy horses. Until thou hadst horses thou wert with us. Now thou art another capitalist more."
>
> "That is unjust," said Pablo. "I expose the horses all the time for the cause."

They argue. " 'I am an old man who is afraid of no one,' Anselmo tells him. 'Also I am an old man without horses' " (15–16).

The burden of eros no longer troubles the old man as it does Jordan and Pablo. While Jordan tries to figure out the reliability of Pablo the horse-lover, his own thoughts wander back to the horses.

> They are awfully good horses, though, he thought, beautiful horses. I wonder what could make me feel the way those horses make Pablo feel. The old man was right. The horses made him rich and as soon as he was rich he wanted to enjoy life. (16)

[15] See Mircea Eliade, *Cosmos and History*, pp. 67 and 70, on the horse as a funerary animal, and James G. Frazer, *The Golden Bough*, abr. ed., pp. 476–479, on the rite of the sacrifice of the horse as a vegetation god.

Jordan thinks of the horses as merely material possessions, but for the reader they grow in meaning. The horses are at once the wealth of and the source of danger to the little community. Yet in their corral they have no function, and Pablo is against Jordan's mission which will require the horses for an escape. Just so the differences between the loves of Jordan and Pablo: Pablo's love is unused, inactive, impotent, hoarded until he becomes sick of it and its loneliness. Jordan's is active, and the more it is exercised the stronger it becomes. When the guerrillas depose Pablo as their leader, he has no one to turn to but his horses—his dream of love rather than the use of it (89). When Pilar recounts the atrocity of the village uprising—that embodiment of hate—she remembers that the dying men " 'were screaming as horses scream in a fire' " (125). When Jordan watches Maria, he sees her walking "like a colt moves" (137).

In order to escape from the darkness, the inactivity, the frustration, and the angers of their cave, the guerrillas need horses—eros. But this commodity, as Philip Rawlings called it, is hard to come by. The lack of this love is the largest obstacle to the guerrillas' success. Jordan, El Sordo, and Pilar discuss the problem (144), and Maria puts it in clear-cut terms.

> "I wish we had horses to ride," Maria said. "In my happiness I would like to be on a good horse and ride fast with thee riding fast beside me and we would ride faster and faster, galloping, and never pass my happiness." (161)

Opposed to this virtue of eros are ideas and uses that indicate its limitations and dangers: the immediate fear of the guerrillas is of fascist cavalry, Pablo's politics are associated with those of horse thieves (163), and the horse tracks that El Sordo leaves lead to his death (257). "We certainly got Sordo into a fine jam with that horse business. How does it go in Spanish? *Un callejón sin salida.* A passageway with no exit" (305). The kind of love symbolized by the horse is not enough. El Sordo's own horse is sacrificed in one last effort on the hill where his band dies. He shoots his horse "quickly, expertly, and tenderly" so that the beast will plug a gap in the defensive perimeter. But having killed the horse of love, the band will die, even though Sordo uses the horse by firing the machine gun over its back (307). One of the images of life that El Sordo thinks of as he awaits the fascists' attack is that "Living was a horse between your legs and a carbine under one leg and a hill and a valley and a stream . . ." (the carbine is phallic and the landscape is female). He pats his dead horse and thinks how he had carefully shot it. " 'Thou wert plenty of horse' " he says (313), and he knows that he will die on that hill that he once imagines as shaped like a chancre (a mark of diseased love) and once thinks of as shaped like the nippleless breast of a young girl (a mark of incomplete or immature love) (309).

A stronger accusation is made when the cursing Agustín tries to provoke Pablo into a fight. Pablo retreats from the cave to care for his horses—he runs from hate to his idea of love, to find some consolation in their animal companionship, to avoid the struggles needed in learning to love.

> "I will be going out to see the horses."
> "Go and befoul them," Agustín said. "Is not that one of thy customs?"
> "No," Pablo said and shook his head. He was taking down his big blanket cape from the wall and he looked at Agustín. "Thou," he said, "and thy violence."
> "What do you go to do with the horses?" Agustín said.
> "Look to them," Pablo said.
> "Befoul them," Agustín said. "Horse lover."
> "I care for them very much," Pablo said. "Even from behind they are handsomer and have more sense than these people. Divert yourselves," he said and grinned. "Speak to them of the bridge, *Inglés*. . . .
> "I have thought you are a group of illusioned people," Pablo said. "Led by a woman with her brains between her thighs and a foreigner who comes to destroy you."
> "Get out," Pilar shouted at him. "Get out and fist yourself into the snow. Take your bad milk out of here, you horse exhausted *maricón* [sodomite]."
> "Thus one talks," Agustín said admiringly, but absent-mindedly. He was worried.
> "I go," said Pablo. (215–216)

Other indications that Pablo's sickness is somehow sexual are contained in Anselmo's view of him:

> And now, he is as finished and as ended as a boar that has been altered, Anselmo thought, and, when the altering has been accomplished and the squealing is over you cast the two stones away and the boar, that is a boar no longer, goes snouting and rooting up to them and eats them. (193–194)

Later when Anselmo calls Pablo's cave the Palace of Fear, Jordan jokingly corrects the name to "the cave of the lost eggs."

> "What eggs?" Fernando asked.
> "A joke," Robert Jordan said. "Just a joke. Not eggs, you know. The others."
> "But why are they lost?" Fernando asked.
> "I don't know," said Robert Jordan. "Take a book to tell you." (199)

After Pablo has stolen the exploders, Jordan thinks of him as a "sod," a sodomite, just as the other guerrillas had, and he also calls him a *cabrón,* a man who consents to his wife's adultery. And finally, after Pablo returns to help Jordan and they shake hands and exchange explanations, Pilar mocks them for acting like *maricones,* homosexuals (404). All three terms, of course, are invectives with a figurative but not a literal truth to them.

Earlier Pilar had confided in Jordan that Pablo had a sickness for Maria, the sickness of romantic love. " 'It is another thing which destroys him. It lies on him like a sickness when he sees her' " (32). In turn, Pablo's views of the other characters are frequently sexually described, but for him, eros is a corruption. When he argues that Pilar is stupid, he says that she has a head of a seed bull and a heart of a whore (53) and that she has her brains between her thighs (215).

Jordan and the symbolic horse have a slightly different relationship. When Jordan wakes from a night in his sleeping bag with Maria, he shoots a fascist cavalryman off his big gray gelding, the very horse on which Jordan in his turn will be injured and consequently be left to die. Though still a horse, the gelding is a maimed horse, "sick" or incomplete, as eros romanticized is and as Pablo the horse lover is; Agustín's accusation was not altogether unfounded, for actual physical contact is enjoyed by Pablo as he mounts the gelding.

> He grinned and patted the nervous horse. Robert Jordan saw him rub his leg along the horse's flank affectionately.
> "*Qué caballo más bonito,*" he said and patted the big gray again. "*Qué caballo más hermoso. . . .*"
> "See what a horse has done for him" [Pilar said].
> "That I should have two horses," Robert Jordan said fervently.
> "Danger is thy horse."
> "Then give me a mule," Robert Jordan grinned. (268)

But in a moment his grin fades when Maria joins him and wants her share of love from her man. Jordan is curt with her. Now is not the time for love. But because she saw the man shot from his horse, she is strangely aroused; once more the gun becomes phallic as Maria associates death and love:

> "Thou," she said. "I saw all."
> "Thou saw nothing. One man. One man from a horse. . . ."
> "I want to go to hold the legs of the gun and while it speaks love thee all in the same moment. . . ."
> He looked at her and smiled through his thinking.
> "When you hear firing," he said, "come with the horses. Aid the Pilar with my sacks. It is possible there will be nothing. I hope so."
> "I go," she said. "Look what a horse Pablo rides."
> The big gray was moving ahead up the trail. (269–270)

Later Jordan thinks, "That horse certainly did things for him" (273). Perhaps the horse moves Pablo to action, for he steals away that night with all the horses and Jordan's dynamite exploders (his potency that he carries in sacks!), but the horses alone do not suffice for any man (361). He returns the next night with more guerrillas and more horses to help in the escape (392). Once more a man thinks he can kill other men, as Pablo plans to kill the new guerrillas, and still use their horses—their love.

This love, these horses, are, however, unreliable because some of them may panic when the fighting at the bridge begins (403). Even so, the two weakest members of the band, Maria and Rafael the gypsy, are assigned to hold and guard them until the fight is over. Maria does not wish to remain behind Jordan, but he tells her, " 'The horses is where thou art most useful' " (394). The requirement of eros alone is little, and the weak suffice to handle it; but after staying with the horses for a long time, Maria finds "they were no comfort to her. Nor was she any to them" (448–449). Her love for Jordan has transcended eros and thus her nervousness among the horses as she prays for his safe return.

Jordan does return from the bridge, but he never makes good his escape. He and Maria are never to live together as man and wife, and the horse again plays a decisive role. Pablo has killed the other guerrillas— " 'They were not of our band' " (456)—so that *his* people will have many horses (455). Jordan rides the big gray gelding whose former rider Jordan had shot—the boy with the Sacred Heart insignia. Jordan thinks sensually of the horse: "it was much horse between his legs and under his hands" (457).

He caressed the gray once with his thigh muscles, and then held him steady as they dropped down fast and sliding through the pines, telling the gray with his thighs as they dropped down what the spurs would have told him if they had been on level ground. (458)

Like El Sordo, Jordan then tries to use a horse for his protection from the gunfire of the enemy, but the horse veers off and a tank-gun shell knocks Jordan and his gelding down. In the fall, Jordan cannot get free of the horse. Earlier Fernando had been wounded in the groin, and his wound and his giving up of his horse to the others foreshadows Jordan's fall (440–442). The horse crushes his left leg; ironically, the gelded (incomplete, undeveloped) symbol of eros administers the symbolically castrative wound. Another shot from the tank hits the horse, which then sits quietly beside him and waits to die (459–461). His "horse" wounded, the hero is only half a man; it is not worth living thus, but one can die well and help his friends escape. In effect, Jordan is a fisher-king, a sacrificial hero, just as the horse has traditionally been a sacrificial embodiment of the god of vegetation. In order to insure fecundity or life, life must be taken. Eros is killed for the sake of eros.[16] (When the horse is identified with the cosmos, as it sometimes is, its sacrifice symbolizes the act of creation, a parallel paradox.)[17]

Pablo looks at the big gray gelding "with true regret on his face" (462). He feels more the loss of the horse than the loss of Jordan. But for Pablo and the rest there are still other horses, enough, in fact, to enable them to carry off their camp utensils and supplies so that life can begin again somewhere else. Eros is clearly life for them. A horse has been sacrificed, and the horses are the means to life. Jordan thinks:

It's wonderful they've got away. . . . Look how different it would be if they were all scattered out across that hill where that gray horse is. Or if we were all cooped up here waiting for it. No. They're gone. They're away. (468–469)

Then more horsemen come, but these are the enemy, Lieutenant Berrendo's cavalry.

He saw the trooper who stopped by the gray horse and shouted to the officer who rode over to him. He watched them both looking down at the gray horse.

[16] Frazer, *The Golden Bough,* pp. 476–479; see also the parallels suggested by Frazer's description of the Hippolytus myth, pp. 4–5.

[17] Mircea Eliade, *Patterns in Comparative Religion,* p. 96.

They recognized him of course. He and his rider had been missing since the early morning of the day before. (471)

The fascists' horses are wet and blown and have to be urged forward to meet the further death that awaits them and eros in the midst of the hate of war.

The role of the horse, the funerary animal and the eros animal, archetypically complements the conscious, overt meaning of the theme of agape. Furthermore, eros is present in much else that is implicit in the novel, in addition to the famous sleeping-bag scenes. For instance, the object of Jordan's mission is to "destroy" a bridge, an erection, over a deep gorge. The "sodomite" Pablo is at first opposed to dropping the bridge into the gorge, but after he has thrown Jordan's "exploders" into the gorge (and vicariously experienced eros with Jordan and Maria) and then returned to humanity (the guerrilla band), he agrees to help. His thoughts always turn to the last symbolically sexual activity that he remembers nostalgically as the "good time" in the past—the blowing up of the train, the destruction of the long powerful phallus spouting white clouds of hot steam, followed by the machine-gunning of the little men, the homunculi, who burst out of the exploded train. Pablo had been a great lover (before the war his trade was working with horses in the bullfights), but since the train, there had been only laziness, sloth, and failure, only living in the past glory of the last destruction, the last moment of eros that literally ended in death for so many.

Except for some connection to the idea of eros and hate, the long passage of Andrés' remembrance of his youthful bullbaiting would be tedious. As the guerrilla remembers the village *capeas*, their similarity to the act of love is apparent. The bull, eros animated and epitomized, engenders excitement, delight, and fear in the youths who bait it. Paradoxically, as with other vegetation sacrifices, the symbol of virility is killed, but only by youths who have *cojones*. Andrés had leaped on a bull, "the bull rocked and bucked under him," and he

drove his knife again and again and again into the swelling, tossing bulge of the neck that was now spouting hot on his fist as he let his weight hang on the high slope of the withers and banged and banged into the neck. (365)

When the bull settled dead under him, the boy was both proud and ashamed, feeling empty and happy (366). He had proven he had *cojones*: " 'That's what it is to have a pair of *cojones*' " (366). Andrés, remembering, equates the war with the bullbaiting, and in spite of his courage, he is glad that his mission as a messenger has relieved him of proving his manhood once more in the blowing up of the bridge. Of course, the libido disappears in the face of great danger, although that other love, agape, can conquer fear, as it did when the guerrillas rescued Maria from the train they blew up (133).

Other allusions to the association of eros with hate, death, and fear range from concrete yet symbolic actions to the abstract thoughts of various characters: nearly all of the Republican *milicianas* get pregnant, because eros flourishes in wartime (399); hate can be "killing" and similar to sexual intercourse with a woman one does not love (370); the messenger Andrés frantically rides his motorcycle through another vaginal landscape (401);[18] Pilar thinks of a destructive man as "a great layer of women" (253); when the hate-filled, foul-mouthed Augustín wants to kill four fascists he pictures himself as a fearful mare in heat (286); and, to repeat, El Sordo imagines his last stand as on a chancre-like hill (Chapter 27).

A special problem is the anger that Pilar feels towards the love of Jordan and Maria. Initially, Pilar acts as a procuress for Maria, but her motive is the unselfish maternal one both of finding a mate for Maria and of completing Maria's emotional cure after the shocks of her parents' murder and her rape. Pilar puts Maria on display: " 'Isn't she pretty?' she asked Robert Jordan. 'How does she seem to thee? A little thin?' " (65). And she sends Maria to Jordan's sleeping bag for a cathartic sexual experience. Jordan says:

> "Dost thou wish?"
> "Yes. Everything. And if we do everything together, the other maybe never will have been."
> "Did you think of that?"
> "No. I think it in myself but Pilar told me."
> "She is very wise. . . ."

[18] Also see how El Sordo images the good life as a ride through a sexually symbolic landscape (313), and see the vaginal landscapes of "Macomber," p. 35, and *Across the River and into the Trees*, p. 153. Like Colonel Cantwell of the later novel, Jordan thinks of his lover's body as a landscape (341).

"She said that nothing is done to oneself that one does not accept and that if I loved some one it would take it all away. I wished to die, you see."

"What she said is true." (72–73)

Pilar sees that her plan has worked, and at first she is happy for Maria and able to jest with Jordan about his "conquest." But then she is also reminded of her youth and of the time when she was a great lover of great men (85–86, 97–98). Now she, like Pablo, is left with her memories and Pablo, the man who was made psychically impotent the night the fascists were brutally executed. Pilar is now too old, and emotions tire her (140). Only in her spirit, and vicariously in Maria, is she still a great lover. Thus she instructs Maria in the art of love; it is something like religious instruction, Maria says as she blushes. But it is different (324). Thus also Pilar must know the quality of their lovemaking, and she has a gypsy power over Maria to get her to reveal that the earth moved for her when she and Jordan made love. Jordan thinks:

There was nothing predatory. Nor was there anything perverted about it. There was a spreading, though, as a cobra's hood spreads. He could feel this. He could feel the menace of the spreading. But the spreading was a domination, not of evil, but of searching. (173)

If it were not for the pervading presence of a mythic dimension in the novel, this scene would be the merest sentimental claptrap. Maria admits that the earth moved. " 'Truly. It was a thing I cannot tell thee' " (174). Pilar warns her not to tell it to her own people (non-gypsies), for they would never believe her. It is a mystery common to the gypsies, but " 'Non-gypsies have a little luck sometimes.' " Jordan's anger and disbelief change in the face of Pilar's strength and faith:

Nobody knows what tribes we came from nor what our tribal inheritance is nor what the mysteries were in the woods where the people lived that we came from. All we know is that we do not know. We know nothing about what happens to us in the nights. When it happens in the day though, it *is* something. Whatever happened, happened and now this woman not only has to make the girl say it when she did not want to; but she has to take it over and make it her own. She has to make it into a gypsy thing. I thought she took a beating up the hill but she was certainly dominating just now back there. If it had been evil she should have been shot. But it wasn't evil. It was only wanting to keep her hold on life. To keep it through Maria. (175–176)

In Chapter 12 that kind of vicarious eros appears to be not enough for

Pilar. She has been angry with Maria because she has been jealous of her, but at the same time that she envies Maria's possession of Jordan, she envies Jordan's possession of Maria. She caresses Maria, and her feeling for her is sexual, though in her own mind she denies it and says her only interest is in Maria's happiness. Like anyone else, Pilar can feel the terrible tension between her own gratifications and an intellectual or ethical commitment that includes, as a corollary reinforcement, the knowledge that free satisfaction of her desires will end as nothing but the smell of death, love's labor lost. Man is caught in something of a dilemma. To be happy, he should reject what would seem to make him happy and achieve his own happiness only through others. The remaining alternative is a longing or a perverse, never consummated approach to the object of love, that once attained immediately turns to nothingness. Pilar is a woman of intense feeling, but she is also wise and honest and strong enough to admit the truth to the somewhat bewildered Maria. Pilar does not "make perversions," but still she both loves Maria—sensually and maternally—and is jealous of her, desiring to have Jordan herself (154–156).

Pilar and Jordan allude to the bridge as a phallic banana that Pilar wishes to devour hungrily. Such talk of destruction is exciting to her, and when Pilar gets up to leave Maria and Jordan alone so that they may make love, some hint of her erotic power is detected. Jordan wants to go with her, presumably because she had looked ill before. It is then Maria's turn to defend jealously her mate from the other woman:

> "Let her go," Maria said, her head still down.
> "I think I should go with her."
> "Let her go," said Maria. "Let her go!" (157)

Pilar is a truly noble woman who is not afraid of facing the truth of her feelings and yet is able to rise above them to an act of agape. She is no *tortillera*, she says, no Lesbian, yet she is a mother reluctantly initiating her innocent child, and at the same time she is a lover of men who sees a good man in her child's husband. She needs both loves, erotic and familial, and she is giving both of them up for the sake of Maria. Her choice, like Jordan's at the end of the novel, is inevitable, hardly a choice at all, yet both Pilar and Jordan sacrifice themselves with the least reluctance and ultimately with a kind of grandeur.

Pilar's example foreshadows Jordan's relations with Maria. At first his great happiness with Maria is, ironically, a source of bitterness to him, for he tends to value love quantitatively and he realizes that this, his first true love, cannot endure (168). Pilar, however, gives Maria to Jordan because she values love qualitatively. Even if Jordan were to die, Maria would have something good and enduring; while eros is repeatedly associated with destruction, agape is indestructible; a three day's experience can last forever.

In Jordan's idealistic talk with Maria in his sleeping bag, he glorifies eros in an image of union, an image corresponding to the mythic ideal of woman as life and the hero as her knower and master.[19] The sexual joining is a type of a spiritual union; Maria takes off her "wedding shirt" and tells Jordan she will not be cold.

> "Afterwards we will be as one animal of the forest and be so close that neither one can tell that one of us is one and not the other. Can you not feel my heart be your heart?"
>
> "Yes. There is no difference."
>
> "Now, feel. I am thee and thou art me and all of one is the other. And I love thee, oh, I love thee so. Are we not truly one? Canst thou not feel it?"
>
> "Yes," he said. "It is true."
>
> "Nor any other legs, nor feet, nor of the body. . . ."
>
> "I would be thee because I love thee so. . . ."
>
> "It is better to be one and each one to be the one he is."
>
> "But we will be one now and there will never be a separate one." (262–263)

One plus one equals one, but when eros combines with agape, one minus one equals one also. " 'As long as there is one of us there is both of us,' " Jordan tells Maria as he lies wounded and tries to explain why he must be left behind during the escape. " 'If thou goest then I go, too. . . . Whichever one there is, is both. . . . Thou wilt go now for us both' " (463).

The scenes of eros have gradually changed and have given Jordan his first true love, which in turn gives him the strength to lose his love and his life. In the first scene (Chapter 7), Maria comes to his sleeping bag ashamed and afraid. She has been practically driven there by Pilar, and she even mistakes his pistol—that other discharger of destruction—

[19] Joseph Campbell, *The Hero with a Thousand Faces*, p. 116.

for his phallus (70). Jordan's assurance that he "loves" her assuages her shame and fear, but when she tells him that she had been raped, she feels a change in his affection. Yet she is pitiful and hopeful and still spiritually innocent, and Jordan says he understands that she is.

Joseph Warren Beach observes that Maria is a sacrificial lamb, or virgin martyr, for humanity. Though she had been raped, she is virginal in the sense that she is the pure-hearted lover of only one man; thus her traditionally sacred name, Maria.[20] Jordan thinks of different names for her: "Sweetheart, *chérie, prenda,* and *schatz.* He would trade them all for Maria. There was a name" (167). Later Jordan says he loves Maria *and* her name. Maria says, " 'It is a common name.'

" 'No,' he said, 'It is not common' " (263–264). Maurice Valency notes that thirteenth-century courtly poetry depicted a love so ideal that it is occasionally difficult to distinguish between Mariolatry and love poems: the Lady is almost indistinguishable from the Blessed Virgin Mary, Maria's namesake and counterpart.[21] When Jordan kisses this deified woman, he is, naturally, "happier than he had ever been" (72). Nevertheless, he accepts her as his woman only temporarily.

> "I love you now."
> "And I can be thy woman?"
> "I cannot have a woman doing what I do. But thou art my woman now."
> "If once I am, then I will keep on. Am I thy woman now?"
> "Yes, Maria." (73)

Later he reiterates the isolation of his love from his other life. He likes women, and drink, very much, but only outside his work. Yet Maria, he is beginning to feel, is something special, and Pilar announces their "engagement" (91–92).

The following day he wonders if perhaps the joy of the night was just another erotic dream, like the many he has had of the movie stars Jean Harlow and Greta Garbo. The dreams were always better than the real thing, and Maria was too good to be true. The dream of romance is latent in Jordan's mind, but Maria is the exception. He reaches out and touches her arm. She *is* the dream come true (137–138).

When they again love each other that afternoon, their love is so in-

[20] Joseph Warren Beach, *American Fiction: 1920–1940,* pp. 91–92.
[21] Maurice Valency, *In Praise of Love,* p. 193.

tense that the earth mystically moves "out and away from under them" and time is "absolutely still . . . having stopped" (159). This rare phenomenon, known before only to the gypsies, is love's transcendence of time and space. Still, Jordan has a trace of romance in his blood, and though the earth moved for both of them, their views are slightly different.

> "Maria, I love thee and thou art so lovely and so wonderful and so beautiful and it does such things to me to be with thee that I feel as though I wanted to die when I am loving thee."
>
> "Oh," she said. "I die each time. Do you not die?"
>
> "No. Almost." (160)

Maria's surrender to love is complete, Jordan's "almost." He praises Maria's body as having some magic power.

> "In a fine body there is magic. I do not know what makes it in one and not in another. But thou hast it."
>
> "For thee," she said.
>
> "Nay."
>
> "Yes. For thee and for thee always and only for thee." (161)

Maria denies any romantic mystery in love. Only the giving of her love has created the magic. For Maria, lying on her back and looking upward to the sunlit sky, eros is "red, orange, gold-red from the sun on the closed eyes," but for Jordan, lying on her and facing the earth, eros "was a dark passage which led to nowhere . . . always and forever to nowhere" (159).

Accompanying the change in Jordan wrought by the special love of Maria is a "clearing of the head" which enables him to see the paradox implicit in a communistic ideal which is to be effected through war and hatred. "Continence is the foe of heresy," Jordan thinks, and eros has made him a heretic. He will still fight for the people, but he will not be bigoted, he will not use the revolutionary and patriotic clichés like "enemy of the people."

> . . . the Communists were always cracking down on Bohemianism. When you were drunk or when you committed either fornication or adultery you recognized your own personal fallibility of that so mutable substitute for the apostles' creed, the party line. (164)

Furthermore, Jordan even begins to think of marrying Maria, a remarkable thought for a Hemingway hero. But one cannot walk down the aisle with a stylization or beget children on a dream. "The real lover tends to make children, not songs . . ."[22] Instead of seventy years, Jordan's whole allotted life span will be seventy hours. Maria is a dream and is very properly meant to be, but she is a tough-minded vision, not an Iseult. On the probability of the love story, Joseph Warren Beach writes that Jordan discovers the absolute importance of the love of a woman.

This affair of Maria is highly romantic. It is a startingly effective instance of the poetic formula of shining love projected against the shadow of death. . . . However true or untrue, however plausible or implausible it may be from the historical point of view, this episode is highly symbolic in relation to the political theme and to what we may call the writer's metaphysic of emotion."[23]

Jordan's pistol, the Tristan sword that could lie between and separate them, is placed, like the tempting Satan, behind Jordan (70). He will not be tempted to indulge in the sickness of romantic love.

I am no romantic glorifier of the Spanish Woman nor did I ever think of a casual piece as anything much other than a casual piece in any country. But when I am with Maria I love her so that I feel, literally, as though I would die and I never believed in that nor thought that it could happen. (166)

Though he is still conscious of the romantic image associating eros with death, he also associates Maria with life forces. He had been willing to sacrifice his life for the abstract Republic of Spain, but now

he would much prefer not to die. He would abandon a hero's or a martyr's end gladly. He did not want to make a Thermopylae, nor be Horatius at any bridge, nor be the Dutch boy with his finger in that dyke. No. He would like to spend some time with Maria. That was the simplest expression of it. He would like to spend a long, long time with her. (164)

If there is not any such thing as a long time, nor the rest of your lives, nor from now on, but there is only now, why then now is the thing to praise and I am very happy with it. Now, *ahora, maintenant, heute. Now,* it has a funny sound to be a whole world and your life. *Esta noche,* tonight, *ce soir, heute abend.* Life and wife, *Vie* and *Mari.* No it didn't work out. The French turned it into husband. There was now and *frau;* but that did not prove anything either. (166)

[22] *Ibid.,* p. 166.

[23] Beach, *American Fiction,* p. 91.

Jordan gropes for sweet life and finds it in Maria's love. He "marries" her:

Two nights to love, honor, and cherish. For better and for worse. In sickness and in death. No that wasn't it. In sickness and in health. Till death do us part. In two nights. (168)

Jordan is dramatically reminded of the contrast of life and love to death when Maria matter-of-factly asks him to teach her how to shoot his pistol (to teach her the masculine art of dealing death) so that either one could kill the other if it were necessary to avoid capture and torture. She also carries a razor blade with which to cut her throat. "You have forgotten this," he tells himself. He has forgotten about the war and hate, and if the reader has too, the relation of love and war to agape must be re-established. Like other great goddesses of religion and myth, Maria possesses simultaneously the opposites of gentleness and dread, fertility and destruction, birth and death and war. (But for a matriarchal goddess, Pilar is better suited as a type of Kali, the protective and at the same time destructive goddess.)[24]

The passage in which the gypsy guerrilla Rafael deserts his guard post to kill two rabbits making love in the snow symbolically complements this relationship of love and war to agape. The rabbits are caught and surprised because of eros, just as Jordan and Maria were almost caught that same morning by the fascist cavalry trooper who rode by Rafael's deserted post. Rafael too was ruled by an appetite, and Jordan tells him he could be shot. Jordan forgives him, however, perhaps because he is unconsciously aware of the coincidence or parallel of the rabbits to Maria and himself. Rafael would never leave his post again; in fact, " 'Never would such an opportunity as the two hares present itself again. Not in the life of one man' " (275). That is to say, such a love as Maria's and Jordan's is unique and ideal.

That night, in the third lovemaking scene, Maria comes to Jordan's sleeping bag without the fear and need for "treatment" that characterized their first night. John Killinger cites the sleeping bag as a womb symbol that accords "with the death instinct and the desire for reversion to the intra-uterine state."[25] Although there is no disputing the po-

[24] Eliade, *Patterns*, pp. 418–419.
[25] John Killinger, *Hemingway and the Dead Gods*, p. 27.

tential use of a sleeping bag for such symbolic purpose, in this context there is not enough supplementary evidence to support such a reading. The guerrilla's cave is also a warm retreat from the hardships of weather and war outside it, but, like the sleeping bag, its activities usually indicate a literal rather than a symbolic role. The guerrillas lose their safe retreat when they involve themselves in mankind by re-entering the war. Jordan has broken away from the Mother. He admires Pilar the matriarch, but he does not want her meddling with Maria. Symbolically he does not return to the protective, destructive womb of her cave, nor does he sleep there at night but rather with Maria outside, even in the snow. In this third lovemaking scene, they are "married," she wears a "wedding shirt," and they are united physically and spiritually—they become as one (262). This time the earth does not move for them, but neither do they romantically "die":

> ". . . it was not as this afternoon" [Maria said].
> "No."
> "But I loved it more. One does not need to die."
> "*Ojalá no*," he said. "I hope not."
> "I did not mean that."
> "I know. I know what thou meanest. We mean the same."
> "Then why did you say that instead of what I meant?"
> "With a man there is a difference."
> "Then I am glad that we are different."
> "And so am I," he said. "But I understood about the dying. I only spoke thus, as a man, from habit. I feel the same as thee."
> "However thou art and however thou speakest is how I would have thee be." (263)

Jordan's decision actually to marry Maria is a monumental one that invites comparison with Lieutenant Henry's decision in *A Farewell to Arms*. The earlier hero who breaks with society's conventions and makes his separate peace by running off with his true love is not as well motivated to desire marriage as Jordan is. Frederic Henry delays his marriage because Catherine regards it of little importance, but the rebel looks forward to it, after the embarrassing pregnancy is over, as a necessary seal of their love. Jordan has *returned* to society and compromised his ideals for the sake of a desirable goal; he does not see only in blacks and whites; he is not blinded by what Arthur Koestler calls the fallacy of the perfect cause, a disease of the mind to which young heroes are acutely susceptible.[26] Accepting other conventions and limitations in society, Jordan can also desire marriage without the faint touch of irony that Lieutenant Henry's desire has.

Jordan will not only care for Maria in a strange way—by sleeping with her—he will also marry her. He and Augustín discuss marriage and Maria and the ways that one person cares for another. Pilar has put Maria in his care, Jordan says, and to *joder* with her all night is a lucky way to care for one so long as there is "seriousness" and responsibility in the lovemaking. Time after time Jordan repeats to Augustín his acceptance of this responsibility:

> "I care for her seriously. . . ."
> "I will care for her. . . ."
> "I care for her greatly" (290–291)

He will also marry Maria as soon as he gets the chance, for the changed Hemingway hero desires the formality, the convention, and his actions have not, like Lieutenant Henry's, run counter to a certain ethical decorum. It is to the tradition of Tristan and romantic love that Jordan is a heretic: he *intends* to marry his lover. Since Frederic Henry had the same intention, the important difference must be seen to lie in Henry's inconsistency of motivation and in Hemingway's solution—Catherine must die.

The last sleeping-bag scene has, however, some Tristan-like elements (Chapter 31). Maria is sore and in pain and does not think she will be any good for Jordan. He is disappointed, but he conceals his hurt and turns down her offer of onanism. He says, " 'We will have our necessities together. I have no necessities apart from thee' " (349). Besides, he cannot afford to waste on the pine needles the virility he will need the next day to perform his chivalric deeds in honor of his lady. He and Maria talk instead; they plan their future together, and Maria tells of her rape at the hands of the fascists. Jordan is angered momentarily, but he is satisfied with the kind of lovemaking that the troubadors recommended as the height of true love—warm embracing without the final act of coition: " 'Lie close against me, rabbit. I love thee as much feeling thee against me in here in the dark as I love thee making love' "

[26] Arthur Koestler, "The Seven Deadly Fallacies," *The Trail of the Dinosaur*, p. 51.

(341). "Then they lay quiet and close together in the night, hot-aching, rigid, close together and holding her . . ." (346).

Under the threat of his death the next day, Jordan dreams impossible dreams that he recognizes as unrealizable, and confesses a love of her that is cosmic in its scope. Maria has come to represent many things.

> "I have worked much and now I love thee and," he said it now in a complete embracing of all that would not be, "I love thee as I love all that we have fought for. I love thee as I love liberty and dignity and the rights of all men to work and not be hungry. I love thee as I love Madrid that we have defended and as I love all my comrades that have died. And many have died. Many. Many. Thou canst not think how many. But I love thee as I love what I love most in the world and I love thee more. I love thee very much, rabbit. More than I can tell thee. But I say this now to tell thee a little. I have never had a wife and now I have thee for a wife and I am happy." (348)
>
> "We are married, now. I marry thee now. Thou art my wife." (354)

The point that Jordan makes explicit—universalizing his love for Maria—has been made in the prior action and characterization, and the point has been made much better and more convincingly than in Jordan's speech that is rich with Lieutenant Henry's obscene abstractions. In hammering the point home, Hemingway almost destroys it, and then returns to the erotic matters at hand. Whatever the ideal of love-making for Tristan, Jordan still wishes they had spent their last night differently (355), and early the next morning he has his wish fulfilled when Maria awakes full of passion and clasps him to her, and they have one final time in *la gloria*:

> . . . one and one is one, is one, is one, is one, is still one, is still one, is one descendingly, is one softly, is one longingly, is one kindly, is one happily, is one in goodness, is one to cherish, is one now on earth with elbows against the cut and slept-on branches of the pine tree with the smell of the pine boughs and the night; to earth conclusively now, and with the morning of the day to come. (379)

This last sacrifice to love will give Jordan the spirit he needs to sacrifice himself this last day. It is the culmination of his seventy-two hour education.

> "You taught me a lot, *guapa*," he said in English.
> "What did you say?"
> "I have learned much from thee."
> "*Qué va*," she said, "it is thou who art educated."

Educated, he thought. I have the very smallest of beginnings of an education. The very small beginnings. If I die on this day it is a waste because I know a few things now. . . . I have been all my life in these hills since I have been here. Anselmo is my oldest friend. . . . Agustín, with his vile mouth, is my brother, and I never had a brother. Maria is my true love and my wife. I never had a true love. I never had a wife. She is also my sister, and I never had a sister, and my daughter, and I never will have a daughter. I hate to leave a thing that is so good. . . .

"I find life very interesting," he said to Maria. (380–381)

Hemingway suggests that his hero's education is not yet finished, but he now knows what he does not know. Nothing is left to be said, for the "nada," the absolute nothing of a Meister Eckhart, has been perceived.[27]

The concept of agape unifies the two stories of love and war. Love is not eros alone, Jordan has learned. His love for Maria partakes of the romantic only if one limits that word to mean an ideal stylization. Maria is not meant to be "real." She is an image, a mythic woman much better than any real woman just as Jordan is an oversized hero, an epic lover and fighter.

But agape is only potential or primitive or budding between Jordan and Maria and the other characters. And thus the paradox of life: Jordan still keeps the life-giving love on the periphery of his death-dealing life. He fights and hates for love. He loses his life and his love in the only way he can find life and love. No greater love has Jordan than the love that lets him lay down his life for his friends. His noble sacrifice is, however, in some ways an avoidance of love's responsibilities. The martyr has it easy. It is the man who lives—a Santiago or even a Jake Barnes—who has it hard. Jordan lines up his sights on another Hector, Lieutenant Berrendo, and thus demonstrates the tragedy of man's fate.

[27] The *nada*'s and *nothing*'s are persistent throughout the text, e. g., pp. 81, 82, 93, 101, 126, 180, 251, 277, 355, 389, 409, 465, 470, and especially 463–464.

# 9 ~ THE NEW ISEULT

Ah, love, let us be true
To one another! for the world, which seems
To lie before us like a land of dreams,
So various, so beautiful, so new,
Hath really neither joy, nor love, nor light,
Nor certitude, nor peace, nor help for pain;
And we are here as on a darkling plain
Swept with confused alarms of struggle and flight,
Where ignorant armies clash by night.

—Matthew Arnold, "Dover Beach"

To catch the unicorn, a maid
Was led by huntsmen to a glade.

—William J. Stevens, "De Casibus
Animalium Illustrium"

ACROSS THE RIVER AND INTO THE TREES (1950) has been among the least well received of Hemingway's novels. Even Hemingway's defenders were hard put to find something good to say about it. Perhaps his readers were expecting too much; they hadn't heard from him since *For Whom the Bell Tolls,* a novel which confirmed a profound change in direction of some of his attitudes, notably those concerning love and women. It had been, perhaps, not so artistically tight as the two earlier novels, *The Sun Also Rises* and *A Farewell to Arms,* but it had had a breadth and depth of feeling that seemed an evolution and a promise of even better books to come. The story of Robert Jordan also seemed to prove that *Green Hills of Africa* and *To Have and Have Not* were only temporary ebbings of Hemingway's talent, not signs of his having written himself out.

In retrospect it is easier to understand the disappointment that many felt with *Across the River and into the Trees.* It wasn't the kind of book that a living legend should write, and compared to *For Whom the Bell Tolls,* it seemed anticlimactic. If *Across the River and into the Trees* was not very good Hemingway, neither was it as bad as the worst reviews claimed it was. And as a statement of the themes of love, it was, contrarily, very good Hemingway. No matter what it did for Hemingway as a novelist, it continued the evolution of the themes of love. Colonel Cantwell's love story should have been and was the next step in Hemingway's ideological maturation. Read, therefore, in light of the love themes, *Across the River and into the Trees* is an important novel with a sustained interest.

The novel is relatively short and structurally simple, even though the few days encompassing the action are enriched by the Colonel's numerous recollections. Thematically, however, the novel is extremely dense in its treatment, both directly and through allusions, of eros and agape. In the unfolding of the story, we see the subtle changing of the Colonel, his steady but sometimes reluctant changing into a latter-day Tristan, a tough-minded Tristan who wants to beget children on his Iseult. Renata, in fact, no matter how idealized she seems, no matter how romantic the setting and action in this novel is, is in revolt against the romantic tradition of love. Her idealization is deliberate and proper, just as the characterization of other Hemingway women had been. To read her as a dream girl, a fairy child, is to miss the point of the novel. Renata is more a Beatrice than an Iseult. She is the very Tristan-like Colonel's spiritual guide, who dramatically teaches him through her actions that eros and agape can be combined in a human relationship. Unfortunately, William Wasserstrom in his thoughtful *Heiress of All the Ages* has not considered this last of the Hemingway heroines but has limited his analysis, as far as Hemingway is concerned, to Lady Brett, Catherine Barkley, and Maria. For Renata, like Henry James' Maggie Verver, blends and represents the achievement of "idealism, sex, love, and civilization," the four qualities that American Woman, the heiress of all ages, combines.

The formal richness of *Across the River and into the Trees* is understood and appreciated in terms of antitheses and ambiguities that circle the theme of love. The novel works itself out through opposition of love and hate, of eros and agape, and of eros-agape and romantic love. Overt conflicts and tensions are minimal; not much seems to happen. The action is internal; the Colonel is being taught, by Renata and through self-therapy, how to love. By extension, since the novel is also about death, the Colonel is getting ready to die; his Beatrice is getting him ready for paradise. The Colonel's education is a clarification of his own notions of love as he moves away from an initially ambiguous position—an ambiguity, one is tempted to add, that is pervasive in our society. The Colonel's position is complemented by "love's" ambiguity in relation to life and death. Hate equals death. Romantic love equals death. Eros and agape equal life. The algebraic extension, "Therefore, romantic love equals hate," is not intended, but at least in a metaphysical sense is nearer the truth than not.

In simple terms, *Across the River and into the Trees* is, of course, a story about death, "one of the subjects that a man may write of," Hemingway had so casually said.[1] The story tells of the last few days in the life of a professional soldier, a U.S. Army colonel. From the first chapter, with its images of light and darkness, of the changing tides, of health and sickness, and of the duck hunt itself with its purpose of death and with the hunter isolated and buried in his shooting barrel, Hemingway foreshadows the Colonel's death and begins the dramatization of his theme.

"You don't know how many more times you will shoot ducks and do not let anything spoil it for you," the Colonel tells himself when his surly Italian guide demonstrates his hatred of the Colonel, for some unknown reason. "Every time you shoot now can be the last shoot and no stupid son of a bitch should be allowed to ruin it."[2]

On his mission of bringing death to some ducks, the Colonel is aware of his own illness and impending death. At the end of the novel, after a long flashback, the reason for the guide's hatred will be revealed. The Colonel, a soldier, a professional killer, is "wearing his hip boots and an old combat jacket" (3) that he might have worn when he was fighting the Italian and his people. It is the battlejacket of the Allies (Moroccans specifically) who raped both his wife and his daughter in an excess of eros without agape (302). (They were also Moroccans who raped Robert Jordan's Maria.)

One final image in this first chapter may be noted. In the sunken shooting barrel in which the Colonel is hidden from the beautiful, free, high-flying ducks, he looks out across the frozen lagoon and the pestilential marsh with its unhealthy water and sees

> the snow-covered mountains a long way off. Low as he was, no foothills showed, and the mountains rose abruptly from the plain. As he looked towards the mountains he could feel a breeze on his face and he knew then, the wind would come from there, rising with the sun . . . (6)

[1] Ernest Hemingway, *Death in the Afternoon*, p. 2.

[2] Ernest Hemingway, *Across the River and into the Trees*, pp. 6 and 7. Subsequent references to this novel in this chapter will be in the text itsef.

Mistaken generalizations about Hemingway's plains versus mountains imagery, are easy to make, as E. M. Halliday has pointed out, but although mountains are the source of death in *A Farewell to Arms* and a place of death in *For Whom the Bell Tolls,* to mention only two of the many works in which Hemingway uses mountain-plains oppositions, the mountains are usually a place of cleanliness, strength, and vigor, as it seems they are meant to be in this passage.[3] The mountains are associated here with a rising sun; in Chapter 3 they are associated with a life-eros "bambini theory" that Jackson, the Colonel's driver, is working out. He sees the Italian Renaissance painters, like all Italians, as big bambini lovers; the Italians love to make babies, literally and artistically. Although Jackson likes the ubiquitous madonna paintings, he wishes that the painters " 'would paint some good pictures of that high country up around the rest center at Cortina.' " The Colonel tells him that Titian, one of the most luxuriant of the bambini painters, came from up there, and he also informs Jackson that the pointed steeples that he likes in the mountains are *campaniles,* bell towers (15–16). The sexual shapes of the mountains, bell towers, and bells complement the sexual subjects of the Renaissance paintings they are talking about.

In short, the reader finds that in *Across the River and into the Trees* Hemingway is developing themes of love with symbolic imagery in much the same way that he had before. Eros continues to be almost obsessive, even though the Hemingway hero is now a man in his fifties. And the function of eros continues to change along the lines indicated in *For Whom the Bell Tolls*; it is being blended with agape. The creative and destructive dualism of eros remains, but the formula for its use without hate and death is being learned by the Hemingway hero.

Still, love keeps its own secrets. Only in action can man know love. It is not analyzable or intellectual. The Colonel tells Renata:

> "I love you."
>
> "Whatever that means," she interrupted.
>
> "I love you and I know whatever that means. The picture [Renata's portrait] is lovely. But there is no word for what you are." (151)

The Colonel said nothing, because he was assisting, or had made an act of

[3] E. M. Halliday, "Hemingway's Ambiguity: Symbolism and Irony," *Hemingway,* Robert P. Weeks, ed., pp. 52–71.

presence, at the only mystery that he believed in except the occasional bravery of man. (153)

At the height of passion, the Colonel directs Renata:

> "Don't think of anything. Don't think of anything at all."
> "I'm not."
> "Don't think."
> "Oh please let's not talk."
> "Is it right?"
> "You know."
> "You're sure."
> "Oh please not talk. Please."
> Yes, he thought. Please and please again.
> She said nothing, and neither did he, and when the great bird had flown far out of the closed window of the gondola, and was lost and gone, neither of them said anything. (153–154)

Love is ignorant, for the Colonel admits to Renata that he does not know how a woman feels during erotic love. Although the language is almost comic and the puns bad, the lovers' view of Renata's body as tactical terrain reveals how "knowing" a woman is a very limited knowledge. Making love in a Venetian gondola (Tristan first made love to Iseult in a boat!), the Colonel reverses the vaginal-landscape imagery of "Macomber" and *For Whom the Bell Tolls.* With one hand he "searched for the island in the great river with the high steep banks," and with the other hand, good tactician that he is, he "holds the high ground" (153) of Renata's breasts. Later he asks her:

> "Where is the island now and in what river?"
> "You are making the discovery. I am only the unknown country."
> "Not too unknown," the Colonel said.
> "Please don't be rude," the girl said. "And please attack gently and with the same attack as before."
> "It's no attack," the Colonel said. "It is something else."
> "Whatever it is, whatever it is, while I'm still on the lee."
> "Yes," the Colonel said. "Yes, now if you want, or will accept from kindness."
> "Please, yes." (155)

The Colonel's knowledge of Renata's "terrain features" is rude ignorance beyond which lies the mystery of true love, whatever it is.

One's powers of eros can be proved by spreading a bedroll and copulating, but that Renata says, would be barbarous; it would be a misuse of love if eros were the only end. Colonel Cantwell, on the same page, refers to diseased eros, in the form of gonococci carried in a matchbox by front-line soldiers to infect themselves and thus be relieved of duty (161). Eros entails the responsibility of duty, and duty, or care for the loved one, is a quality of agape.

At the same time, without eros there can be no agape between man and wife. Cantwell contrasts Renata to his former wife. With Renata there can be "movement"—eros—but women like his former wife had been taught not only how to count and put their hair in curlers, but also how to keep their legs together. Renata's hair is dark and loose; she is beautiful for Cantwell here and now, not for somebody else tomorrow morning in an everlasting sexless beauty contest (178–179). It is implied that Renata is pregnant (110), and the Colonel wishes he could have five sons by her. Their erotic love is productive, it functions; the Colonel's former marriage was sterile: his former wife had "hired out" for childbearing but she "could not even make a child." With Renata, love is orgasmic and organic; it works because it is a combination of eros and agape.

The role of the female is symbolized in the passages about the hen duck that the Colonel uses as a hunting decoy. The live hen is tied near the shooter's blind, and as she calls out, passing curious drakes fly down to their deaths. Cantwell thinks of the hen as a bitch, but then reverses his judgment (288). It is in the nature of the female to lure the male through eros, he muses, and if the destruction of love—its romantic "death"—is the only value the drake finds, that is not the hen's fault alone. The Colonel too is a "bird"—a full colonel with eagles on his shoulders—and he knows that he too is near death. His death, however, will be a literal one, not a romantic image, and his love has led him to his capture by the female, not to his death. So it is that when Cantwell has winged a drake and his dog has retrieved it, he decides not to kill the beautiful mallard "with his heart beating and his captured, hopeless eyes," but to put him in the sack with the hen who lured him. Cantwell will use the drake with the hen as another caller or perhaps even let him go when he has recovered. If the drake and the hen "marry" and work together, they will lure other ducks to their domestic tranquility, or to death. Such are the alternatives of eros.

The kind of eros that does not lead to death but to life is innocent and gentle and does not get its ideas of sex from *The Ladies Home Journal* (85–87). It requires judgment too, like the judgment one needs in avoiding the loss (the death) of men in battle. The Colonel had lost three wives and three battalions through a lack of judgment and also through brutality (95). This lifegiving eros is not possessive. "I don't want to own you," the Colonel says, and Renata answers, "That's one more reason why I love you" (100). Love is giving—of the bodies and of presents, such as a Moor's-head statue or an emerald heirloom that the lovers exchange. Love may also hurt one—the Colonel is tough minded enough to know that hurt comes even with the good love—but when two people are lucky, they become as one in the same way that Robert Jordan and Maria of the previous novel were united in a bond that even real death could not sever (156).

Parting is not Tristanized sweet sorrow for these lovers. It is a sadness at the thought of separation that is inevitable (269).

> "So now we stand up and kiss each other and say good-bye."
> "What's that?"
> "I don't know," the Colonel said. "I guess that is one of the things everybody has to figure out for themselves."
> "I'll try to figure it."
> "Just take it as easy as you can, Daughter."
> "Yes," the girl said. "In the vehicle without the shock-absorbers."
> "You were tumbril bait from the start."
> "Can't you do anything kindly?"
> "I guess not. But I've tried."
> "Please keep on trying. That's all the hope we have." (276–277)

The Colonel's Beatrice wants her Dante to be kind and good—to have agape, the only hope we have. (There are numerous allusions and references to Dante and his *Commedia,* e.g., 124–125, 129, 218, 246, 269, 280–281.) Renata is not a predator, like the Colonel's former wife, or a trap, like the hen mallard (285). Here is a love that is inexplicable to the Colonel as he contemplates his naked ugliness in a mirror:

"how could she love a sad son of a bitch like you?

"I do not know, he thought truly. I truly do not know" (289).

Her love is the agape that passes all understanding. In part, she loves him because in spite of all his anguish and sorrow he is never sad. And Tristan is the model of the sad lover. Renata wants no part of that myth.

She is the agape-eros blender, no Iseult but a Beatrice to whom one can give everything and know that the gift will be honored. The Colonel is a "poor" man with little to give, but he can give her love (290–291).

This decision of his follows, however, the bulk of the novel in which, while he has been loving her, he has been also telling her of his military adventures. Philip Young has criticized the war anecdotes as one of the "basic difficulties" of the novel. "The unintentional delusion under which Hemingway labors throughout the novel is that he is being interviewed."[4] While some of the stories the Colonel relates may be impertinent or intrusive, the "interviewing" suggests a fruitful comparison and affords a link between the themes of love and death. When Renata asks the Colonel to put his arms around her and encourages him to tell her of his "oldest and best" trade of war, and when the Colonel readily responds throughout the novel, the distinct impression is that here is another Othello and Desdemona in the same city of Venice (114, 231, 235, 253). Comparison also reveals that like Othello, Cantwell was a soldier all his life and that Desdemona was carried off to Othello by a gondolier. Does Renata then love the Colonel for the dangers he had passed, and does he love her because "she did pity them," as Othello thinks?[5] The Colonel denies it:

> They were not Othello and Desdemona, thank God, although it was the same town and the girl was certainly better looking than the Shakespearean character, and the Colonel had fought as many, or more times than the garrulous Moor. (230)

But if Shakespeare could regard his hero as "a bogus great man, whose masterfulness and nobility" were simply veneers for egotism and insane passion, then it is likely that the repeated allusions could lead to a corresponding regard of Cantwell by Hemingway.[6] Such a view would be, in effect, the view of the novel held by most of its detractors, who saw the less heroic side of the hero's nature. Both authors could sympathize with their heroes and still be critical of them. Furthermore, when the Colonel and Renata exchange gifts, Renata asks him to buy her a small statue of a Moor's head. She has given the Colonel a portrait of herself;

[4] Philip Young, *Ernest Hemingway*, p. 89.
[5] William Shakespeare, *Othello: The Moor of Venice*, Act. I, Scene iii.
[6] John Bayley, *The Characters of Love*, p. 129.

if the exchange is of equivalent items, the Moor's head is a direct remembrance of the Colonel as an Othello (259, 267, 268, 290).

The soldiers who had raped Maria in *For Whom the Bell Tolls* and the soldiers who had raped the Colonel's Italian guide's wife and daughter were all Moors. The erotic success of the Moors is hated by Iago as well as Jordan and the Italian guide. Their reactions vary from the infamy of Iago to the nurtured bitterness of the guide to the acceptance of Jordan and his rehabilitation through love of the victim. Desdemona's father likewise cannot understand how his daughter could betray herself and her family to the outlandish Moor. Her father thinks Othello has charmed her, and so he has, but not with a magic potion.

Renata pins the Moor's head on her shoulder. "It was about three inches long, and was quite lovely to look at if you liked that sort of thing. And if you don't you are stupid, the Colonel thought" (268). Later he thinks of other things he could give her—a duck-down jacket, guns, his war medals.

> I never give her anything, as she pointed out. There was the small moor's head. But it does not mean anything. She selected it and I bought it. That is no way to give a gift.
>
> What I would like to give her is security, which does not exist anymore; all my love, which is worthless; all my worldly goods, which are practically non-existent. . . .
>
> With all my worldly goods I thee endow, he thought.
>
> And she gave me her love, some hard stones, which I returned, and the picture. . . .
>
> I better just give her my love. (290–291)

This warrior in Venice, though not a Moor, is a foreigner who has wooed and won a girl as ideal as Desdemona. One can agree with Philip Young that in *Across the River and into the Trees* the Hemingway heroine is "never less real," but reality is not the object.[7] Renata is like the Lady of *stilnovisti* love poetry whose influence on her lover was very great; she radiated charity and led the way to his salvation. She was perfect and led the true lover to strive for perfection in order to become worthy of her.[8] Unlike Othello, the Colonel in this scene seems to realize how undeserved her love for him is. He has simply told her,

[7] Young, *Ernest Hemingway*, p. 90.

[8] Maurice Valency, *In Praise of Love*, pp. 239–240.

without sadness, of his sufferings, and she loves him with a love that is unfathomable to him, the love that passes all understanding.

Colonel Cantwell strains to find an answer that his own life has already demonstrated. Just as Desdemona had said, "I saw Othello's visage in his mind," so could Renata explain why she loved Cantwell. For beneath his gruff exterior, as beneath the Moor's dark skin, beats a heart of gold, and the continuation of the previous scene in which the Colonel wonders what to give Renata clearly demonstrates how agape has influenced their love.

In the very same paragraph in which the Colonel wonders how to keep his love fresh, he also wonders how to get a jeep engine to an old boatman whom he has befriended. The Italian's life depends on his boat, and its engine, like the Colonel's heart, is dying. In a selfless gesture of kindness the Colonel promises to get a condemned Army jeep engine for the boatman. Yet as the duck hunt continues, hatred and death surge through the Colonel's mind when he thinks of the Italian guide who for some unknown reason is making his last hunt miserable. He would gladly kill "that son of a bitch," but he checks himself.

> Stop that, he said to himself, and think about your girl. You do not want to kill anyone anymore; ever.
>
> Who are you feeding that to, he told himself. You going to run as a Christian? You might give it an honest try. She would like you better that way. Or would she? I don't know, he said frankly. I honest to Christ don't know.
>
> Maybe I will get Christian toward the end. Yes, he said, maybe you will. Who wants to make a bet on that?
>
> "You want to bet on that?" he asked the calling duck [the live hen decoy]. But she was looking up at the sky behind him and had commenced her small chuckling talk. (291)

It is clear that Renata has led the Colonel to something besides a Tristan's tryst in a gondola. Like Dante's Beatrice, she leads him away from his baser thoughts to paradise; she prepares him for his fast approaching death. His faith in her, reflected in his self-control with the moody Italian guide, is rewarded and verified when he treats the boatman well, not showing his anger, helping him to pole the boat through the ice-bound marsh ("they worked together in complete co-ordination"), sharing his gin with him on the cold trip back, accepting the boatman's apologies, and then learning from his friend how the boatman had been affected by the Allied uniform worn by both the Colonel and the Moroccans who had raped his wife and daughter during the war (295–302). The patterns of eros and agape overlap once more.

He tells his hunting companion to give his love to Renata, he climbs into his automobile—his "tumbril" (288)—and after another brief spat with his comic-book–reading driver Jackson, the bathetic namesake of Stonewall Jackson (307), he quickly apologizes and gets ready to die. He writes a will and thinks he is ready: "Any further concern you may have is about yourself and that is just a luxury" (306). His education has taught him to overcome self. He dies.

Just as eros is ambiguous, being both creative and destructive, so is death. The title of this novel, part of the dying words of Stonewall Jackson, is a funerary one, as was *For Whom the Bell Tolls.* Throughout the novel the awareness of oncoming death weighs heavy on the Colonel's mind, informs his last days on earth, and similarly determines many of the images and allusions. As part of the game of life, death is a natural end, to be accepted with whatever dignity a man can muster, but there are bad deaths too. They are deaths associated with hate—the condition of nonlove—and loneliness. The drake that is lured to his death by the call of the hen is a lone drake, and the Colonel is an isolated man except for the five-member "Order" and Renata, his "last true love."

All of his former wives were presumably American, and America is the land of loneliness and death, although loneliness is found in the middle of crowds and death is known only by euphemisms. When the Colonel speaks to his driver Jackson about Titian's paintings of women, Jackson tells him such a symbol of creativity and passion would be out of place in his home town, even in the museum, where all the "art" is of death rather than life:

"Arrow heads, war bonnets, scalping knives, different scalps, petrified fish, pipes of peace, photographs of Liver Eating Johnston, and the skin of some bad man that they hanged him and some doctor skinned him out." (16)

Yet the Colonel himself is a professional killer who can say at one time that war " 'is not a dirty trade' " (114) and later that it is a butchery (188) in which good soldiers die hard (230). Among good soldiers, agape strengthens in the time of war. Bad leaders are loveless leaders, who lead their men to death unredeemed by love. The facts of life and death are unimportant, one should conclude, for all that matters is the manner in which people approach them (114). The Colonel is dying well, without too many regrets, without tears. He is dying tough in a tough town that has manners, in Venice, the best of cities (36). He would like to be buried there too.

> I could be a part of the ground where the children play in the evenings, and in the mornings, maybe, they would still be training jumping horses and their hoofs would make the thudding on the turf, and trout would rise in the pool when there was a hatch of fly. (35)

The children, horses, and fish are symbols of life and fertility; the "Order" the Colonel has founded is "de los Caballeros"—the Colonel and all good men are horsemen, knights, chevaliers (56). The Colonel again thinks of horses as an appropriate gift from Renata to him (261), and he also thinks of Renata's portrait as lovely, " 'But it is like skinning a dead horse' " in comparison to the real thing (114). Another possible allusion to the horse as symbol is the Colonel's contempt for the use of cavalry in modern war, where it is worthless (232). Eros and war as an honorable profession have both been debased. Creative eros is gone and war is a matter of atomic bombs and biological warfare (197).

This real eros and the picture of it are different things, and agape can be similarly viewed. In fact, if there is a conflict in the novel, it is within the Colonel and is his struggle to love broadly and well. Being a man—that is, being human—and more particularly being the man of violence that he is, he will never completely achieve that desired goal of universal love. Even in his love for Renata he can be cruel, and outside the small circle of personal friends who are in his quasi-religious "Order," he is sometimes as irrationally wrathful as he is irrationally beneficent.

This interior conflict is symbolized by the Colonel's old war wounds, particularly one in his hand, which make the Colonel into a demi-Christ figure, one half of him bearing the wounds of Christ and living a life of love, the other half unmarked, human, and living without agape. Once, in fact, his "other, good, side" says, "You love them"—that is, men who have been hit solidly, men who have received castigation, and cripples (71). Renata likes to feel Colonel Cantwell's hand, and she wants her affection for it to be taken seriously because she often dreams that this very hand, misshapen and distasteful to the Colonel, is " 'the hand of Our Lord'" (84). He mocks her dream and the hand, but though she is frightened by the sacrilegious implications, Renata insists that his hand and her dream-Christ's hand are one and the same. When they are momentarily saddened at the thought of their coming separation, Renata tells Cantwell to put his right hand, "the split hand," in his pocket to feel the emeralds that Renata has given him. This ritual restores Renata's happiness (132). Later, by himself, he repeats the stone-handling ritual to sustain his own spirits—sliding the emeralds "from his bad hand into his good hand" (165). The right hand, the wounded hand, is the "bad" hand, the hand that Renata wants the Colonel to caress her with.

"Please put your hand here."
"My good or my bad?"
"Your bad," the girl said. "The one I love and must think about all week. I cannot keep it like you keep the stones." (226)

It is the hand to run through her hair (151–152), and then the one to find Renata's "island in the great river with the high steep banks" (153). The hand of Christ is the hand of love, but that love includes eros. It is the hand she wishes to hold while they are talking:

"Tell me very low and soft and put your bad hand in mine."
"The hell with my bad hand," the Colonel said. "Since when was it so bad."
"It's bad," the girl said. "Badder, or worse, than you will ever know." (244–245)

But it is also a hand used to beat the two sailors who whistle at Renata. Fittingly, the bad right hand of agape becomes "a good right hand" of violence when it is shot into the bodies of the sailors in a most un-Christlike action which the Colonel regards as an "accident" the sailors brought on themselves (284). Renata does not understand fighting. "'Shouldn't I have stayed and cared for them?'" she asks. "'Never,' the Colonel told her" (286). After he explains the ethics of street fighting, Renata asks if he has hurt his bad hand.

"No," he explained. "I only threw it once to the head. The other times I punched to the body with it."
"May I feel it?"
"If you will feel very softly."
"But it is terribly swollen."
"There is nothing broken in it and that sort of swelling always goes down."

"Do you love me?"

"Yes. I love you with two moderately swollen hands and all my heart." (287)

The Colonel no doubt intends the juxtaposition ironically, but the repeated allusions to his injured hand as bearing a stigma-like mark makes the juxtaposition an excellent symbolic focus of the theme of the novel: Colonel Cantwell achieves erotic love with Renata through frequent and good use of the same hand that establishes him as a part-time, apprentice Christ. Through eros, this man aspires to agape, and the hero who Can't-get-well, who is dying, is having a last, great, true love affair that is all of paradise that he expects to know. " 'Would you ever like to run for Queen of Heaven?' " he asks Renata (83). And she asks to hold his hand again as a remembrance of him for the times when they will be apart and she will go to mass and read Dante (218). " 'I love your hand and all your other wounded places,' " she says, almost prayerfully, in partial answer to the Colonel's request to tell him of her love (141).

The Colonel acquired his wounded hand " 'Very honorably. On a rocky, bare-assed hill' " (135, 128–129, 256). The point is made several times, and if there is any doubt as to the hill being a Calvary, the Colonel also tells Renata that the trees in the woods around the hill were Christmas trees (255). Further, the Colonel is so tough that he can rest on his feet or " 'against a God damned tree' " (197); he too has his agony (198); and he too works a "miracle" by beating the sailors and declaring his love for Renata "with two moderately swollen hands and all my heart.' "

> So that was that, and maybe it was that day or maybe it was another that made the miracle. You never knew, he thought. There was the great miracle and he had never consciously implemented it. (287–288)

The miracle is Renata's love for him, a beaten, wounded, scarred "son of a bitch."

But perhaps the surest indications of agape in the Colonel's character are the repeated instances in which he expresses or shows his love for his enemies. These indications culminate in the understanding and sympathy he has for the embittered boatman who almost ruins his last hunt (294–298). While the Colonel has a certain lack of tolerance for all those people outside the "Order"—the noble, military, and religious mock Order of Brusadelli made up of the Colonel, Renata, and a few Italian friends—an enemy who fights well should not be hated. During World War I, the Colonel as a young lieutenant had "never hated" the enemy (33), and he could even like many of them who fought well or were, like him, mutilated (71). The Germans may have been in the wrong, " 'But who has not been?' " the Colonel forgivingly asks (122; also 150 and 231).

> I can't hate Fascists, he thought. Nor Krauts either, since unfortunately, I am a soldier.
>
> "Listen, Portrait," he said. "Do I have to hate the Krauts because we kill them? Do I have to hate them as soldiers and as human beings? It seems too easy a solution to me." (176)

German General Erwin Rommel he liked "very much." " 'But he was your enemy,' " Renata says. " 'I love my enemies, sometimes, more than my friends' " (286), the Colonel answers. As a soldier the Colonel would be prepared to fight, "Our potential enemy" (the Russians), but, he says, " 'I like them very much and I have never known finer people nor people more as we are' " (70).

In fact, when the "good side" of the Colonel is in power, he hates nothing at all (232), but the other side of his nature is full of the violence of hunting and war and the hatred of men who cheat, who are selfish, who are cowardly, who are phony, who are perverted, or who are merely ignorant (184, 187, 217, 223–225, 227, 236, 237–238). No matter how justified, however, giving vent to his anger is not good for him (281)—it will bring on a heart attack; it will weaken the seat of the affections that has been so sorely tried by his warrior's life.

Of course, the Colonel does die of a heart attack. If followed long enough, every story ends in death, Hemingway had written earlier.[9] But if he has not completely lived his last days in love both erotic and brotherly, he has at least been as good as he was able. He is no Christ, but he has taught himself through his own Passion enacted on a bare-assed hill in the Huertgen forest, in bad marriages, and in countless other agonies of his violent life, that concern for oneself is a luxury (306).

He has reached a pinnacle of earthly love that includes doing all

[9] *Death in the Afternoon*, p. 122.

things with love and care. Sometimes this love is ridiculous in isolated detail—as when they kiss "true," or when he opens doors with rites, or reaches "accurately and well" for a champagne bucket, or closes a car door "carefully and well" (109, 154, 307)—but in sum and in context the details are an extension of love to all of life. And it is sound in reality as well as in principle that, for instance, a good shopkeeper should cut a paper-thin slice of sausage for the Colonel "ferociously and lovingly" (190) and the Colonel himself should in admiration of a good wine recork it "carefully, precisely, and lovingly" (164). If the Colonel had lived to an old age, he would, perhaps, have even further subdued his ego and lived the love-full way of Hemingway's last hero, the old man of the sea.

# 10 ~ THE LAST HERO

*Dayadhvam:* I have heard the key
Turn in the door once and turn once only
We think of the key, each in his prison
Thinking of the key, each confirms a prison
Only at nightfall, aethereal rumors
Revive for a moment a broken Coriolanus
DA
*Damyata:* The boat responded
Gaily, to the hand expert with sail and oar

—T. S. Eliot, *The Waste Land*

The first thing God made is love
Then comes the blood
And the thirst for blood
Goaded by the body's seed as if by salt.
The first thing God made is the long journey;
That house is waiting
With its blue smoke,
With the dog grown old
Waiting, that he may die, for the homecoming
But the dead must give me guidance . . .

—George Seferis, "Stratis the Sailor
among the Agapanthi"

COLONEL CANTWELL, a professional soldier, speaks of his trade only in retrospect, in the fragmentary conversations in which he tells Renata of his wartime deeds and agonies. In the dramatic action of the novel, slight as the action is, the ideal of living lovingly in all things is thus reduced to bathos when the living is reduced to the opening of doors and bottles "lovingly and well" rather than, perhaps, soldiering that way. Although the same ideal of perpetual loving expressed even in mundane acts is carried over into Hemingway's last novel, *The Old Man and the Sea* (1952), the emotional pitfall that occasionally traps the Colonel is avoided by the fisherman Santiago because the action of his story is mainly in the present, when he is still pursuing his trade. Like the Colonel, the fisherman is a hard worker, a careful craftsman, a man who honors the dignity of work and performs his task well, trusting to skill rather than luck. But Santiago's simple devotions are in the context of a simple trade followed by a simple man. They are, in fact, functional acts relatively more important to his life than are the Colonel's opening and closing of doors to his.

Santiago is also like the Colonel in being a demi-Christ figure: Santiago also has one bad hand that symbolizes his internal struggle or his divided nature, a man who is half divine and half too too mortal. The central action similarly reflects this division. Santiago, like Coleridge's Ancient Mariner, knows that

> He prayeth well, who loveth well
> Both man and bird and beast.
>
> He prayeth best, who loveth best
> All things both great and small . . .

In the daily round of humdrum life, one kills a bird or catches a fish too noble to die and then pays for one's pride. Santiago can recognize the ideal of brotherhood in nature and can almost achieve it—he knows the creatures of the air and the sea are his brothers—but there is the necessity to live as a fisherman who preys on his brothers, and there is also the shark, the rapacious beast that comes out of darkness to ravage beauty and confound skill. The shark in man will not be stilled either.

It has been pointed out that Santiago "is Spanish for Saint James—the fisherman, apostle, and martyr"[1]—and that the description of Santiago that uses Christ symbols and allusions suggests "solidarity and love and humility as opposed to individualism and pride."[2] But to note ways in which Santiago is not a martyr or a Christ is just as important if one is to see him as a man torn between two worlds, two ways of life—one the way of the shark, of hate and destruction, the other the way of love, the brotherhood of man in and with nature. Santiago has gone out "too far," and when he catches the huge marlin, he is completely alone, completely without help, completely isolated from his fellow man. After the initial thrill and happiness of hooking the fish, he gradually comes to regret his "luck": "he began to pity the great fish."[3] The marlin's

> choice had been to stay in the deep dark water far out beyond all snares and traps and treacheries. My choice was to go there to find him beyond all

[1] Melvin Backman, "Hemingway: The Matador and the Crucified," *Hemingway and His Critics*, Carlos Baker, ed., p. 256. Mr. Backman also indicates the Christ parallels.

[2] Clinton S. Burhans, Jr., "*The Old Man and the Sea:* Hemingway's Tragic Vision of Man," *Hemingway and His Critics*, Carlos Baker, ed., p. 264. My conclusions closely parallel those of Burhans and also of William J. Handy, who says: "Hemingway's theme is clear: Success in the achievement of being carries with it the most valued of man's possessions, the capacity for love" (see "A New Dimension for a Hero," *Six Contemporary Novels*, William O. S. Sutherland, Jr., ed., p. 66). Carlos Baker's chapter on the novel has many complementary points, such as observing the parallels between the novel and Coleridge's "Ancient Mariner" (see Carlos Baker, *Hemingway: The Writer as Artist*, p. 301).

[3] Ernest Hemingway, *The Old Man and the Sea*, p. 53. Subsequent references to this novel in this chapter will be made in the text itself.

people. Beyond all people in the world. Now we are joined together and have been since noon. And no one to help either one of us.

Perhaps I should not have been a fisherman, he thought. But that was the thing that I was born for. (55–56)

Man's fate is to love and respect the very things that he must kill. Santiago speaks of being "with a friend" (61); "He is my brother. But I must kill him . . ." (65). They are joined together by the long taut line, and they suffer greatly together—both of these old, male fighters (53–54); the fish are "not as intelligent as we who kill them; although they are more noble and more able" (70).

The two brothers contend with each other.

He jumped almost as though to show me how big he was. I know now, anyway, he thought. I wish I could show him what sort of man I am. But then he would see the cramped hand. Let him think I am more man than I am and I will be so. I wish I was the fish, he thought, with everything he has against only my will and my intelligence. (70–71)

And the marlin's courage and strength is a glory that Santiago now regrets having to destroy. His pride outweighs what he sees as an injustice.

"I'll kill him though," he said. "In all his greatness and his glory."

Although it is unjust, he thought. But I will show him what a man can do and what a man endures.

"I told the boy I was a strange old man," he said. "Now is when I must prove it." (73)

After the kill he admits to himself:

You killed him for pride and because you are a fisherman. You loved him when he was alive and you loved him after. If you love him, it is not a sin to kill him. Or is it more? (116)

Santiago's sin is hardly pride in usual human terms, for he had also attained a humility that "was not disgraceful and it carried no loss of true pride" (14). But finally Santiago concedes that he has sinned:

"I wish it were a dream and that I had never hooked him. I'm sorry about it fish. It makes everything wrong." He stopped and he did not want to look at the fish now. Drained of blood and awash he looked the color of the silver backing of a mirror and his stripes still showed.

"I shouldn't have gone out so far, fish," he said. "Neither for you nor for me. I'm sorry, fish." (121)

Santiago's recognition is of the pride of tragedy.

When he finally kills the marlin—and then he is not sure who is killing whom (102)—he realizes that the victory is the fish's: "'I have killed this fish which is my brother and now I must do the slave work'" (105). The fish had fought with his heart while Santiago had used his body and head, but not his heart. It is also the heart that Santiago must harpoon in order to kill the marlin, but the marauding sharks are stabbed in the brain and eyes and clubbed on the head. When Santiago feels the marlin's heart with his harpoon, the phallic symbol penetrates to the seat of love and kills. It is the Hemingway hero's lesson repeated. For Santiago it is a religious revelation: as the silvery marlin's blood spreads like a cloud in the water, "The old man looked carefully in the glimpse of vision that he had" (104).

After the vision, he sails home, and as he sails back to mankind, the half-god is crucified by the sharks:

> "Ay," he said aloud. There is no translation for this word and perhaps it is just a noise such as a man might make, involuntarily, feeling the nail go through his hands and into the wood. (118)

Even after reaching port, Santiago suffers as a Christ—climbing with his cross (the boat's heavy mast) up his Calvary (the hill to his shack) to sleep "with his arms out straight and the palms of his [cut] hands up" (133–134). He suffers like a god for acting a god—a self-sufficient, monolithic being. Yet he fights to the limit of his strength and ability to protect the body of the marlin he has violated. He tells the marlin he is sorry because of the sharks, i.e., the instruments of destruction had been unleashed by his own action of going out too far (121).

The sole sign of a change in Santiago is his concession that, like Harry Morgan who also sailed the Gulf Stream waters, no man alone has a chance. Santiago will accept the help of Manolin, the boy who had once sailed with him before his luck turned bad and who now demands that he take him to sea once more. Manolin will bring his own luck with him, and Santiago will teach him the ways of the wind and sea and all their creatures, who are Santiago's brothers. Like the fisherman St. Peter (116) and Santiago's namesake, St. James, he will teach the gospel to the boy (138–139).

In spite of all the concern with love between man and woman in the earlier novels, there is remarkably little affection between men in Hemingway's work. Hemingway's heroes work, fight, and die in masculine trades, but until *The Old Man and the Sea,* not one of the novels describes a male relationship with the warmth and completeness of Manolin and Santiago's. It is something special, and it plays an important role in this novel by showing agape at work and agape uncorrupted by the selfishness and destruction that too often mark eros.

Because Santiago has been unlucky, Manolin is sad for him (9). He shares the old man's grief, and he wishes to sail with him again to help him. Both men are uncomplicated. "The old man had taught the boy to fish and the boy loved him" (10). In turn, the old man looks at Manolin "with his sunburned, confident loving eyes" (13) when the boy urges his help on Santiago. Although others have lost faith in Santiago, the boy has not. And while it is the old man who teaches Manolin, the boy has something to give Santiago too, for he goes along with Santiago's little fictions that save his pride, he fetches bait for him, he covers him when he is sleeping, and he even begs food for him when Santiago out of pride would rather starve (17–22); and the old man is conscious of his dependence on the boy who literally keeps him alive (117). It is while Santiago is out "too far" fighting the marlin that he realizes most sharply his need for help, and particularly the aid of the boy. As soon as he hooks the big fish, he says aloud, " 'I wish I had the boy' " (49), and he repeats that wish later, adding " 'To help me and to see this [fight]' " (52)–that is, their relationship is reciprocal, each giving and taking something. Four times more in the long fight Santiago wishes for the boy, twice in a general plea and twice for specific aid, like rubbing the "humiliating" cramp out of his arm and wetting the coils of line that are burning and cutting his hands (57, 62, 68, 91).

After the victory over the marlin, Santiago continues to think of the boy who makes him happy simply because of his faith in his skill (25). Because Manolin is becoming a man (28), Santiago has had to catch the marlin, in part to prove his own manhood to the boy, to guarantee, as it were, Santiago's right to teach him. Santiago looks forward to displaying his great catch and to repairing his lines with the boy's help (106). After the marlin is destroyed by the sharks and he is "crucified" by them, the old man thinks:

> I cannot be too far out now. . . . I hope no one has been too worried. There

is only the boy to worry, of course. Many of the older fishermen will worry. Many others too, he thought. I live in a good town. (127)

After his voyage out of mankind, Santiago has returned to it through the boy.

But, ironically, the boy had needed no proof of Santiago's virtues as a teacher. Manolin finds Santiago:

> He was asleep when the boy looked in the door in the morning. It was blowing so hard that the drifting-boats would not be going out and the boy had slept late and then come to the old man's shack as he had come each morning. The boy saw that the old man was breathing and then he saw the old man's hands and he started to cry. He went out very quietly to go to bring some coffee and all the way down the road he was crying. (134–135)

The other fishermen are more interested in the skeleton of Santiago's huge marlin than they are concerned with Santiago's condition. Manolin nurses the exhausted old man, and he tends his spirit as well.

> "They beat me, Manolin," he said. "They truly beat me."
> "*He* didn't beat you. Not the fish."
> "No. Truly. It was afterwards." (136–137)

Manolin's only request is for the symbolically phallic, lifegiving, lifetaking spear of the marlin:

> "Pedrico is looking after the skiff and the gear. What do you want done with the head?"
> "Let Pedrico chop it up to use in fish traps."
> "And the spear?"
> "You keep it if you want it."
> "I want it," the boy said. "Now we must make our plans about the other things."
> "Did they search for me?"
> "Of course. With coast guard and with planes."
> "The ocean is very big and a skiff is small and hard to see," the old man said. He noticed how pleasant it was to have someone to talk to instead of speaking only to himself and to the sea. . . .
> "Now we fish together again."
> "No. I am not lucky. I am not lucky anymore."
> "The hell with luck," the boy said. "I'll bring the luck with me." (136–137)

Manolin, Santiago's closest link with his community, is a true friend who accepts the old man's weakness and lack of luck as well as his skill, respect, and love. From another point of view, Manolin is being initiated, and the giving of the marlin's spear is one of the several symbolic images of eros. This last novel, with an aging hero, would realistically have little to do with eros in the action, characterization, and language, and in fact, if a transition of emphasis from eros to agape had not been gradually established and clearly indicated in the previous two novels (*For Whom the Bell Tolls* and *Across the River and into the Trees*) a radical difference in theme would have to be noted. In a sense, the importance of eros has continued to deteriorate as the Hemingway hero has aged, and the question of whether or not Santiago is a different kind of Hemingway hero can only be answered negatively if one sees the obvious similarities in the personal codes of Santiago, Cantwell, and Jordan. He is different in age, and quite simply his physiological change is symbolic of the author's reduction of the role of eros to its pleasantly animal, livegiving function. Eros remains, literally, only as a dream—the old man's recurring dream of the lions. When he had been a youth like Manolin, he had seen young lions playing on the beaches of exotic Africa, and the lions have come to symbolize a past strength, his virility, that he no longer has except in his pleasant dreams of the lions. The lions of youth and vigor are very close to being simply symbols of eros. In explaining the subtitle of his book, *The Mind and Heart of Love: Lion and Unicorn, a Study in Eros and Agape*, M. C. D'Arcy writes:

> The Lion symbolizes that noble and ignoble love which is leonine and lordly and asserts itself in pride and self-respect and honour. In other words it stands for self-centered love.[4]

Further connection between symbol and idea is indicated by the term "pride" to describe a group of lions and the obsolete meaning of "pride" as sexual desire. (Carlos Baker notes the close link between Manolin and the lions.)[5] Santiago tells Manolin about the lions, following the apparently oft-repeated story with reflections on John J. McGraw and his association with horses (another erotic beast), and then he sleeps to dream about the lions once more.

> He no longer dreamed of storms, nor of women, nor of great occurrences, nor of great fish, nor fights, nor contests of strength, nor of his wife. He only

[4] M. C. D'Arcy, *The Mind and Heart of Love*, p. 17.
[5] Baker, *Hemingway, The Writer as Artist*, p. 307.

dreamed of places now and of the lions on the beach. They played like young cats in the dusk and he loved them as he loved the boy. He never dreamed about the boy. (27–28)

At sea, when he sleeps briefly during the fight to land the marlin, Santiago dreams of the lions again, "and he was happy" (90). During the day, he wishes that he could sleep and dream about the lions. "Why are the lions the main thing that is left? Don't think, old man, he said to himself" (73). And finally, when he has returned home with his mast to struggle up the road to his shack with no one there to help him in the night, he sees a cat "going about its business" (134). Apparently his first exhausted sleep is dreamless, but after the boy has brought him coffee and talked to him about the marlin and about preparing to go fishing together once more, the old man falls asleep again. "He was still sleeping on his face and the boy was sitting by him watching him. The old man was dreaming about the lions" (140). Those are the last words of the story.

Santiago's erotic necessities have been sublimated into a symbol; the conscious mind would revolt at substituting Manolin in the dream, but the unconscious asserts the relationship. (Once when he falls asleep in the boat he does not immediately dream of the lions but of "a vast school of porpoises . . . in the time of their mating" [89].) This is not to say that Santiago's love for the boy is sexual, but simply that the boy is becoming sexually mature and is about the same age as Santiago was when he lived in Africa. Manolin's age is not precisely given; he is simply "the boy" throughout the novel. But he is old enough to work regularly on the fishing boats and to be of real assistance. He is also old enough to realize the mutual responsibility and care and knowledge that he and Santiago share. In short, he has reached the age of puberty. Like those other lovers of water, Huckleberry Finn and Ishmael, he is ready to be initiated, to become a lover in the broadest sense of that word.

The sea itself is a woman and an object of eros to Santiago and to all others who love her.

He always thought of the sea as *la mar* which is what people call her in Spanish when they love her. Sometimes those who love her say bad things of her but they are always said as though she were a woman. Some of the younger fishermen, those who used buoys as floats for their lines and had motorboats, bought when the shark livers had brought much money [the materialistic, the uninitiated, the nonlovers, the destructive ones who live off the destructive sharks], spoke of her as a contestant or a place or even an enemy. But the old man always thought of her as feminine and as something that gave or withheld great favors, and if she did wild or wicked things it was because she could not help them. The moon affects her as it does a woman, he thought. (32–33)

When Santiago is being towed by the marlin and passes a mass of Sargasso weed, he sees it heaving and swinging "in the light sea as though the ocean were making love with something under a yellow blanket . . ." (79–80).

Santiago also regards the creatures of the sea as creative or destructive lovers. The Portuguese man-of-war with its stinging filaments is a whore to him—beautiful to see but deadly and "the falsest thing in the sea" (39–40). He liked to see the big turtles eating them.

He loved green turtles and hawks-bills with their elegance and speed and their value and he had a friendly contempt for the huge, stupid loggerheads, yellow in their armor-plating, strange in their love-making, and happily eating the Portuguese men-of-war with their eyes shut. (40)

The turtles are strange, and some people view them mystically because their hearts will beat for hours after they have been butchered. The old man feels no mysticism about them because "I have such a heart too" (41). Both he and the turtles are strong hearted—strong, strange lovers.

He likes the porpoises too, and he can tell the difference between the males and females.

"They are good," he said. "They play and make jokes and love one another. They are our brothers like the flying fish." (53)

The marlin's love, however, is even more "human" than the turtles and porpoises'. Santiago believes his marlin is a male, and he is reminded of the time he hooked one of a pair of marlin:

The male fish always let the female fish feed first and the hooked fish, the female, made a wild, panic-stricken despairing fight that soon exhausted her, and all the time the male had stayed with her, crossing the line and circling with her on the surface. He had stayed so close that the old man was afraid he would cut the line with his tail. . . . When the old man had gaffed her and clubbed her . . . and then with the boy's aid, hoisted her aboard, the male fish had stayed by the side of the boat. Then, while the old man was clearing the lines and preparing the harpoon, the male fish jumped high into the air beside the boat to see where the female was and then went down deep, his lavender wings, that were his pectoral fins, spread wide and all his wide lavender stripes showing. He was beautiful, the old man thought. The boy was sad too and we begged her pardon and butchered her promptly. (54–55)

Even if Santiago humanizes unintelligent animals, no artistic flaw can be thus arbitrarily attributed to the author who wishes to picture a man unnaturally, almost supernaturally, conversant with nature. Robert P. Weeks has attacked Hemingway as going "soft" in thinking and style in *The Old Man and the Sea* as well as being unrealistic and thus violating his own standards for good writing. Weeks cites, seriously it would seem, the Miami Weather Bureau as one authority on Hemingway's lack of verisimilitude. Such an attack reveals a serious misreading not only of this novel but also of all of Hemingway. Very little of his work is "realistic" in the plodding feeling of actuality one might find in Howells or Galsworthy. Weeks' statement that Santiago's "friendly" stars are really "cold" and "remote" is as much a matter of point of view as is Santiago's—and the story is Santiago's.[6] As the stars are humanized, so the creatures of the sea are emblems of water: they are infused with its power, and they govern the fertility of the world. Mythically, water is of sacred importance and has consecrating power. And at rest, at least, the sea has the feminine qualities of undulating seductiveness and lazy pleasure.[7] The water itself is purifying. Just as Santiago washes his cut hands in it to cure them, so he baptizes himself in a way like the archetypal "Old Man [who] dies by being immersed in water and gives birth to a new, regenerate being."[8]

Like many myths, *The Old Man and the Sea* grew out of a historical event, which Hemingway briefly wrote of in an article on deep-sea fishing in *Esquire*, April 1936. Mircea Eliade points out that a combat between a heroic figure and a fabulous sea monster or a gigantic serpent is a familiar paradigmatic myth (see Beowulf and St. George) and that in the struggle the hero often undertakes a journey to heaven or hell. While serpents and sea monsters are phallic and fertility symbols, they

[6] Robert P. Weeks, "Fakery in *The Old Man and the Sea,*" *College English*, 24 (December 1962), 188–192.

[7] Mircea Eliade, *Patterns in Comparative Religion*, pp. 207, 210, 205.

[8] *Ibid.*, p. 197.

also symbolize "the involution, the preformal modality of the universe, the undivided 'One' of pre-Creation" whom man must conquer.[9] In the hero's struggle, he is often aided by a woman, and although Santiago is alone and "not religious," he prays " 'ten Our Fathers and ten Hail Marys that I should catch this fish, and I promise to make a pilgrimage to the Virgen de Cobre if I catch him' " (71). Later, he promises to pray one hundred Our Fathers and one hundred Hail Marys (96), and, significantly, "Hail Marys are easier to say than Our Fathers, he thought" (72). It is to the female—the virgin, the creative woman, the object of eros—that the hero turns.

The necessity of eros is underlined in the subsequent fights with the sharks (110 ff). They too are sea monsters, and the first one, the great mako shark from "deep down in the water," from the center of being, is very fast and strong and beautiful except for his destructive jaws. The other later sharks of a different species are lesser beasts, vicious and contemptible. The first shark is the biggest one Santiago has even seen—a fit retributor for the greatest marlin. As Santiago thinks of it, the shark will destroy *him*, "hit" him, for Santiago has identified himself with his noble victim. "He did not like to look at the fish anymore since he had been mutilated. When the fish had been hit it was as though he himself were hit" (113). For a moment Santiago is sorry he ever hooked the marlin, and he fights the shark "without hope but with resolution and complete malignancy" (113). Although he had harpooned the marlin's heart, Santiago strikes at the sharks' brains and eyes, the seats of intelligence rather than love. His own diminished sexual powers may be symbolized in the harpoon he loses in the first shark, in the stone he wishes he had brought to sharpen his knife (121–122), in that knife which he next loses in the head of another shark (123), in the makeshift weapons of tiller and club that he wields until they too are broken or carried away (130–131), in his brother the marlin's spear that he would have cut off to kill more sharks had he been able to (127), in that same spear which he presents to the boy as a remembrance and also as a sign of his sexual maturity (137), and in the new lance, the better, stronger lance that Manolin and Santiago plan to fashion before they go fishing together again (138). Like the marlin, who is first mutilated above the tail, Santiago's vigor and weapons are steadily diminished;

[9] Mircea Eliade, *Cosmos and History*, pp. 37ff.

he too is mutilated while the sharks rape the beautiful marlin: "The skiff was still shaking with the destruction the other shark was doing to the fish . . ." (120). So too is Santiago "destroyed" though not defeated: " 'But man is not made for defeat,' he said. 'A man can be destroyed but not defeated' " (114).

This metaphorical use of "destruction" used elsewhere by Hemingway in sexual contexts is the only remnant of ideas of romantic love in the novel. In place of the romantic dream is a development of agape to, and perhaps beyond, the limit to which a fallible, imperfect human being may aspire. The quest that has taken Santiago "too far out" has made him a wonderful figure of solitary man who discovers the limits of the ego, the self, and yet who comes to know the untapped power of the self.

The very first sentence of Santiago's story draws attention to his loneness: "He was an old man who fished alone in a skiff in the Gulf Stream . . ." (9). Although he lives in a fishing village, only Manolin visits him and cares for him. He had even put away the photograph of his dead wife "because it made him too lonely to see it . . ." (16–17), and for lack of a companion on his boat, he talks to himself and the creatures of the sea. Once he has hooked the marlin, he is towed out of sight of land to do lonely battle, and once he realizes the nobility of the fish he has hooked, he repeatedly wishes for Manolin and thinks, "No one should be alone in their old age. . . . But it is unavoidable" (53). There is a real conflict within him as he ponders his fate and that of the marlin, the strange yet only other friend that he now has: "Now we are joined together. . . . And no one to help either one of us" (55).

Like the other Hemingway heroes, Santiago still has to cope with loneliness, but unlike the others, he realizes that his pride has, in part, brought the loneliness on himself. This knowledge has the power to reverse his feelings; understanding his sin, he masters it. The fertile, feminine undulating waters renew his spirit.

> He looked across the sea and knew how alone he was now. But he could see the prisms in the deep dark water and the line stretching ahead and the strange undulation of the calm. The clouds were building up now for the trade wind and he looked ahead and saw a flight of wild ducks etching themselves against the sky over the water, then blurring, then etching again and he knew no man was ever alone on the sea. (67)

Whether he will land the marlin and whether he can keep it from the sharks does not matter to him now. He has *seen.* The persistent use of sight-and-light imagery indicates that the strangeness of the old man is in his supernatural sight, his affinity to the animals that also see well (including the marlin and the horse [74]), and his friendship with the light-giving stars, sun, and moon (82–83). He will hope and fight and endure to the limit of his will and strength, but the outcome will not greatly matter as long as he can endure with grace. "Perhaps it was a sin to kill the fish," he thinks, because pride was one reason for his long battle (116). But loving the marlin is an important extenuation, and if he pays by losing the marlin to the sharks, he can return from his journey into hell (where all the punishment is self-punishment) to live with men. Like Ulysses, Dante, Ishmael, and the Ancient Mariner, a sadder but a wiser man and a teacher of Manolin.

Unlike the real fisherman, the model for Santiago, whose battle ended in a rescue at sea, Santiago is alone even after he reaches port. He beaches his boat late at night, unaided, and carries his cross of a mast alone to his shack. It is only early the next morning that Manolin discovers him and with his tears receives Santiago back into mankind. Once he is within easy range of his home, he thinks, "I cannot be too far out now . . ." (127), but in order for his agony to be complete, being near home and friends is not close enough. He must be completely humiliated before he can emerge from the sea as the new man. Just as the medieval view of love ranged from eros to romanticism to agape and the Franciscan view of the good man as the great lover of God's creation, so does the old man signify the brotherly lover of the marlin, other fish, the stars, the wind, and the very sea itself. "In the Franciscan view . . . man's highest good was the ecstatic union with God, and love alone was the key to this beatitude."[10] The rebaptized Santiago has that key, and it is important to see that the change in him is not in regard to the creatures and elements of nature, but in regard to the rest of humanity as epitomized in Manolin, in Martin, the benevolent owner of the restaurant who gives Manolin food for Santiago, and in other fishermen like his friend Pedro. Throughout the brief narrative, Santiago regards nature as friendly (or evil as are the robber birds and the sharks), and

[10] Maurice Valency, *In Praise of Love*, p. 235.

it is only toward his fellow man that he finally knows, like Harry Morgan, that no man alone has a chance.

Pier Francesco Paolini has good points to make on Hemingway's themes, including observations on his Franciscan sentiments, man's ultimate isolation, and the self versus anti-self antithesis that can be seen in the conflicts of the dilettante and the professional (e.g., Harry of "The Snows of Kilimanjaro" versus Santiago), and nihilism versus social consciousness or engagement. The commitment of the Hemingway hero in *For Whom the Bell Tolls* was not completely satisfactory because it was political and partial; the commitment of Santiago "signifies . . . man's creative integration in the drama and mystery of Nature."[11] (Nature, I take it, includes Santiago's human as well as animal and elemental society.)

*The Old Man and the Sea* is a story of the victory of faith and of the endurance of the man who loves both great and small. No matter what happens to a man, if he can love, he can overcome himself; suffering and even physical isolation will be endurable; man will be "well adjusted" without surrendering his individuality to the tyrannical mass; he will be a part of his world, not an addition to it, not an outlander, not a pitiable excresence on it. He will be no Adam, but neither will he be a feared, outcast Cain. He will love his brother, even as he loves the birds and fish of the sea he loves. He has been a long time learning (if we extend his spiritual chronology back to the youth of the early stories and novels), and eros has helped him learn. Too old for sexual love, eros lives on in him as his dream of the lions of his youth. "Anyone can be a fisherman in May," he says (15); it takes a strong man to catch the "great fish" of September, the autumn of life. The eros of May or youth is no test for the love of men that outlives eros.

Unlike *To Have and Have Not* and *For Whom the Bell Tolls*, the "social context" of *The Old Man and the Sea* is tenuous, and it is easy to see why, to the Soviet critics who were enthusiastic about the Hemingway of *The Fifth Column*, it was "disturbing."[12] Hemingway's last, and climactic, statement about man's condition was not to pursue the

[11] Pier Francisco Paolini, "The Hemingway of the Major Works," *Hemingway and His Critics*, Carlos Baker, ed., p. 144.

[12] Deming Brown, "Hemingway in Russia," *Hemingway and His Critics*, Carlos Baker, ed., p. 153.

tentative probings of a narrowly social or political solution, but it was a predictable conclusion that saw man's fate as tragic but potentially noble, as, of course, all tragedy is. And man the Lover was the ultimate form of the hero. The role was unstable, dubious, impractical perhaps, but it was the only possible role for the man who *thought,* as Santiago repeatedly does, as well as felt.

Jake Barnes refuses to think about his condition; his self-pity would burst his heart; instead he turns to ritual—to the church, the bullfight, fishing—as a substitute for thought. When Brett tells the de-sexed, therefore de-loved Jake, " 'Jake, . . . we could have had such a damned good time together,' " and the phallic baton of the nearby policeman rises, Jake's answer is agonizingly ironic: " 'Yes. . . . Isn't it pretty to *think* so?' "[13]

Jake has yet to think out his problem. Frederic Henry sentimentalizes and isolates his love for Catherine (who obligingly dies). The political and military context is too utterly chaotic to be thought about; escape is the only solution. The experiment in social commitment is an illy tested failure, but the heroes who follow at least have a precedent to consider. And they begin to think—Harry Morgan when it is too late, Robert Jordan and Colonel Cantwell just in time, and then Santiago, an old man a long time learning, the least sophisticated and most humble of the lot of heroes, but the toughest one, the most durable one, and the only one tough enough to deal with abstract thought: "he liked to think about all things that he was involved in . . ." (116). He tests the limits of the self by going "too far out," and he learns that mankind is one other thing that he cannot help but be involved in. That, simply, is a lesson of agape.

[13] Ernest Hemingway, *The Sun Also Rises*, p. 247, my emphasis.

# 11 ~ BLACK CHRIST

It is good to be merry and wise,
It is good to be honest and true,
It is best to be off with the old love,
Before you are on with the new.

—Anonymous

If we are directed only by our particular Natures, and regulate our inclinations by no higher rule than that of our reasons, we are but Moralists; Divinity will still call us Heathens. Therefore this great worke of charity, must have other motives, ends, and impulsions.

—Sir Thomas Browne, *Religio Medici*

FROM THE POINT OF VIEW of this study, what tremendous irony there is in Hemingway's posthumous *A Moveable Feast*. Here Hemingway tells us that in the twenties he was practicing with his wife Hadley the kind of love he later understood was best for any man. He had to lose this love in order to find it, and the rest of his life was perhaps lived in some regret over what he had lost and in making attempts to recapture it. The understanding came gradually, and in *A Moveable Feast* he does in fact tell us that it began after he fell in love with another woman, presumably his second wife, Pauline Pfeiffer, and was on the point of leaving his first wife though he still loved her too! Thus Hemingway looks back at those intense years of found love and ironically writes of lost love. Apparently his own early love of Hadley was more like the loves of his later "happy lovers" Robert Jordan and Colonel Cantwell than it was like the loves of the "sad lovers" Jake Barnes and Frederic Henry. Later art imitated earlier life while earlier art imitated an ideal, an abstraction of love; when Hemingway practiced this mythic love, it proved to be unsatisfactory and a sham.

Of course such a line of thought is highly speculative, and neither is this study biographical, but it seems that Hemingway's life does here give us hints by which to interpret his writing. Having divorced his wife, it really didn't matter how many more Hemingway had, for he had tacitly accepted the possibility of attaining "true love" within the bonds of marriage. Yet because his last marriage was his longest and most durable, may it not have been a biographical complement of Santiago's endurance and love? With the rejection of his first wife, the search for Iseult was on. That he began it was his personal problem; that without the search we might be without the literature, and certainly without the particular emphasis that occasions this book, was his triumph. Because *A Moveable Feast* now makes the beginning of this search public, it is easier and no longer improper to discuss it.

This latest book, *A Moveable Feast,* balances *Green Hills of Africa,* that other work of nonfiction that also tells a love story. The African book is pivotal in that it is the first extended story of Hemingway's struggle to conquer the self, to transcend the role of the "four-letter man" that he sometimes played in the safari drama that became a morality play. *A Moveable Feast* tells the end of that struggle as well as some causes for its beginning. Hemingway's ability and desire to write such a book, which required moral courage, evokes the same sort of admiration that the first autobiographical book did.

The author of *A Moveable Feast* is no saint, but neither is he the defamer of character that one reviewer called him.[1] He is, rather, one of the most painfully honest of writers who does not flinch from what he sees as the truth, whether it is about Gertrude Stein, Scott Fitzgerald, or, the difficult part, himself. And he knew what he was doing; Mary Hemingway wrote of her thoughts after reading some of the book-in-progress:

> "It's not much about you," I once objected. "I thought it was going to be autobiography."
>
> "It's biography by *remate,*" Ernest said. *Remate* idiomatically is used to mean a two-wall shot in jai alai. "By reflection."[2]

So was *Green Hills of Africa* autobiographical. So was it an attempt "to write an absolutely true book." And so they both have a curious ambiguity in Hemingway's Foreword in the earlier book and Preface in the latter about each book's fictional quality. "Unlike many novels," Hemingway wrote in *Green Hills,* "none of . . . this book is imaginary." In *A Moveable Feast* he concludes the Preface:

[1] Brooks Atkinson, "Hemingway Turns to Defamation of Character," *Houston Chronicle,* July 8, 1964, Sec. 7, p. 6.

[2] Mary Hemingway, "The Making of the Book: A Chronicle and a Memoir," *New York Times Book Review,* May 10, 1964, p. 27.

If the reader prefers, this book may be regarded as fiction. But there is always the chance that such a book of fiction may throw some light on what has been written as fact.[3]

In addition to calling it one of Hemingway's better works, Lewis Galantiere thought that *A Moveable Feast* was not fragmentary and "should be read as a novel"[4]—a judgment equally appropriate for *Green Hills of Africa.* The four parts of the African book were entitled "Pursuit and Conversation," "Pursuit Remembered," "Pursuit and Failure," and "Pursuit as Happiness" (with a play on the "pursuit of happiness" in the Declaration of Independence). The continuity was climactic and led to the conclusion that only in the pursuit—the attempting, the fighting, the struggling for what one believes in, even when one knows the attainment is impossible—only in that pursuit is there happiness.

A distinction must be made between this kind of striving or becoming and romantic yearning. The hunter seeks the prey knowing it is desirable. Tristan seeks his lady knowing instinctively that she is but a woman, though they both act, as the common expression would have it, as if her ass *were* a gold mine. Accepting pursuit-through-agape as happiness requires a tremendous effort of will and self-denial, because it is only through self-denial that one becomes an individual and also transcends self. The hunter paradoxically concedes the elusiveness of his natural goal; the lover acts as though his seeking were the sheerest agony, and perhaps his suffering is real in terms of impeded circulation, tasteless or neglected meals, and, in general, life missed or passed by. The hunter—and Santiago is the climactic embodiment of that allegorical role—anticipates no trophy, though he must believe in the worthiness of it and in the virtue of action (not passion), and the happiness of being, becoming, and pursuit.

The hunter metaphor is absent in *A Moveable Feast,* but here Hemingway suggests a source for the demi-Christ metaphor that occurs in *Across the River and into the Trees* and *The Old Man and the Sea.* One winter while he and Hadley Hemingway were skiing in the Alps, he grew a beard and let his hair grow long, and the peasants who saw him

[3] Ernest Hemingway, *A Moveable Feast,* p. ix. Subsequent references to this book in this chapter will be in the text itself.

[4] Lewis Galantiere, "There Is Never Any End to Paris," *New York Times Book Review,* May 10, 1964, p. 26.

one night skiing down a mountain called him "the Black Christ" (206). What a wonderfully poetic phrase! What suggestions of bitterness and struggle and hope it conveys; and what electric insight into Colonel Cantwell and Santiago and surely Hemingway himself, whose personal generosity and warmth could be clouded in an instant with hate and rage. For instance, in an incident reported by Morley Callaghan, the Canadian author and Hemingway had been boxing, and Callaghan was getting the better of the larger Hemingway, whose mouth was bleeding. Then Hemingway spat a mouthful of blood in his friend's face and solemnly explained it was merely a bullfighter's gesture. Callaghan rather suspected that the "barbarous gesture" had come from some "strange nocturnal depths of his mind" that drew him unnaturally close to destruction and yet could exist at the same time with a "sweet and likable" nature that strangely drew Callaghan "closer than ever to him."[5] Or as Lewis Galantiere put it:

> Two natures struggled in the breast of this Faust—and they died in each other's grasp, so to say, the lower nature resisting with its last breath. Because there was this struggle, we must speak of tragedy, not of pathos.[6]

Black Christ indeed.

Thus, while the setting of *A Moveable Feast* is in Hemingway's first period of the twenties, thematically and developmentally it belongs with his last fiction of the fifties. In it Hemingway looks back with the experience and wisdom of his maturity to work out on paper what he was then; and knowing that younger man, the older man instructs us of the final fruit that his youth was inevitably to bear. Being of Santiago's years, the author is physiologically no longer driven by eros or obsessed by romance. A coolness in writing about these feverish forms of love might be cynically read as stemming solely from organic causes, but there is more to Hemingway's detachment than that.

Eros is not here merely in an impotent man's memory, although the tenor of his attitude is modulated. Eros is no blind Cupid now, but a fairly well disciplined handservant of agape. This return of the old writer to his youth provides an instructive double or comparative focus, and Hemingway was perhaps aware of the value of it. In any case, his

[5] Morley Callaghan, *That Summer in Paris*, pp. 122–123.
[6] Galantiere, "There Is Never Any End," p. 26.

wife Mary has written that before he began *A Moveable Feast* he gave her the manuscript of a novel set in southern France in the twenties, at least indicating the time and place of his current thoughts.[7]

Tracing the theme of eros with this double focus in mind, one finds sexual love as vital as ever for the author. There is no nostalgia or mourning for something lost; eros is still alive and productive, the functional opposite of the destructive love that Hemingway saw in the relations of Zelda and Scott Fitzgerald. "A Matter of Measurements" tells the partly comic, partly pathetic story of Fitzgerald's agony caused by his wife's telling him that his "measurements" made him sexually inadequate and led to her mental breakdown. Hemingway inspects and assures Fitzgerald and then takes him to the Louvre for further anatomical study and reassurance. Though there is a comic absurdity in this picture of the three-years-senior Fitzgerald (who had made a fortune as the "historian" of a sex-hungry jazz age), our knowledge of his romantic and idealistic nature and his adulation of Hemingway's "know-how" verifies the poetic truth of the story. Hemingway felt that Zelda was jealous of Fitzgerald's art and tried to destroy it. She was trying to put Scott "out of business." Hemingway urges Scott to cultivate an unnamed girl who likes him and forget the crazy Zelda who " 'just wants to destroy you' " (190–191).

The bitch-wife corrupts eros and uses it as a tool, though I do not mean to judge Zelda personally, for her reasons were no doubt complex, and one can readily imagine this Golden Girl, a descendent of Iseult, waking up to the loss of her Tristan to—not another woman but—his art. What an insult.

Contrasted with the Fitzgeralds' corruption of eros from a productive to a destructive power is the Hemingways' frankness and warmth. He is very much in love with his wife, and yet he notices and admires the beautiful women around him (5–6, 102–104, 199, 205); he greatly enjoys good eating, that other lifegiving activity; he takes great pleasure in the rebirth of nature in the spring and in the excitement of horse racing. As always, he puts in what might seem merely incidental information—the Kansas City whores "who were marked for death" swallowed semen "as a sovereign remedy" (126)—and he compares Fitzgerald's excitement at drinking wine from a bottle to a girl's excitement

[7] Mary Hemingway, "The Making of the Book," p. 27.

at swimming nude for the first time (163). In another comparison, he says that "After writing a story I was always empty and both sad and happy, as though I had made love" (6); and unless he was careful in what he did between writing sessions, he would become impotent (13). Whether it was eating or writing or making love, there were organic connections between these productive pleasures.

Making love "with whom you loved," in fact, was "better than anything" to keep the goodness in his writing (25), and at that time in his imagination making love was the natural end of other activities, for other people (100) as well as for Hemingway (38, 57). If one kept this balance between work, play, eating and drinking, and talking with friends, and if the culmination of this balance was the act of love, then one was happy. When Hemingway occasionally lost this productive balance, he called himself stupid, and when he threw it off for good, he began the tortuous life that was simply his payment for the ultimate recovery of the moveable feast, the Paris of his youth before his own corruption of love.

He knew of certain corruptions, like Zelda's and Gertrude Stein's. Miss Stein had undertaken to instruct Hemingway on sex, and she tried to weaken what he admitted were certain prejudices against homosexuality—meaning, presumably, that in Stein's view Hemingway's dislike of homosexuality without first trying it was like refusing to taste snails. Her argument on behalf of toleration of homosexuality and her picturing of it between women as in no way leading to criminality or unhappiness, however, stemmed from an argumentative position made suspect by her personal involvement, which Hemingway later accidentally discovered. Perhaps his dislike of homosexuals stemmed also from a personal experience, and perhaps it was involved, like his sports, with some inner fear or doubts of his own masculinity. *A Moveable Feast* clearly supports the first supposition and gives no evidence for the second, which flourishes best from the nourishment of legends rather than direct evidence. After Gertrude Stein's "instruction," he returns to love his wife in a happy rejection of that attitude described and practiced by Miss Stein.

His "corruption" was not the perversion of eros, but of agape into romance, and against that change he was defenseless. Gertrude Stein initially liked the Hemingways so much that she could even forgive them for being in love, for she knew "time would fix that" (14–15), and she could always pretend that Hadley didn't matter (54). Hemingway's bitter irony can be appreciated fully only in light of its composition thirty-five years and three wives later. " '. . . we'll read and then go to bed and make love,' " Hemingway says. And he has that first wife answer:

> "And we'll never love anyone else but each other."
> "No. Never."
> "What a lovely afternoon and evening. . . ."
> "We're always lucky," I said and like a fool I did not knock on wood. There was wood everywhere in that apartment to knock on too. (37–38)

His foolishness was more than neglect of a superstition. It becomes a longing, a "hunger," for people and times lost. " 'Memory is hunger,' " Hadley reminds him, and " 'We should live in this time now and have every minute of it' " (57, 55). As Hemingway creates a woman of great attraction with simple womanly wisdom, he remembers that he "was being stupid," and he describes his "stupid" longing in memorable language:

> It was a wonderful meal at Michaud's after we got in; but when we had finished and there was no question of hunger any more the feeling that had been like hunger when we were on the bridge was still there when we caught the bus home. It was there when we came in the room and after we had gone to bed and made love in the dark, it was there. When I woke with the windows open and the moonlight on the roofs of the tall houses, it was there. I put my face away from the moonlight into the shadow but I could not sleep and lay awake thinking about it. We had both wakened twice in the night and my wife slept sweetly now with the moonlight on her face. I had to try to think it out and I was too stupid. Life had seemed so simple that morning when I had wakened and found the false spring and heard the pipes of the man with his herd of goats and gone out and bought the racing paper.
>
> But Paris was a very old city and we were young and nothing was simple there, not even poverty, nor sudden money, nor the moonlight, nor right and wrong nor the breathing of someone who lay beside you in the moonlight. (57–58)

That passage is at the heart of the book, and in a later chapter, the greatly comic one about an automobile trip with Fitzgerald, Hemingway subtly indicates how carefully these Paris "sketches" are organized. As Lewis Galantiere suggests, the book should be read as a novel. And the study of love is this novel's chief concern. While we can laugh at the telling of this insane journey taken by two of our greatest authors, Hemingway also prepares us for the quite natural conclusion of the chapter which returns us to Hemingway and his relations with his wife. On the trip Fitzgerald had been telling Hemingway the sad love story of his life with Zelda. He paradoxically enjoys their brief separation; he is "happy with the tragic implications" of the separation, and he even tells modest lies about it to Hemingway in order to heighten the drama of it.

With this distorted, comic romance on his mind, Hemingway returns to his wife, having learned " 'Never to go on trips with anyone you do not love' " (175). In contrast to the Fitzgeralds, the Hemingways feel they are " 'awfully lucky' " in their love, but their happiness has already been infected by some canker that hints at Hemingway's longing for the unattainable; perhaps it is a longing generated in the racial subconscious that neither logic nor conscious desire can suppress.

> But what we wanted not he [a waiter] nor anyone else, nor knocking on wood or on marble, as this café table-top was, could ever bring us. But we did not know it that night and we were very happy. (176)

Yet while eros and romance are important to *A Moveable Feast*, agape is at the heart of the book. The full pleasure of eros is attained with one you love, and in part *A Moveable Feast* tells a warm story of the fine practice of a love which is eros and agape combined. From the first chapter to the last we feel the respect, delight, care, and admiration of Hemingway for his wife:

> She had a gently modeled face and her eyes and her smile lighted up at decisions as though they were rich presents. (7)

> In the night we were happy with our own knowledge we already had and other new knowledge we had acquired in the mountains. (21)

> . . . it was very good to make love with whom you loved. That was better than anything. (25)

> We ate well and cheaply and drank well and cheaply and slept well and warm together and loved each other. (51)

And when his wife speaks, the feeling continues and is expanded by her mundane remarks in a warm and idyllic tone:

> "The Sion wine was even better. Do you remember how Mrs. Gangeswisch cooked the trout *au bleu* when we got back to the chalet? They were

such wonderful trout, Tatie, and we drank the Sion wine and ate out on the porch with the mountainside dropping off below and we could look across the lake and see the Dent du Midi with the snow half down it and the trees at the mouth of the Rhône where it flowed into the lake." (55)

. . . it was wonderful to see my wife. . . . We were happy the way children are who have been separated and are together again . . . (175)

. . . and I was very happy to see my wife who had the villa running beautifully . . . (185)

. . . Hadley and I had all the new country to learn and the new villages, and the people of the town were very friendly. (199)

Hadley and I had loved skiing. . . . She had beautiful, wonderfully strong legs and fine control of her skis, and she did not fall. (200)

And finally, climactically, the point of the last long sketch that ends the book, that ends the moveable feast, that begins the loss and destruction, then the seeking and rebuilding of his life that shaped the mastering theme of his literary career: Hemingway had fallen in love with another woman, a friend of Hadley, who had "unknowingly, innocently and unrelentingly set out to marry" him (209). It is his bad luck to be in love with two women—the "new and strange" one and his wife. Whatever the truth of the moment was, the truth of his bitter recollection is clear:

When I saw my wife again standing by the tracks as the train came in by the piled logs at the station, I wished I had died before I ever loved anyone but her. She was smiling, the sun on her lovely face tanned by the snow and sun, beautifully built, her hair red gold in the sun, grown out all winter awkwardly and beautifully, and Mr. Bumby standing with her, blond and chunky and with winter cheeks looking like a good Vorarlberg boy.

"Oh Tatie," she said, when I was holding her in my arms, "you're back and you made such a fine successful trip. I love you and we've missed you so."

I loved her and I loved no one else and we had a lovely magic time while we were alone. I worked well and we made great trips, and I thought we were invulnerable again, and it wasn't until we were out of the mountains in late spring, and back in Paris that the other thing started again.

That was the end of the first part of Paris. Paris was never to be the same again . . . (210–211)

True to the spirit of Nick Adams, Jake Barnes, and Frederic Henry, he learned that what was at first "stimulating and fun" was caused only by his and his lover's wicked innocence. Tristan and Iseult had not known the power of the love potion, but Hemingway says he cannot plead his ignorance, for "All things truly wicked start from an innocence. . . . You lie and hate it and it destroys you and every day is more dangerous, but you live day to day as in a war" (210). Like his early heroes, Hemingway needed to learn to avoid romantic wickedness, which tended ignorantly to trade the grace of love for the misery of "true love."

Of course the proportion of the book devoted to his wife Hadley is slight, but one can see a pattern in the chapters that may seem to be independent episodes about random events and people, and the pattern dramatizes the theme of love. Each episode in one way or another shows an aspect of love at work, as indeed any narrative involving two or more persons may. The "characters" can be loosely grouped into those whom Hemingway likes and those whom he dislikes. In spite of the reviewer who saw mainly defamation of character and loathing, Hemingway's friendships, or at least admirations, are as numerous as his enmities, and the latter are usually tempered by a humor that converts loathing into laughter, for him as much as for the reader. And not only does Hemingway have friendships with Sylvia Beach, "Chink" (Eric Edward Dorman-Smith), Mike Ward, Pascin, Ezra Pound, Evan Shipman, and the waiter Jean, but he also has friendships with Gertrude Stein and Scott Fitzgerald, although relations with them were not so simple and were often strained. The fact is that Hemingway purposely elaborates on the two relationships not only to "set the record straight," but because they are the chief complementary illustrations for the problems of loving which he has been concerned with. On the one hand is the illustration of Gertrude Stein's egotism and perversion, on the other Fitzgerald's idealism and tragic involvement with a bitch wife. Even if Hemingway's evaluation of these people were inaccurate or distorted or ungenerous, the depictions would be thematically right. His sardonic frankness is refreshing in an age of innuendo and false flattery, and his courage in assuming and defending an esthetic or ethical position should likewise be welcomed, even applauded, in an age of hypocrisy and ego-serving caution.

Fitzgerald and Stein are transitions between the other more stable friendships (Ezra Pound's for example) and the less than cordial relationships between Hemingway and Ford Madox Ford, "Hal," Wyndham Lewis, Ernest Walsh, Zelda Fitzgerald, and the anonymous figures of the German ex-naval officer and the "pilot fish" who leads the corrupting rich to the innocent Hemingway. Appropriately enough, the "enemies" are sometimes described through sexual images. Hemingway asks Hal (who may be a homosexual) if he went to Greece or used it (grease), and he decides the best way to describe the supercilious, cruel, vain, nasty-looking Wyndham Lewis is to say that his eyes were "those of an unsuccessful rapist" (93, 109). Fitzgerald's prostitution of his writing talent in his *Saturday Evening Post* stories Hemingway calls "whoring," and Fitzgerald agrees (155). Zelda Fitzgerald tries to destroy the sexually naive Scott by criticizing his sexual shortcomings. Gertrude Stein is a Lesbian, and Ernest Walsh is a con man with two wealthy, innocent "nice" girls in tow.

But even with the incitement toward alienation provided by these deviations that Hemingway could not tolerate, the burden of his self-examination is maintenance of a demanding standard that often made him regret his cruelties and stupidities, no matter how much justified. Ezra Pound provided a standard in his kindness and "beautiful" loyalty to his friends.

> Ezra Pound was always a good friend and he was always doing things for people. . . .
>
> Ezra was kinder and more Christian about people than I was. His own writing, when he would hit it right, was so perfect, and he was so sincere in his mistakes and so enamored of his errors, and so kind to people that I always thought of him as a sort of saint. He was also irascible but so perhaps have been many saints. (107–108)
>
> Ezra was the most generous writer I have ever known and the most disinterested. He helped poets, painters, sculptors and prose writers that he believed in and he would help anyone whether he believed in them or not if they were in trouble. (110)

For the sake of Pound, Hemingway even tried to like Wyndham Lewis, but it was easier to like someone like the modest and kind Evan Shipman who "knew and cared about horses, writing and painting"—the things Hemingway cared about too (135). A key difference between

Hemingway and Fitzgerald is indicated through their differing attitudes toward Shipman's friendship with Jean, a French waiter. Hemingway also liked Jean and was concerned about his future and a petty assault on his dignity: "I thought of telling Scott about this whole problem . . . but I knew he did not care about waiters nor their problems nor their great kindnesses and affections. At that time Scott hated the French" and the Italians and the English too (168). Fitzgerald's personal relations were almost abstract; even his animosities were generalized to include whole nationalities, and his likes were perhaps not so much of individuals as of groups, like writers.

But Hemingway "could not be angry with Scott" (66), and he had "no more loyal friend than Scott when he was sober" (184), and when Fitzgerald was drunk or otherwise difficult, Hemingway accepted, in spite of his own anger, the painful necessity of helping him and defending him, of "riding herd on Scott" (167) and trying "to be a good friend" (176). No matter what the record of letters or other accounts might objectively indicate (such as Morley Callaghan's account of the year 1929 that climaxes in the angry rupture of Callaghan, Fitzgerald, and Hemingway's friendship), the *last* Hemingway here looks back and convinces us, after all, that his heart was in the right place. He is above making excuses, and he is neither sentimental nor nostalgic.

But *A Moveable Feast* is in the nature of an apologia. It contains no surprises. It is humorous and bitter by turns, and it informs us of facts we might not have known, but the author is a familiar figure consistent with the image that evolved through his previous work. The one lasting impression that it leaves is of the courage Hemingway had in perceiving his divided, conflicting emotions and then in writing of them with an honesty presumably not even masked in the form of fiction, and sparing himself least of all.

# A SELECTED READING LIST

In addition to sources cited, this list includes those works consulted that are of some significance to the subjects of Hemingway and love. It is by no means a complete bibliography of either subject. The best checklist of Hemingway criticism is in Carlos Baker's *Hemingway and His Critics;* the best descriptions of Hemingway's writings are in Baker's *Hemingway: The Writer as Artist,* 3d ed., and Lee Samuels' *A Hemingway Check List,* all cited below.


*Across the River and into the Trees.* New York: Charles Scribner's Sons, 1950.

*Death in the Afternoon.* New York: Charles Scribner's Sons, 1932.

*A Farewell to Arms.* New York: Charles Scribner's Sons, 1929.

*The Fifth Column: A Play in Three Acts.* New York: Charles Scribner's Sons, 1940.

*For Whom the Bell Tolls.* New York: Charles Scribner's Sons, 1940.

*Green Hills of Africa.* New York: Charles Scribner's Sons, 1935.

*A Moveable Feast.* New York: Charles Scribner's Sons, 1964.

*The Old Man and the Sea.* New York: Charles Scribner's Sons, 1952.

"On the Blue Water," *Esquire,* 5 (April, 1936), 31, 184–185.

*The Short Stories of Ernest Hemingway.* New York: Charles Scribner's Sons, 1953.

*The Sun Also Rises.* New York: Charles Scribner's Sons, 1926.

*To Have and Have Not.* New York: Charles Scribner's Sons, 1937.

Adam, August. *The Primacy of Love.* Westminster, Maryland: Newman Press, 1958.

Aldridge, John W. *After the Lost Generation.* New York: Noonday Press, 1958.

Algren, Nelson. "The Dye That Did Not Run," *Nation,* 193 (November 18, 1961), 387–390.

Aronowitz, Alfred G., and Peter Hamill. *Ernest Hemingway: The Life and Death of a Man.* New York: Lancer Books, Inc., 1961.

Atkins, John W. *The Art of Ernest Hemingway: His Work and Personality.* London: Peter Nevill, 1952.

Atkinson, Brooks. "Hemingway Turns to Defamation of Character," *Houston Chronicle,* July 8, 1964, Sec. 7, p. 6.

Bache, William B. "*Nostromo* and 'The Snows of Kilimanjaro'," *Modern Language Notes,* 72 (January 1957), 32–34.

Backman, Melvin. "Hemingway: The Matador and the Crucified," *Hemingway and His Critics.* Carlos Baker (ed.). New York: Hill & Wang, Inc., 1961.

Baker, Carlos. *Hemingway: The Writer as Artist.* Princeton: Princeton University Press, 1956, 2d ed; 1963, 3d ed.

——— (ed.). *Hemingway and His Critics.* New York: Hill & Wang, Inc., 1961.

——— (ed.). *Ernest Hemingway: Critiques of Four Major Novels.* New York: Charles Scribner's Sons, 1962.

Barrett, William. *Irrational Man: A Study in Existential Philosophy.* Garden City, New York: Doubleday & Company, Inc., 1958.

Barzun, Jacques. *Classic, Romantic, and Modern.* Garden City, New York: Doubleday & Company, Inc., 1961.

Bayley, John. *The Characters of Love.* New York: Basic Books, Inc., 1960.

Beach, Joseph Warren. *American Fiction: 1920–1940.* New York: Macmillan Company, 1942.

Beach, Sylvia. *Shakespeare and Company.* New York: Harcourt, Brace & Company, 1959.

Beck, Warren. "The Shorter Happy Life of Mrs. Macomber," *Modern Fiction Studies,* 1 (November 1955), 28–37.

Bédier, Joseph. *The Romance of Tristan and Iseult.* Hilaire Belloc and Paul Rosenfeld (tr.). Garden City, New York: Doubleday & Company, Inc., 1953.

Beebe, Maurice. "Criticism of Ernest Hemingway: A Selected Checklist with an Index to Studies of Separate Works," *Modern Fiction Studies,* 1 (August 1955), 36–45.

Booth, Wayne C. *The Rhetoric of Fiction.* Chicago: University of Chicago Press, 1961.

Bowden, Edwin T. *The Dungeon of the Heart.* New York: Macmillan Company, 1961.

Breit, Harvey. "Talk with Mr. Hemingway," *New York Times Book Review,* September 17, 1950, p. 14.

Brinin, John Malcolm. *The Third Rose: Gertrude Stein and Her World.* Boston: Little, Brown & Company, 1959.

Brooks, Cleanth. *The Hidden God.* New Haven: Yale University Press, 1963.

Brown, Deming. "Hemingway in Russia," *Hemingway and His Critics.* Carlos Baker (ed.). New York: Hill and Wang, Inc., 1961.

Brown, Norman O. *Life Against Death.* New York: Random House, 1959.

Burhans, Clinton S., Jr. "*The Old Man and the Sea:* Hemingway's Tragic Vision of Man," *Hemingway and His Critics.* Carlos Baker (ed.). New York: Hill & Wang, Inc., 1961.

Burnam, Tom. "Primitivism and Masculinity in the Work of Ernest Hemingway," *Modern Fiction Studies,* 1 (August 1955), 20–24.

Callaghan, Morley. *That Summer in Paris: Memories of Tangled Friendships with Hemingway, Fitzgerald and Some Others.* New York: Dell Publishing Company, Inc., 1964.

Campbell, Joseph. *The Hero with a Thousand Faces.* New York: Pantheon Books, Inc., 1949.

Coomaraswamy, Ananda K. *The Transformation of Nature in Art.* New York: Dover Publications, Inc., 1956.

Cowley, Malcolm. *Exile's Return.* New York: Viking Press, Inc., 1951.

D'Arcy, M. C. *The Mind and Heart of Love.* New York: Meridian Books, Inc., 1956.

DeFalco, Joseph M. *The Hero in Hemingway's Short Stories.* Pittsburgh: University of Pittsburgh Press, 1963.

Dworking, Martin S. "A Dead Leopard and an Empty Grail," *Humanist,* 13 (July–August 1953), 164–165.

Eastman, Max. *Art and the Life of Action.* New York: Alfred A. Knopf, Inc., 1934.

———. *Einstein, Trotsky, Hemingway, Freud and Other Great Companions.* New York: Collier Books, 1962.

Eliade, Mircea. *Patterns in Comparative Religion.* Rosemary Sheed (tr.). New York: Sheed & Ward, Inc., 1958.

———. *Cosmos and History: The Myth of the Eternal Return.* Willard R. Trask (tr.). New York: Harper & Brothers, 1959.

Eliot, T. S. *The Complete Poems and Plays.* New York: Harcourt, Brace & Company, 1952.

Engstrom, Alfred G. "Dante, Flaubert, and 'The Snows of Kilimanjaro'," *Modern Language Notes,* 65 (1950), 203–205.

Fenton, Charles A. *The Apprenticeship of Ernest Hemingway: The Early Years.* New York: Viking Press, Inc., 1958.

Ferguson, George. *Signs and Symbols in Christian Art.* New York: Oxford University Press, 1959.

Fieldler, Leslie A. "From Clarissa to Temple Drake: Women and Love in the Classic American Novel," *The Griffin*, 6 (July 1957), 13–24.

———. *Love and Death in the American Novel.* New York: Criterion Books, Inc., 1960.

Frazer, James G. *The Golden Bough.* Abr. ed., New York: Macmillan Company, 1949.

Freud, Sigmund. *On Creativity and the Unconscious: Papers on the Psychology of Art, Literature, Love, Religion.* Benjamin Nelson (ed.). Joan Riviere (tr.). New York: Harper & Brothers, 1958.

Frohock, W. M. *The Novel of Violence in America.* 2d ed. Dallas: Southern Methodist University Press, 1957.

Fromm, Erich. *The Art of Loving.* New York: Harper & Row, 1962.

Galantiere, Lewis. "There Is Never Any End to Paris," *New York Times Book Review*, May 10, 1964, pp. 1, 26.

Geismar, Maxwell. *Writers in Crisis.* New York: Hill & Wang, Inc., 1961.

Gourmont, Remy de. *The Natural Philosophy of Love.* Ezra Pound (tr.). New York: Collier Books, 1961.

Halliday, E. M. "Hemingway's Ambiguity: Symbolism and Irony," *Hemingway.* Robert P. Weeks (ed.). Englewood Cliffs, New Jersey: Prentice-Hall, Inc., 1962.

Handy, William J. "A New Dimension for a Hero: Santiago of *The Old Man and the Sea,*" *Six Contemporary Novels*, William O. S. Sutherland, Jr. (ed.). Austin: University of Texas Press, 1962.

Hecht, Ben. "The Myth about Marilyn Monroe's Death," *Family Weekly*, September 30, 1962, pp. 4–5.

Hemingway, Leicester. *My Brother, Ernest Hemingway.* Cleveland: World Publishing Company, 1962.

Hemingway, Mary. "The Making of the Book: A Chronicle and a Memoir," *New York Times Book Review*, May 10, 1964, pp. 26–27.

Hewlett, Maurice Henry. *The Forest Lovers: A Romance.* New York: Charles Scribner's Sons, 1907.

Hoffman, Frederick J. *The Twenties.* New rev. ed. New York: Collier Books, 1962.

Huizinga, J. *The Waning of the Middle Ages.* Garden City, New York: Doubleday & Company, Inc., 1954.

Johnson, Edgar. "Farewell the Separate Peace," *Ernest Hemingway: The Man and His Work.* John K. M. McCaffery (ed.). Cleveland: World Publishing Company, 1950.

Kazin, Alfred. *On Native Grounds: An Interpretation of Modern American Prose Literature.* Garden City, New York: Doubleday & Company, Inc., 1956.

Killinger, John. *Hemingway and the Dead Gods: A Study in Existentialism.* Lexington: University of Kentucky Press, 1960.

Knoll, Robert E. (ed.). *McAlmon and the Lost Generation: A Self-Portrait.* Lincoln: University of Nebraska Press, 1962.

Koestler, Arthur. "The Seven Deadly Fallacies," *The Trail of the Dinosaur.* New York: Macmillan Company, 1955.

Krutch, Joseph Wood. *The Modern Temper.* New York: Harcourt, Brace & Company, 1956.

Lania, Leo. *Hemingway: A Pictorial Biography.* Joan Bradley (tr.). New York: Viking Press, Inc., 1961.

Levin, Harry. "Observations on the Style of Ernest Hemingway," *Hemingway and His Critics.* Carlos Baker (ed.). New York: Hill & Wang, Inc., 1961.

Lewis, C. S. *The Allegory of Love: A Study in Medieval Tradition.* New York: Oxford University Press, 1958.

Lewis, Wyndham. *Men Without Art.* London: Cassell and Company, Ltd., 1934.

Loeb, Harold. *The Way It Was.* New York: Criterion Books, Inc., 1959.

*Love and Violence.* George Lamb (tr.). London: Sheed & Ward, Inc., 1954.

Machlin, Milt. *The Private Hell of Hemingway.* New York: Paperback Library, 1962.

Materlinck, Maurice. *The Life of the Bee.* Alfred Sutro (tr.). London: G. Allen, 1901.

Marcuse, Herbert. *Eros and Civilization.* New York: Random House, 1962.

Maurois, André. *Seven Faces of Love.* Haakon M. Chevalier and Bert M-P. Leefmans (tr.). Garden City, New York: Doubleday & Company, Inc., 1962.

McCaffery, John K. M. (ed.). *Ernest Hemingway: The Man and His Work.* Cleveland: World Publishing Company, 1950.

Mizener, Arthur. "The Two Hemingways," *The Great Experiment in American Literature.* Carl Bode (ed.). London: William Heinemann, 1961.

Moseley, Edwin M. *Pseudonyms of Christ in the Modern Novel: Motifs and Methods.* Pittsburgh: University of Pittsburgh Press, 1962.

Moynihan, William T. "The Martyrdom of Robert Jordan," *College English,* 21 (December 1959), 127–132.

Neumann, Erich. *Armor and Psyche.* Ralph Manheim (tr.). New York: Harper & Row, 1962.

Nygren, Anders. *Agape and Eros, A Study of the Christian Idea of Love.* Philadelphia: Westminster Press, 1953.

Ortega y Gasset, José. *On Love.* Toby Talbot (tr.). New York: Meridian Books, Inc., 1957.

Paolini, Pier Francesco. "The Hemingway of the Major Works," *Hemingway and His Critics.* Carlos Baker (ed.). New York: Hill & Wang, Inc., 1961.

Parcheminey, Georges. "The Problem of Ambivalence," *Love and Violence.* George Lamb (tr.). London: Sheed & Ward, Inc., 1954.

Plimpton, George. "Ernest Hemingway," *Writers at Work: The "Paris Review" Interviews.* Second series. New York: Viking Press, Inc., 1963.

Ross, Lillian. "How Do You Like It Now, Gentlemen?" *New Yorker*, May 13, 1950, pp. 57–60.

———. *Portrait of Hemingway*. New York: Simon and Schuster, Inc., 1961.

Rougemont, Denis de. *Love Declared: Essays on the Myths of Love*. Richard Howard (tr.). New York: Pantheon Books, Inc., 1963.

———. *Love in the Western World*. Rev. ed. Montgomery Belgion (tr.). Garden City, New York: Doubleday & Company, Inc., 1957.

Rovit, Earl. *Ernest Hemingway*. New York: Twayne Publishers, Inc., 1963.

Samuels, Lee. *A Hemingway Check List*. New York: Charles Scribner's Sons, 1951.

Sanderson, Stewart F. *Ernest Hemingway*. New York: Grove Press, 1961.

Sanford, Marcelline Hemingway. *At the Hemingways: A Family Portrait*. Boston: Atlantic-Little, Brown, 1962.

Scott, Arthur L. "In Defense of Robert Cohn," *College English*, 18 (March 1957), 309–314.

Seferis, George. *Poems*. Rex Warner (tr.). Boston: Little, Brown & Company, 1961.

Shapiro, Charles (ed.). *Twelve Original Essays on Great American Novels*. Detroit: Wayne State University Press, 1958.

Singer, Kurt. *Hemingway: Life and Death of a Giant*. Los Angeles: Holloway House, 1961.

Spilka, Mark. "The Death of Love in *The Sun Also Rises*," *Twelve Original Essays on Great American Novels*, Charles Shapiro (ed.). Detroit: Wayne State University Press, 1958.

Stein, Gertrude. *The Autobiography of Alice B. Toklas*. New York: Harcourt, Brace & Company, 1933.

Stein, William Bysshe. "Love and Lust in Hemingway's Short Stories," *Texas Studies in Literature and Language*, 3 (Summer 1961), 234–242.

Stendahl, M. de. *On Love*. Tr. by H. B. V., under the direction of C. K. Scott-Moncrieff. Garden City, New York: Doubleday & Company, Inc., n.d.

Stephens, Robert O. "Hemingway's Don Quixote in Pamplona," *College English*, 23 (December 1961), 216–218.

Strassburg, Gottfried von. *Tristan: With the* TRISTRAN *of Thomas*. Translated with an Introduction by A. T. Hatto. Baltimore: Penguin Books, Inc., 1960.

Tedlock, E. W., Jr. "Hemingway's 'The Snows of Kilimanjaro'," *Explicator*, 8 (October 1949), Item 7.

Thurber, James, and E. B. White. *Is Sex Necessary*? New York: Harper & Brothers, 1929.

Trilling, Lionel. "Hemingway and His Critics," *Hemingway and His Critics*, Carlos Baker (ed.). New York: Hill & Wang, Inc., 1961.

Twain, Mark. *Adventures of Huckleberry Finn*. New York: Charles L. Webster, 1885.

Valency, Maurice. *In Praise of Love*. New York: Macmillan Company, 1961.

Walcutt, C. C. "Hemingway's 'The Snows of Kilimanjaro'," *Explicator*, 7 (April 1949), Item 43.

Warren, Robert Penn. "Introduction," *A Farewell to Arms*. New York: Charles Scribner's Sons, 1953.

Wasserstrom, William. *Heiress of All the Ages: Sex and Sentiment in the Genteel Tradition*. Minneapolis: University of Minnesota Press, 1959.

Weeks, Robert P. "Fakery in *The Old Man and the Sea*," *College English*, 24 (December 1962), 188–192.

—— (ed.). *Hemingway: A Collection of Critical Essays*. Englewood Cliffs, N. J.: Prentice-Hall, Inc., 1962.

West, Ray B., Jr. "Ernest Hemingway: The Failure of Sensibility," *Forms of Modern Fiction*. William Van O'Connor (ed.). Minneapolis: University of Minnesota Press, 1948.

White, Victor. "Anathema-Maranatha," *Love and Violence*. George Lamb, tr. London: Sheed & Ward, Inc., 1954.

Wilson, Edmund. *The Shores of Light*. New York: Farrar, Straus & Young, Inc., 1952.

——. *The Wound and the Bow: Seven Studies in Literature*. Boston: Houghton Mifflin Company, 1941.

Wright, Austin McGiffert. *The American Short Story in the Twenties*. Chicago: University of Chicago Press, 1961.

Young, Philip. *Ernest Hemingway*. New York: Rinehart & Company, Inc., 1952.

——. "Our Hemingway Man," *The Kenyon Review*, 26 (Autumn 1964), 676–707.

# INDEX